STRONG AT THE BROKEN PLACES

a memoir

Sherry O'Neill

Generations

My parents did the best they could…or did they?
They handed me their pain, along with a heavy dose of misery.
They imparted emotional complications and flaws as well,
but they also gave me long eyelashes and a sense of humor.
And to whom do I owe my grit and determination?

Like an unremitting whirl, wretchedness is passed from
one generation to another without awareness or understanding.
But that is how it is and will ever be.
So cast off the chains of anger and hurt
and pick up the scepter of resilience.
The world is waiting to embrace you.

Sherry O'Neill

To my beloved sons, Chris and David,
Who saved my life
And to Jim,
Who made that life worth living

Contents

AUTHOR'S NOTE

"There is no greater agony than bearing an
untold story inside you."
—Maya Angelou

A few summers ago, three of my girlfriends and I took a vacation to the beach in North Carolina for a few days. Sitting on the second-story porch till noon, watching the goings-on below, we shared our stories. In the evening before dinner, we lounged on the porch with our gin and tonics and kept up a running dialog, captivated by each other's tales. At what turned out to be a pivotal moment, one of my friends leaned over to me and said, "You need to write a book."

I'd known for many years I would eventually write a memoir, but something had stopped me. Once home, the same friend asked, "Have you started your book yet?" I confessed I hadn't. One morning before I could think of an excuse, I sat down at the computer and started to write. Memories came flooding in—happenings from long ago. At last, I'd reached a point in life where the fear of judgment no longer held me back; my past didn't haunt me anymore.

This is the first time I've revealed, even to family and closest friends, all the details of my struggles. Mine is a classic human story of dysfunction, addiction, narcissism, and character flaws, but it's also a story of hope, resilience, hard-earned knowledge, and deliverance.

Reality is relentlessly complex, and memories are shaded by one's psyche and personal perspectives. This is *my* side of the story—the way I remember it. Others would undoubtedly tell it differently, but all my words are true to the best of my recollection. My sister and brother fact-checked the manuscript along the way and corrected me when I got something wrong. Some dialogue I recall close to verbatim; in other places I've recreated it to provide readability, but always with a commitment to truth in depicting the real people in my life. The names of a few characters have been changed to protect privacy.

The re-telling of personal experiences has the potential to transform both the writer and the reader. I hope this book will empower those who share my experience of growing up with parents who failed to protect you, wounded you, and abandoned you. Change is possible. No matter how deep the hole, or how hard the world pushes against you, there is a primal determination and strength that can push back even stronger. As Camus once wrote, "In the depths of winter, I finally learned that within me there lay an invincible summer."

PART I

My mother and father. Jim and Christine Knoche.
Wedding Day—May 2, 1946

THE DAY THE WORLD SHIFTED
Jacksonville, Florida
1962

"Life on earth has sharp teeth."
—*Unashamed* by Lecrae Moore

The year was 1962, late August, and the day, like most summer days in the South, had arrived in a cloud of blazing heat and sweat. I'd completed sophomore year in high school, and we were living in Love Grove Acres, the last place we would ever live as a family. I was fifteen years old. Before this ordinary day would end, my life would change forever.

My best friend, Allison, and I rode our bikes to a nearby shopping center that morning and spent a few hours sampling lipsticks and eye shadows and browsing through the small department store. We ignored the disapproving looks of salesclerks as the sound of our laughter and giggles erupted like barks from a kennel.

"Did you see that lady behind the makeup counter?" Allison whispered to me. "She looks like her teeth were wadded up and thrown in her mouth." We doubled over with peals of giggles. Standing at the bargain jewelry bin, I held up a pair of chartreuse, feathery earrings to my ear.

"Hey, Alli, how do these look?" I asked.

"Oh my God. Those are the ugliest things I've ever seen," she answered, and we proceeded to dig around in the bin, posing for each other with one pair after another and cackling. At the perfume counter, Allison spritzed cologne on her wrist and waved her arm under my nose with a wicked smile.

"Nice, huh?" she said, and I made a gagging sound as I jerked my face away.

"Whew! That smells like swamp gas. Let's get out of here."

As we walked toward the front door, I scanned the walls for a clock. *What time was it anyway? Probably after noon.* Time had a tendency to fly when you were with your best friend, but I had to get home to make sure my younger sister and brother had eaten their lunch. Since my older sister, Jo, had left home, I'd become the de facto overseer. Everything had been fine when I left, but I didn't like to leave my mother alone too long.

Allison and I raced out the door and jumped on our bikes, pedaling hard to move through the heavy, sultry air, each movement tugging against us like quicksand. Splitting off at Love Grove Acres Road, we agreed to meet up later that afternoon at her house. Under porcelain, cloudless skies, the sun burned like an acetylene torch on my back as I pushed the pedals with all my strength, trying to ignore a growing anxiety. Rolling up into the yard, I hopped off the bike and laid it in the grass, wiped the sweat off my face with my shirt, and opened the front door. The dark house was eerily quiet.

"Mom! Where are you? Hey, is anybody home? Pammie, Freddy!" I called. Silence. The stillness was unnerving as I walked through the living room and down the hall. The first and second bedrooms on the left were empty, and I moved to the guest bathroom on the right. Butterflies flapped in my stomach as I pushed the door to the large bathroom open. In the dark, I sensed someone sitting at the dressing table. Groping around for the switch, my fingers landed on it, and I flipped on the lights.

I gasped. There was so much blood. Everywhere. It looked as if the room had been painted with it. Mother was slumped in the chair wearing only her bra and underpants, covered in blood, her head on her chest. The surface of the dressing table overflowed with dark red, bloody syrup that spilled onto the floor creating a lake, threatening to breach the hallway. Crimson streaked the chair, her face, her arms, legs, the walls, even the mirror. My brain struggled to catch up with my eyes, and a voice in my head shouted, *Get out. Go back where you were. This didn't happen.*

The ferric smell of blood mixed with vodka filled the room. I stepped through the slippery gore and touched her shoulder. "Mom! Mom!" I said. "Wake up! Oh my God! What have you done?"

Her hands slipped off the dressing table into her lap, and blood poured from bone-deep cuts in her wrists. *You've really done it this time, Mom.* I ran from the bathroom to the kitchen phone. It was 1962—before 9-1-1, so I dialed the only number I could remember. Allison's mother, Mrs. Johnson, answered.

"It's my mother, please help!" I screamed, breathless as I attempted to explain.

"I'll be there in five minutes. We need to rush her to the hospital."

I hung up and stood still, my body trembling, heart beating like a drum in my ears. Sweat snaked down my armpits and I sucked in a deep breath, swallowing the long, loud scream gathering in my chest. A rip in the fabric of time and space existed in that bathroom. I couldn't go back in there alone, so I stood at the front door and waited for Mrs. Johnson.

Within two minutes, her car screeched to a stop in front of the house, and I threw the door open. We flew into the dressing room and tried to lift my mother, but her slippery, dead weight made the task almost impossible. Struggling to move her across the lawn in the bright sunshine, we exposed our drama to the entire neighborhood. The three of us were bathed in blood, and as I attempted to place her in the front seat, a tug at my shirt brought my eyes directly into the horrified face of my six-year-old brother.

"What happened? What's wrong with Mom? Where are you going?" he cried.

Frantic, I looked around and, like an angel, our next-door neighbor, Mrs. Kajawa, came running over. She placed her arm around his small shoulder and turned him toward her house.

"Come with me, Freddy. I've got some cookies just out of the oven," she said in a gentle voice as she whisked him away.

Mrs. Johnson raced through traffic, laying on the horn and swerving between lanes. Terrified, I watched my mother pump her hands into fists, sending geysers of blood pouring onto the seat like a broken levee.

"Stop, Mom, stop!" I screamed as I grabbed her by the shoulders from the back seat, but even in a semi-conscious state, she wanted to finish the job.

Please hurry, please hurry, I silently repeated as my heart began an arrhythmic lurch. Mrs. Johnson peeled into the emergency entrance, hand holding steady on the horn, and the hospital attendants rushed out to take her from us.

As we sat in the waiting room, I felt a numbness, a blank nothingness wash over me. I blurted out, "I'm sorry my mother ruined your new car, Mrs. Johnson."

She took my hand and in a soft voice reassured me, "It's not a problem, honestly. It can be cleaned up like new."

Disembodied, I gazed down at my bloody clothes and extremities. Even the insides of my socks and tennis shoes were soppy. The gore had taken on a multi-dimensional quality, one I could not only see, but smell, touch, and feel deep inside.

Hours later, the doctor came out to explain that my mother was stable and resting. It had been a lengthy, intricate surgery, reconnecting arteries and repairing tendons. They'd put thirty-six stitches in each wrist and were transfusing her with blood.

"She'd lost a tremendous amount of blood. It was touch and go. You saved her life by reacting as quickly as you did," the doctor said.

"What will happen now?" I asked. His stern features softened as he looked down at me and explained she would be transferred to the psychiatric ward for sixty days, a legal mandate for attempted suicide. I told him my mother had been admitted to this same hospital three months prior for an overdose of sleeping pills, and he recommended she be hospitalized longer.

"But after sixty days," he added, "the decision to stay is voluntary."

She'll never go for that. I let out a long, deep sigh, relieved that at least I wouldn't be the one in charge of her for a while.

Walking back to the car, Mrs. Johnson and I were silent as leaves crunched under our feet. At their house, as if in a dream, I watched Mr. Johnson remove the seats from the front of the car and hose them down in the yard. Mrs. Johnson encouraged me to stay for a while. She wanted to keep an eye on me, but as I stood in the gathering darkness, my mind raced to Pam and Freddy. At six and seven, they were too young to be alone. "I need to get home right away and check on my sister and brother," I explained. My father was expected home from his travels that day, but I couldn't be certain when.

Sitting in the driveway back at my house, Mrs. Johnson said, "Call me if you need anything or maybe to talk. You've been through a lot today." She patted my hand.

"Thank you for everything, Mrs. Johnson."

"I think you should call me Vivian," she said, kindness and concern radiating from her eyes.

I rounded the kids up and tried to minimize the scene Freddy had witnessed, explaining that Mom had had an accident, but she would recover after a stay in the hospital. Once they were in bed, I wandered through the house looking at the trail of blood leading to the front door, smeared on the walls and door frames, and congealed on the carpet—scenes from a nightmare. I opened the bathroom door and recoiled—the space still vibrated with horror, like screams in a cavern. An unimaginable sea of blood.

Cleanup now, but where do I start? Gathering a bucket, mop, rags, and towels, I set to work. But like a vat of spilled ink, the more I wiped and mopped, the more the blood spread and streaked. A job like this would take days, maybe even a week—it couldn't be knocked out in one night.

I stripped off my clothes and tossed them in the washer along with the towels and rags. Standing in the shower, hot water pelted down on me as I scrubbed off dried blood and watched the russet-colored water swirl down the drain with my tears.

PART II

Beginnings - Sherry O'Neill

BEGINNINGS
Panama City
1950s

"Not even the brightest future can make up for the fact that no roads lead back to what came before—to the innocence of childhood ..."
—Jo Nesbo

"**M**y *vowels* are running off. My *vowels* are running off!" I yelled as I ran up to the group of adults, my parents included, gathered on colorful blankets in the sun.

"Whaaat?" My mother smiled and tilted her head. "Say that again," she said, and I repeated it louder.

A roar of laughter went up from the grown-ups. I stamped my bare foot in the dirt and clenched my hands. "No, dammit! Don't laugh. It isn't funny—my *vowels* really are running off!" I was four and confronting my first episode of diarrhea at a remote state park with no bathroom facilities. "What should I do?" I pleaded.

My father stopped laughing, took a big swig of beer, and backhanded some foam from his mouth. Pointing with his Schlitz can to the expansive body of water in front of us, he said, "Go in the lake." Then he added with a snicker, "But make sure you go *waaay* over there," and he motioned to the far side of the lake. More hoots and giggles from the adults, all half lit by this point. Ignoring me, they turned back to the party.

My very first memory, something I recall like a forgotten, lost baby tooth, insignificant at the time, feels weightier today—a harbinger of sorts—for I would spend years chasing their elusive attention.

I was born in 1947 to Jim and Christine ("Cricket") Knoche, two people woefully ill-suited to parenthood. Daddy, twenty-seven, and

Mother, twenty-six, brought their squirmy bundle home to a tiny, white clapboard rental house on Shady Place in Jacksonville, Florida. My mother said I looked Chinese with a full head of dark hair and slanted eyes, nothing like my sister, who'd made her debut four years earlier as a beautiful, pink Gerber Baby.

Around the time I was two, my father moved us to the small, seaside town of Panama City on the panhandle of Florida. Combining his love and knowledge of boats and the water with a natural aptitude for electronics, he launched James Electronics in 1950 at the foot of the St. Andrews Bridge in a little green house.

In the fifties, life in the torpid stability of the suburbs was all about conformity. For middle-class families like ours, society's standards for acceptable behavior were rigid—appearances were much more important than reality. In the South, good manners and a refined comportment could disguise a boatload of moral turpitude. Adults acting badly and family scandals were locked away and never discussed.

The advent of television only reinforced an unrealistic obedience to conformity. When I was five, watching shows like *Father Knows Best*, *Leave It to Beaver*, and *The Adventures of Ozzie and Harriet* with my sister Jo, I concluded that our family didn't measure up. June and Ward did not party and get drunk, and Ozzie and Harriet never fought or were harsh with their children. I adored my parents and believed they were the most glamorous couple on earth, but I longed to be in a family like that—a *normal* family.

Panama City, a veritable Eden in the fifties, was a beautiful little burg and an idyllic place to grow up. Over fifty years later, the place lingers fresh in my mind—the smell of cut grass on a hot summer day; ripe wisteria dripping in clusters from fences; the perfume of white, velvet magnolia blossoms mingled with damp, decaying woods, loamy soil, and a dash of salt air. Forget-me-not blue skies that turned to soft corals, pinks, and purples at dusk, deep shades of midnight at high noon under the canopy of ancient live oaks, and an astounding spectrum of wildflowers and greens gave the small town a feel of paradise. Bays, bayous, canals, and lakes were a bloodstream through the city, and the Gulf of Mexico our playground.

I spent my days outside with the boys in the neighborhood climbing trees, building forts, catching minnows for bait, and fishing, while the other girls played dolls and had tea parties. In the summer, we were outside from sunup to sundown; feral children, barefoot and unsupervised. Our parents had no idea where we went or who we were with. We lived in a safe place and a safer time, and without the glut of twenty-four-hour news, an uninformed innocence (some call ignorance) defined the era.

My sister Jo, four years older, provided the constancy I craved. She was my role model, and, like a puppy, I followed her lead. My mother's words, "Yes, you can go, but take Sherry with you," brought a disgusted sigh and a glare in my direction as my sister accepted her fate. Only the two of us for seven years, we faced the tumultuous weekends together.

In the early days, our parents strove to do the family thing (if they weren't too hungover), and Sunday nights meant going to the drive-in movies. Located in a rural area, the ride took us by the Holy Pentecostal Emanuel Church, and I'd crane out the window to get a glimpse of the parishioners with their arms up in the air, shouting and chanting, singing, and swaying trance-like.

"Daddy, don't forget to drive slow when we pass the church," I would call out from the back seat.

My father would laugh and yell, "Get your head in the car, Sherry."

Jo and I bounced with excitement in the back seat, straining to be the first to spot the drive-in marquee and yell, "I see the picture show!"

Our neighborhood teemed with kids so there was no shortage of playmates. My sister and I walked to the movie theater downtown on Saturday or Sunday and, for fifteen cents, sat in the air conditioning and watched a double feature.

The fifties were a boom time, but not everyone enjoyed prosperity.

We lived in a small, lily-white town during the time of hard-core segregation. Colored people lived on a different side of town, and not a single black or brown face could be seen in our schools, churches, or any position of power. The "Whites Only" signs over drinking fountains and the back-of-the-bus protocol told me white people deemed coloreds beneath them. My parents, who leaned a little to the left, remained mute on the unpleasant topic. Any of my questions went unanswered, but I do remember my father cautioning Jo and me, "If I ever hear the word *nigger* come from your mouth, I will wash it out with soap." Further confusing the issue, the few black people I encountered appeared happy, affable, and accepting of their status. With the cruelty of segregation hidden, the times took on a patina of the natural order.

But one Sunday afternoon when I was five, Jo and I stood waiting to buy tickets to the latest Robin Hood movie. Four well-dressed adults wearing hats and gloves, most likely coming from church stood in a separate line. When the group had purchased their tickets, they entered the theater through an unmarked door on the side.

Tugging at Jo's sleeve, I asked her, "Hey, where are they going?"

"Hush," she whispered as she swatted my hand away. "I'll tell you when we get in the movies."

Once we were inside, I asked her again. "Where did they go?"

"They *have* to sit in the balcony, and that's the door to the balcony."

"Why?"

She gave me that withering look she favored when addressing me. "Because they're *Nigras*, stupid, or didn't you notice that?" She rolled her eyes and stomped away from me.

When the movie ended, I tried to catch a glimpse of the family in the balcony. "It isn't right," I told Jo as we walked home. "They were dressed better than anyone else in line, so why couldn't they sit where they wanted?" To a young, developing mind that understood the concept of fair, it didn't seem fair at all. As I contemplated it, an unpleasant feeling I recognized as guilt came over me.

Jo shook her head and whispered under her breath, "Moron, you just don't get it."

One afternoon as I sat on the floor coloring, my mother called to Jo, "I'm taking Cora home now."

"Oh, can I go too?" I asked, scrambling to put on my shoes and socks.

Cora, our maid, came once a week to wash and iron. Tall and thin, with skin like brown-black satin, she had hair that reminded me of one of my mother's silver, stainless-steel scrubbing pads. Quiet and hard-working, Cora had a grandmotherly demeanor toward Jo and me, but when my mother spoke to her, she looked down, submissive and fawning. No one else seemed to notice, but it made me sad for her.

Arriving in Cora's neighborhood, I stared in wonder at the party atmosphere—people standing on the corner, laughing, joking, and waving to each other. Kids played in the street, music wafted in the air from one of the establishments, and men congregated, talking and sharing a smoke.

"When I grow up, I'm going to live in this neighborhood," I said. Cora chuckled to herself as she got out of the car and waved goodbye.

My mother took a long, slow drag on her Kool, and I watched the tip grow redder and the long ash dangle, threatening to fall at the slightest movement. "Do you see any white faces over there?" she asked me, blowing a gray river of smoke and stretching her arm out the window to knock off the ash.

I looked around. "Well, no, but I don't care."

"Well, everybody else *would*."

"Why?"

My mother eased the car into gear and we began to roll away from the curb. Clearly exasperated, she looked at me, sighed and said, "That's just the way it is.

We lived near some of the most beautiful beaches in the country on the Gulf Coast, or Redneck Rivera, as it's called. Mother and Daddy loved the water, and almost every weekend they would throw some towels, blankets, and coolers filled with beer into the trunk of the car and we'd take off for the beach. It's a myth that native Floridians are born with gills and a natural ability to swim, but it's nearly true. Jo and I, innate swimmers, had been tossed in as little tadpoles and were unafraid of the water. Our parents would lie on a blanket in the fine, sugar-white sand tanning and drinking beer all day while Jo and I played in the crystal-clear, aqua-green ocean waters.

Daddy had taught us to bodysurf on top of the big, foamy white waves all the way to shore. Oblivious to the dangers inherent in a churning ocean, we went out in water over our heads and dog paddled anticipating the next wave. Half the time I missed the exact second to move to the top of the crest, and the powerful wave slammed me under water and tossed me around like a ragdoll, scraping my knees on the sand and forcing salt water into my nose, mouth, and ears as it washed me to shore. I would struggle to my feet, readjust my bathing suit, and pull plastered hair off my burning eyes so I could scan the horizon for the next big wall of water to ride.

By lunchtime, my parents would be sloshed and arguing, unaware they even had children. One afternoon as I dog paddled in the water, I saw my mother jump up from the blanket in a snit and run down the shore and into the water, heading for the deep. A moment later, Jo followed her, swimming with all her might to catch up. They were way too deep in a matter of minutes, and terror gripped me as I stood at the shore seeing their heads bob up and down and disappear altogether, their screams for help far away and muted by crashing waves. Before I could run to get Daddy, out of nowhere two men dashed into the water and swam rapidly toward them. I'd heard of people drowning in the ocean but never thought it could be us. By the time I'd raced back for my father, the men were coming from the water, carrying my mother and sister.

Riding home, I sat in the back seat with Jo, who, despite being wrapped in towels, trembled forcefully. Her lips were blue against ashen skin, and I could hear her teeth chatter. My mother, sitting in the front with my father, was slack-jawed and whimpering, her eyes closed and head resting on the window. Daddy yelled drunkenly and slammed his hand on the steering wheel, lecturing about the dangers of swimming in water too deep, about undertow and the results of getting caught in a riptide. Without a daring rescue by two strangers who happened by, my mother and sister both would have been washed out to sea that day.

Most summers, our parents rented an oceanside cottage (a rustic, four-room shack with sandy floors and sparse furniture), and we led the carefree lives of beach bums for three weeks. After swimming all morning, Jo would sit on the blanket reading my mother's *Photoplay* movie magazines while I stood bent into a U-shape at the shoreline, peering into the shallows in pursuit of a seahorse skeleton, a rare find since their delicate, lacy carcasses seldom make it to shore in one piece.

In the late afternoon, skin-shriveled and exhausted, we played on the soft, white sand dunes, sea mist dampening our berry-brown faces as the waning light painted the sky purple and pink. No hotels, fast-food joints, or junky shops cluttered the view—only sea oats, sparkling sand dunes, and beaches dotted with small cottages as far as the eye could see.

My dad worked in town during the week but came out to the cottage on the weekends and brought trouble with him. By Friday night, my parents' rowdy drinking friends took over our little piece of heaven. The festivities began on a high note with laughter and music, my father dancing my mother across the sidewalk to Patti Page's *Tennessee Waltz*, but as the night wore on, Jo and I could feel the ground falling out from under us as the people in charge lost control and fights broke out.

Forced into a maturity beyond her years, my sister kept me preoccupied in the tiny cabin bedroom. We listened to the serials, *Fibber McGee and Molly* and my personal favorite, *The Shadow*, on a big console radio. A deep, eerie voice, accompanied by dramatic organ music, announced, "Who knows what evil lurks in the hearts of men... The Shadow knows," and goose bumps danced up and down my arms.

Early Sunday morning as Jo and I headed for a swim, we crossed the sidewalk in front of our cottage and stepped into the sand. Glistening in the sun, amber glass shards and the jagged neck of a beer bottle lay on the ground in front of us. A large circle of dried blood trailed off into the sea oats.

"Careful," Jo said, grabbing my hand. "Don't step on the glass. Someone got hurt here last night." Nights like those ate into all the fun we'd had during the week.

Sunday evening, the four of us sat alone again on the sand watching the setting sun, my parents hung over and brooding. The rest of the summer, Jo and I were packed off to stay with our grandparents in Jacksonville.

MOTHER'S PARENTS:
GRAM AND DADDY MAC

"The greatest wealth is to live content with little."
—Plato

Ida and A.D. McCord, circa 1915

My sister and I made our first eight-hour journey alone on the Greyhound Bus from Panama City to Jacksonville when I was five and she was nine. In the past, our parents had driven us over for the summer, but Mother said we were old enough now to travel unaccompanied. Jo would be in charge. We climbed on the bus with our basket lunch, and she helped me up the big steps to our seats.

As we pulled out of the station, my mom waved to us from the sidewalk. I waved back, but all I could think of was the giant dill pickle packed in our lunch, vacuum-sealed in its own see-through bag, floating in green, briny juice with small slices of garlic dancing in the liquid. Mother had relented, letting Jo and I buy one as a special treat for the trip. I'd have a hard time holding off till lunch, but my rigid taskmaster had control of the basket. I would do what she said, but I didn't have to like it.

The driver and most of the passengers stepped off the bus when we rolled into Tallahassee (halfway), but we stayed in our seats as my mother had instructed and set up our picnic—sandwiches, carrots, chips, and that long-anticipated pickle. I pulled the little tab at the top and began to sip the juice as my eyes watered from the sharp, vinegary taste. Yummy. It had been worth the long wait.

At last, the bus jerked and swayed into the station in Jacksonville. Daddy Mac, at over six feet, towered above my petite grandmother in front of their black 1942 Ford coupe. I jumped up on the seat and waved from the window.

"Look!" I sang out. "There they are! There they are!" We didn't care that they were backward, country people; they were ours and they loved us.

My grandparents looked the same at seventy as they had in their forties—old and gray. A hardscrabble existence and manual labor had left them both worn down at a young age; my grandmother stooped over from the hump on her back. With a "forty acres and a mule" economy, frills were rare. Daddy Mac worked at Moore's Dry Kiln, a lumber yard in town, and Gram spent the day in the garden plowing, planting, or picking. The rest of her day was consumed with cooking, washing, ironing, or attending church. Any social life centered on family and church. According to Gram, God didn't make us to wallow in pleasure; pleasure was the devil's workshop. She had only two indulgences—*The Guiding Light* and *As the World Turns*, TV soaps that aired at noon, each lasting fifteen minutes.

The garden covered over an acre and flourished under the caring hands of my grandparents. Each year they both tilled it with push plows, hand-planting each painstaking seed and watering and fertilizing by hand. Once the planting was finished, my grandmother took over the weeding, watering, and fumigating. In the spring and summer, she stood bent over, harvesting for hours in the blistering sun. Jo and I picked too, and for each bushel of tomatoes, we'd wipe a few off with our shirts and eat them right there in the garden, warm from the sun and dripping with deep, summer flavor.

On the side of the yard, a flower garden full of bountiful blooms in all colors swayed in the afternoon breeze. Thick azaleas loaded with purple and pink flowers surrounded the small house. Blue blossoms the size of dinner plates grew on the hydrangeas, and pear and fig trees bent under their bounty. Long vines of jasmine, wisteria, and honeysuckle hung off the fence, filling the evening air with sweet perfume.

One year when we arrived for the summer, the gardens were withered and brown, rotting in the ground.

"Gram," I called, dashing into the kitchen from outside. "What happened to the garden?"

She wiped her hands on her apron. "Floods from the rains came and took the garden out; it's all gone this year. We never got the first bean." Her eyes watered, but she turned away and went on with her chores. Losing such a valuable asset, not to mention all the gut-busting work they'd put into it, must have been devastating, but neither of my grandparents whined or complained at the random savagery of life.

My memories of Gram are synonymous with the things that were hers: the pink, scratchy living room chair in the corner; little tins of snuff and delicate hankies; her Bible with its black vinyl cover and onion skin pages, and her gaudy Sunday church dresses—taffeta creations in the colors of the rainbow and sweat-stained under the arms. I loved her with the deep, uncomplicated love a child has for a grandparent.

My grandfather built the house in the 1920s according to a blueprint bought from Sears, Roebuck and Co. The lumber came from the sawmill where Daddy Mac worked. I begged to go with him on Saturdays to collect his paycheck and lingered, spellbound by the powerful action of the mighty saws, breathing in the smell of raw, fresh-cut wood stacked miles high. My grandfather sacrificed much of his hearing in that high-decibel, cavernous building.

Their house had two bedrooms, a living room, dining room, and kitchen. Daddy Mac added the inside bathroom in 1935, bringing the square footage to around six hundred. He built a detached garage behind the house where they kept the wringer washing machine. On laundry day, Jo and I watched in awe as Gram fed big, wet wads of clothes into its roller lips to be sucked in and spit out the back as flat as cardboard.

Much of the yearly harvest ended up frozen or in jars. Vegetables filled the chest freezer, and Mason jars with vegetables, fruits, soups, stews, jams, and jellies lined the floor-to-ceiling shelves in the garage. A canning project that massive had to be done in the canning kitchen, a giant carnival tent set up on the fairgrounds nearby. The place was filled with tables, and enormous cauldrons fired up full blast on oversized gas stoves. We loaded the car with bushels of fruits and vegetables, drove over to the fairgrounds, and sat at the tables under the tent, shucking, peeling, and slicing as rivers of sweat poured from us.

Several years after moving into the house, Daddy Mac built the "little house," a one-room dwelling about twenty feet from the back of the main house. Created to house overnight guests, it had three double beds, a table with an oil lantern, and a chest in the corner where Gram stacked the colorful quilts she made at her quilting bees. Old, oxidized sepia portraits of relatives hung on the walls in oval frames, and a single eye-hook latch held the door closed. An imaginary world existed in the brown paper ceiling where water stains, much like clouds, created all kinds of fanciful images. When the cousins came, we begged to sleep together in the little house. Freedom from the prying eyes of adults allowed us to jump on the beds and tell ghost stories late into the night.

The little house had no insulation or heating, and in the winter, you could see puffs of your breath inside, but we didn't mind. We cuddled together, sleeping under mounds of Gram's warm quilts with a toasty-warm water bottle at our feet.

My fondest memories of childhood are the summers with my grand-parents. They were calm, trustworthy, and predictable, elements in short supply at home. Attendance at Macedonia Baptist was mandatory, but the rest of the time, we roamed as free as alley cats.

Diminutive in stature, Gram had a Goliath impact on her family. She wore the pants, and no one wanted to get on her bad side. Quiet but mighty, with a will of iron, she never raised her voice, but if you crossed her moral or religious line, she froze you out and left you begging for forgiveness. When it came to her beliefs, that woman could be rigid and punitive.

When she was younger, my grandmother must have turned heads with her long, lustrous dark hair, sparkling blue eyes, creamy-smooth, white skin, and—as she was proud to tell us—an eighteen-inch waist. But even in his youth, Daddy Mac wasn't a handsome man. Photos of the two of them when they were young begged the question: What had attracted my tiny, winsome grandmother to this Ichabod Crane-like man with big, projecting ears and sunken eyes? His sad, silent presence indicated an invisible burden, but in an unspoken way, he showed infinite patience and kindness to all his grandchildren.

Neither of them was much for talking, but Daddy Mac rarely spoke at all, and when he did, it was in response to Gram's nagging. Each morning, without fail, at 5:30 a.m., the tinkling sound of my grand-father's spoon hitting the sides of the ceramic cup and the odor of propane gas mixed with frying bacon woke me, and I moseyed into the kitchen. Daddy Mac sat at the oil-cloth-covered kitchen table, drinking coffee and waiting for his breakfast. His long, thin crossed legs and angular, lanky upper body resembled a praying mantis as he stirred four rounded teaspoons of sugar into his coffee. My grand-mother, dressed in one of her faded work dresses and an apron, stood at the stove stirring grits and turning bacon.

"Mac, you need to get out in that branch and clear them trees that fell, and I told you yesterday to clean out the garage where you made a mess and how many times do I have to tell you ..." On and on she whirred.

After a few minutes of this, Daddy Mac interrupted and said, "Now that's enough, Ida. I'll get to it directly." Those words and his tone silenced her, but when the chores were untouched a few days later, the exchange turned déjà vu—same words, same reaction.

I watched in fascination when my grandfather chewed his food. His face collapsed, and sometimes the pink ridges of his toothless gums were apparent.

"Gram, why doesn't Daddy Mac have any teeth? Where are they?" I asked her one evening as she fried stew beef for dinner.

She grabbed a dish towel, wiped her hands, and pulled out a kitchen chair. "Well, I'll tell you a story. When Daddy Mac and I was young, we had to have our teeth pulled. That's what they did back then—yanked 'em out. They didn't baby nobody neither. As quick as that last tooth come out, they slapped them hard dentures right in on bleedin' gums." She got up and moved to the sink, spit snuff juice, rinsed it down, wiped her mouth on a hankie, and came back to the table. "When we got in the elevator to go home, as soon as that door shut, Mac reached in his mouth and took them teeth out. He put 'em in a handkerchief, jammed 'em in his pocket, and ain't never put 'em in agin."

"Why did you leave yours in, Gram? Didn't it hurt too much?"

"You bet it hurt, but I wuden about to be a young woman with no teeth."

After that, I watched in amazement as Daddy Mac crunched down on crispy bacon, toast, and even apples and pears. My eyes watered thinking about how painful it must have been in the beginning, teaching gums to be teeth.

Once he retired, my grandfather sat for untold hours, either on the front porch in one of the rockers or on the metal glider in the yard under the pear tree, legs crossed, smoking his roll-your-own Prince

Albert cigarettes, and staring into space.

One afternoon I sat with him on the glider, breathing in the smell of Vitalis and tobacco, and watched his long, leathery fingers roll a cigarette, completing the process with the rapid grace and precision of a flying acrobat. Not even a tiny shred of tobacco escaped as he formed the flawless cylinder in the wink of an eye. The pungent smell of sulfur filled the air as he scratched a Diamond Head match on the underside of the glider, lighting the cigarette with the flame. He drew in a long pull as the paper and tobacco crackled and burned. Unlike the cigarettes of today, the smell was toasty and enticing. It was a magical process—a lost art to my parents' cigarette-package-buying generation.

Many years later, when my sister Pam was in college, she visited me in South Florida, and we sat in my kitchen toking on a joint she'd just rolled. The memory of my grandfather far from my consciousness, I complimented her impeccable rolling skills.

"Well," she said with a smile, "I learned at the feet of the master." We both laughed remembering those days with Daddy Mac.

Our favorite pastime at Gram and Daddy Mac's was hanging out at the swimming hole—a large sinkhole dug eight feet into the earth with steep sides. About a half-mile from their house, it was set back off the road down a woodsy, gravel path that led to an opening and a small bridge over the dark brown water we swam and played in. Black, unctuous soil and tall, moss-draped trees surrounded the swimming hole, keeping it dark even on the sunniest of days. Snakes zigzagged on the ground and in the water sometimes, but they slithered away at our sounds. All the kids from the area were there at one time or another, daring each other to higher feats. Dewey Lee, the neighborhood bad boy who was several years older than me, could be counted on to instigate the boldest challenges, and most of the boys followed suit.

With no adult supervision, parents relied on older siblings to care for the little ones.

One warm, sunny morning, Jo and I were the first to arrive at the swimming hole. Halfway across the bridge, I stopped. The sun beat down through an opening in the trees onto a gigantic pile of black tires.

"Hey, look at all those tires," I said, pointing in the pile's direction.

As we moved closer, Jo screamed, "Oh no! Those aren't tires; they're snakes piled up sunning themselves. They look like moccasins—let's get out of here!" Grabbing me by the arm and turning, she started to run.

"Wait, wait," I said, pulling back and wrangling my skinny wrist away. "Let's go poke them with sticks. Come on, we won't get that close."

Her face twisted in revulsion and she slapped my arm. "Get going, you idiot. Do you want to die today?" When we got home, Jo told Gram about the snakes and what I'd wanted to do. My grandmother chuckled, shaking her head.

Another morning as we reached the small bridge, some of the kids began yelling. "Go back, go back! Dewey Lee's nekked. He's done took all his clothes off."

In my young mind, something powerful and perilous was going on and I tried to twist away from Jo, but she spun me around.

"Don't you dare look at that. You'll go to hell!" she screamed as she began dragging me off the bridge, but not before I caught a glimpse of Dewey Lee and that mysterious, small triangle of dark hair.

Jo, miss goody-two-shoes, bought into all that religious twaddle, but I admired Dewey Lee's gumption and adventurous spirit, and I couldn't understand why my sister always spoiled my fun and kept me on such a short leash. Sometimes she tried to make me feel bad or dumb by controlling me with righteous superiority. Disgusted by my behavior, she walked ten feet ahead all the way home while I grumbled under my breath.

We didn't tell Gram about Dewey Lee. Poking at moccasins was one thing, but seeing a naked boy? Definitely the devil's work. And if she caught a whiff of the devil at the swimming hole, our fun would end on the spot. Several years later, it was a gloomy day on Lenox Avenue when the county closed down the swimming hole for good due to the encroaching polio epidemic.

For a while, in addition to growing all kinds of vegetables, Gram and Daddy Mac also raised chickens. Early in the morning while the mist rolled in, Jo and I would sneak into the henhouse to collect eggs, sometimes removing them from under the hen's warm bottom. But there were two monumental drawbacks to the chickens. One was the malodorous stench that invaded my nostrils at dawn when the dew landed on the chicken shit—a smell that took hours to release its grip on my nose. The other was a nightmarish scene that unfolded on a given Saturday when Gram came from the henhouse with a squawking, flapping chicken under her arm, swung it around by the head, snapping its neck, and laid the carcass on a large tree stump. One precise blow with the axe separated the chicken from its head. But still undead, the headless chicken flew off the stump and ran around the yard, blood spurting up out of its neck.

The platter of crispy fried chicken sitting on the dining room table on Sunday did nothing to erase the memory of the chicken's gruesome demise. We were glad when Gram took down the henhouse and started buying her chicken already butchered from Mr. Griffin's store.

The store—Griffin's, as we called it—sat next door to my grandparents' house and was a one-pump, Pure gas station as well as a butcher shop and a country store. Along with meats and groceries, Mr. Griffin also carried a marvelous variety of candy bars and soft drinks, Moon Pies, and Little Debbie cakes—the basic food groups for a sugar-craving kid. Having a candy emporium next door added to our summer fun since Daddy didn't allow sweets or Cokes in our house.

After swimming all day, Jo and I would take the fifteen cents Gram gave us to Griffin's to make our purchases—a Baby Ruth, PayDay, or Zero candy bar, but always RC Colas. We even adopted the local favorite: a bag of Tom's Salted Peanuts poured into the mouth of your RC Cola for a bubbly, sweet, and salty creation.

Summer afternoons the sky turned indigo and winds whipped in, lowering the temperature several degrees, bending the branches on the tall oak trees, and sending leaves swirling and dancing across the lawn as birds screamed and scattered. From our front-row seats on the porch, we watched lightening split the sky and thunder rumble and crash. Between the sugar rush and the electric charge from Mother Nature, we were wild with exhilaration, rocking in the chairs my grandfather built, rolling back far enough to suspend them on their two back rocker points and flying down into a forward thrust, all the while belting church hymns with the fervor of gospel singers on Sunday morning.

Griffin's store also provided a social destination for kids. We sat out on the split-rail fence talking and teasing while, at one time or another, everyone in the vicinity came and went. Mr. Griffin made moonshine in stills hidden in the woods behind the store, cooking up whiskey, gin, and white lightning. Even though Prohibition ended in the thirties, his pure, strong brand of hooch was popular far and wide.

Although sweet to us, when Mr. Griffin hobbled out from the back of the store where he did his butchering wearing a blood-soaked T-shirt and apron, his florid face set off by wild, snow-white hair, his peg leg thumping on the wooden floors, we approached him with quiet deference. He kept his heavy, molded prosthesis hanging in a prominent spot on the wall, and I beamed with pride at being the lone girl brave enough to touch it. Made of hard, unforgiving material, the straps and buckles crisscrossed in a complicated fashion. Wearing that contraption over his stump must have hurt too much; it reminded me of Daddy Mac's dentures in the soda glass way up on the top shelf in the bathroom....*Some things just weren't worth the pain.*

34

A gentle giant, gracious and accommodating to his customers, Mr. Griffin had a temperament that never changed. But his wife, Mrs. Griffin, who stood shy of five feet, packed a lot of fierceness in her squat presence. Word had it she'd been in an accident and had a steel plate in her head. Her pale-white, saggy face looked clown-like framed with iodine-orange hair, fried and sticking up in all directions. She wore bright fuchsia lipstick painted outside the lines, and a flaming circle of rouge on each cheek. Clumps of black mascara bobbed from her few lashes. One of her blue eyes moved normally, but the other sat disturbingly motionless in the far-left corner. I could never figure out which eye to focus on, and my eyes darted from eye to eye trying to decide.

Occasionally, Gram sent us over to buy her Three Thistles Snuff after closing hours, necessitating a trip to the Griffins' house beside the store. A knock on the door brought Mrs. Griffin and a blue streak of curse words and threats delivered in mind-blistering vocals. Lumbering over to the store, yelling and swearing as we followed, she removed two little round cans from under the counter as we slid two dimes across to her. Slamming the cans down, she yelled, "Now get outta here, you goddamned, sorry-ass young'uns, and don't come back!"

We ran home as fast as we could and flew into the house begging Gram not to send us over there again. "Oh, don't pay her any mind. She can't help it since the accident. She's harmless."

"Well, she may be harmless, but she's as scary as Satan himself," Jo answered.

On the other side of Gram and Daddy Mac's property, Mr. Grobin, a real-life hermit, had no running water or electricity in his shack and went about his chores in the back yard with a safari helmet on his head and nothing else. According to Gram, he was of German ancestry and had returned from the war bad in the head. But she assured us he too was harmless. As a child, I added Mr. Grobin to my detective fantasies, imagining all kinds of covert bomb-making, spying, or traitorous scenarios. By the time I grew into adolescence, peeking at him through the overgrown bushes took on a more voyeuristic purpose for my friends and me.

Years later, after smelling a dead odor emanating from his property, Gram called the police. We all watched as the attendants loaded his exposed body—a slab of meat, black as a raven and decaying—into the ambulance.

Most evenings Gram would sit in the nubby, pink upholstered chair in the living room curled into a "C," the hump on her back like a turtle's shell, and put on her bifocals, careful to wrap the rounded ends behind her ears. Her snuff, spitting jar, and hankie by her side, she'd open her Bible. She told me she'd already finished it once and this was her second attempt. The Bible? An arcane tome that even scholars misinterpreted? Gram, who had left school in fifth grade to help support the family, had rudimentary reading skills. How was it possible? I asked her about that one day and she said the Lord guided her through it and provided understanding. The Bible was the literal truth, every "jot and tittle," she said. If it said Jonah swallowed the whale instead of the other way around, she would still believe it. Never one to miss church on Sunday, she had a long length of pins she attached to her Sunday dresses, each signifying a year of perfect attendance. Despite all this, she kept her faith a personal matter, unlike many of her fellow Baptists who were forever yammering on about "Jesus this" and "my savior that." I respected her take on it.

DADDY'S PARENTS:
GRAMMA ELIZABETH,
BIG POP, AND THE HOUSE
ON THE RIVER

"Let me smile with the wise and feed with the rich."
—Samuel Johnson

Dr. Karl Knoche, DDS
Circa 1950
Big Pop

Elizabeth Daugherty Gilbert Knoche
Circa 1950
Gramma

*M*y paternal grandmother lived with my step-grandfather in a gracious manor on the river in Jacksonville. Gram and Daddy Mac would drop us off sometime during the summer to stay with Gramma Elizabeth and Big Pop for a week. We loved our Gramma Elizabeth, but the fancy, way-too-quiet house required a decorum I found taxing. My grandmother preferred poised, ladylike etiquette— Jo's normal demeanor—but it took great effort for me to squelch my natural exuberance. Making matters worse, Jo and I had no other playmates, and after a few games of Jacks or pick-up-sticks, the squabbles began.

The large house, forged from split logs, didn't resemble your typical log cabin in any way. My grandmother had furnished it with refined, expensive appointments that gave it an elegant, old-money ambiance.

I escaped to the outdoors and spent my days learning to play alone. Phenomenal gardens graced the imposing acreage—terraced aisles of camellias covered in flaming orange, pink, and red flowers; gardenias laden with perfumed blossoms; creamy white magnolias; myriad azaleas; and beds of snapdragons, roses, and peonies. I danced among the long, symmetrical rows of dazzling yellow, aqua, blue, and coral, drinking in the living color. Aged sculptures of nymphs, cherubs, obelisks, and gazing balls dotted the grounds, all resting under the canopy of giant, ancient oaks, captivating in their moss boas.

Delightful smells wafted in the air from the smokehouse, and a separate bakery staffed by their chef who made fresh, organic baked goods. A full-sized, furnished doll house, a swimming-pool-sized fish pond, and the river provided hours of entertainment. Flying high on the rope swing or climbing to the top branch of one of the oaks gave me a view of the entire estate.

Gramma Elizabeth's first husband had abandoned the family when my father was six, leaving her with four children under the age of seven. Daddy, the oldest, took on the role of man of the house, delivering newspapers early in the morning and prescriptions for the local pharmacy after school. The desertion by his father left a hole in Daddy, and he never forgave or forgot, or came to terms with it, holding onto that hurt and rage all his life.

Gramma's well-to-do parents took them in and helped with the kids. Divorced and alone for ten years, my grandmother struggled to raise the children. She met her future husband when Daddy was fifteen and married him a year later. Dr. Knoche ("Big Pop" to us) was a prominent dentist in Jacksonville and a well-known raconteur about town. He moved my grandmother into the house on the river and spared no expense for her. They had a live-in housekeeper, Beulah, a dear woman, as well as a maid who came in twice a week. Their staff also included the cook, the baker, and a battery of gardeners.

An eccentric man, Big Pop was known to be a brilliant, outstanding leader in the world of dental discoveries. He was also a star in The Actors' Theater of Jacksonville and his office at home held a multitude of dramatic awards he'd won over the years. After the marriage, he and my grandmother often appeared as castmates, playing off their chemistry on stage. She adored him, and they were devoted to each other. Considered an interesting couple, their names topped the list of sought-after dinner guests in the homes of the upper crust in Jacksonville.

Tall and stout, Gramma Elizabeth had a mien that suggested breeding and money. Judging from youthful pictures, she'd been naturally pretty, but as she remarked, she'd chosen to grow old gracefully, maintaining the quintessential grandmother look—white-haired and plump. Kind and loving to Jo and me, she even allowed us to explore her jewelry chest and admire the dazzling gems. We whispered as we fingered the opals, diamonds, and emeralds, many of them set in custom designs. Jo had a sense of propriety that I lacked and would slap my arm, saying, "Don't throw those around. You need a gentle touch when placing them back in the chest the way you found them. God, you're impossible."

A skilled seamstress, Gramma made exquisite clothes for Jo's dolls fashioned from leftover scraps of satin, silk, and fur. I had no use for dolls, but I adored the beautiful red and green taffeta Christmas dresses she made us every year. I felt like a princess in her creations and fought to wear them long after the holiday.

Sitting in her lap, the most comfortable seat in the house, I rested my head on her shoulder as she read to me. But her beautiful, dark-brown eyes would flare when I misbehaved. "Act like a lady this minute," she'd say, "and stop 'showing the burnt side of your shirt.'"

My step-grandfather, a robust character, had a habit of running his fingers through his wavy, reddish-white hair and wiping his flushed, sweaty face with a monogrammed hankie. Fond of oration, he spoke with dramatic flair in a loud, booming voice and had a large, strident presence. Though we had to sit and listen, his discourses were lost on me. I'd overheard my parents' whisperings about his genius status and his membership in the Communist party. Maybe that explained his weirdness.

With a prescient passion for healthy eating, he had us carve open our drumstick bones and suck out the marrow, the most nutritious part, he said. The bakery-fresh wheat bread in their house was shot full of all kinds of weird seeds and nuts, but Jo and I longed for the Merita white bread waiting for us at Gram's.

We sat for dinner at the long, polished dining room table while the cook served us a variety of unusual foods, things we'd never heard of and didn't like. I pushed my food around, mashed it together, and slipped it under the table to the dog or into my napkin. One evening, a strange disk of eggplant sitting alone on my plate had begun to take on the appearance of human flesh and I couldn't bear to bring it to my lips.

"Eat your eggplant," Big Pop bellowed.

A meek little mouse, I looked up and said, "I don't like it."

"Yes, you do. You haven't even tasted it," he said, and he slapped his massive hand down on the table. "Now go on and take a bite."

Conversation ceased. All eyes on me, I put a small piece of the nasty-looking thing in my mouth. Biting down, I gagged and vomited my dinner onto the plate. Despite my grandmother's objections, Big Pop sent me to my room. Silent tears slid down my face as I sat shamefaced on the bed. From that point on, I made myself as tiny as a seed in his presence.

When our days there came to an end, Gram and Daddy Mac would drive over in their black Ford to take us back to the other side of the tracks. I can still picture Gram sitting in Gramma Elizabeth's grandiose living room waiting for Jo and me. The chair she sat in was an expensive, turn-of-the-century behemoth, flared on the sides and back, upholstered in embroidered gold brocade, and adorned with carved maple rose motifs. Lost in the sheer volume of the chair, Gram's feet dangled in the air. Clad in a discount-store dress and run-down shoes, gripping her plastic purse to her chest, she looked self-conscious and out of place. I ran over, jumped in her lap, and hugged her tightly. It hurt to think how hard they worked and how little they had.

At the end of summer, our parents drove over from Panama City to take us home. Jo and I waved to Gram and Daddy Mac out the back window, sad to leave. We would miss our grandparents, the Faulkner-ish surroundings, and the calm and stability of Lenox Avenue.

PANAMA CITY
1949–1960

"Buildings go up and structures come down. New streets and lanes appear, landscapes transform and people depart, but a hometown never changes in the mind and heart."
—Sherry O'Neill

I was four the spring we moved into our first house, a small, three-bedroom, one-bath, red-brick box on Fairland Avenue. Every house in the neighborhood had the same layout—a simple plan born in the post-war construction era that took the guesswork out of finding your neighbor's bathroom when you visited. But the metal cut-out of a white flamingo standing in long, wavy, white metal grass affixed to our front screen door gave our little box cachet in a sea of little boxes. A tiny patch of yard and three concrete steps led up to the front door. Most families on the block had three or four kids, and a gaggle of us played tag, Red Rover, and Simon Says in the field of weeds and tall reeds across the street from our house.

The following September, Mother and I took Jo to school on the first day. St. Andrew Elementary, a vast, ancient two-story building covering a city block, looked decrepit and foreboding. I had turned five a few months before and was glad I had another year at home with my mother.

I waved to Jo as her teacher took her hand and led her to the classroom while Mother smiled and chatted with the one-armed principal, Dr. Milam. I stood to the side studying the complicated yet precise way his pressed and creased shirt fastened in the back to create a clean, custom look on his stump.

"Sherry!" my mother said, calling me over. "Yes, Dr. Milam, this is

Sherry, Jo's sister. This will be wonderful. They're inseparable, and she'd be lost at home without her. She's very bright and I know she'll do well. I'll get those papers to you in a few weeks."

I grabbed her shirt in alarm, "What, what are you talking about?"

She smiled her most June Cleaver smile and said, "You're starting school today too. Isn't that wonderful? Thank you, Dr. Milam. I'll take her to her room now." She swept me up and out of the crowd of mothers trying to have a moment with the handsome Dr. Milam.

By the time we arrived at the classroom, I was in full-throated screaming, crying, and snot-slinging mode, pleading with my mother not to leave me. Ignoring my hysterics, she kept the TV smile plastered on her face.

"You'll be fine," she said in dulcet tones. "School is fun and you'll love it. You'll see."

The enormous classroom and towering ceiling reduced the children to tiny dolls. A few of them sniffled, but I took the award for most out-of-control first grader. I sobbed and clung to my mother with a death grip while she grappled to extricate my fingers and place me in the small desk. My wailing had set off a few of the other children, and the pinched-faced teacher glared at us.

"She'll calm down when you leave," she said to my mother. "Please go." I howled even louder, arms outstretched in an attempt to call back my last bastion of security. To this day, the sounds and smells of an elementary school can transport me back to that vast, uncontrollable world of first grade.

To enroll me in school, Mother had lied about my age, telling Dr. Milam I was six (birth certificate or another legal document to be provided later). After a few weeks, the entire episode became a fait accompli, any need for a birth certificate lost in the shuffle. But my mother reminded me to smile when the class sang "Happy Birthday" to me on my "start-school-early," pretend birthday in December.

I cried all day long in school for two weeks, but by the third week, the tears drained off around lunchtime when Daddy picked me up in front of the school. Jo preferred to lunch with the other fourth graders in the cafeteria, but I couldn't wait to fling the car door open and bounce into the seat next to my father.

"Daddy! Quick! Put on *Helen Trent*," I exclaimed. It was a fifteen-minute soap opera we listened to on the way home. The over-the-top promo, "…*when life mocks her, breaks her hopes, dashes her against the rocks of despair, she fights back bravely*…" wiped away my teary morning.

Despite a shaky start, by the end of first grade, I had grown to love school and learning. In the third grade, after reading my first *Nancy Drew* chapter book, I developed a wolfish appetite for the printed word. "An early reader," the teacher called me with pride. Words held a fascination for me, and once I discovered the pleasure of sinking into a story surrounded by words, the outdoors no longer beckoned.

On a freezing day that December of first grade, I rode the city bus alone for the first time. I was five. My mother had an appointment and couldn't pick me up from school, but that morning she breezed through the explanation, emphasizing how easy it would be.

"Once you get on the bus for home, all you have to do is stand on the seat and pull the buzzer overhead one block before our street. How tough can that be?" she asked. "Now don't make a production out of this."

I couldn't read yet, but I recognized the word "Harris," the block before our street. Jo and I had taken the bus many times together, and Mother assumed I could do it, but I begged and cried, "Please, please don't make me ride the bus by myself. I can't do it. I'm too scared."

She smiled. "Yes, you can. It's a snap. No more arguing. You're a big girl now."

On the bus that afternoon, jittery with anticipation as my street approached, I froze and hesitated a second too long. We whizzed by Fairland Avenue and I watched, paralyzed. Collapsing into the corner of the seat, I rode all afternoon, quiet and still so as not to be found out. As dusk approached, one by one, passengers rang the buzzer and stepped off the bus. When we pulled into the dark bus station parking lot—the end of the line—I was the lone passenger. The driver parked and sat in his seat writing on a piece of paper. I walked slowly down to the front of the bus.

"Where'd you come from?" he said as he looked up, startled. Through tears, I attempted to explain what had happened. He patted my head like I was a puppy and said, "There, there, it's okay. We'll get you home for supper. Let's go in and see if anyone has called in a missing little girl. I bet your mom and dad are frantic. How old are you, anyway?"

I sat in the hard plastic chair, sniffling and choking back sobs as I tried to listen to the muffled voices from the adjacent office. The driver came around the corner smiling.

"Yep, like I said, your mom called and they're coming to get you."

When Daddy opened the glass doors, I jumped up and ran to him. "I was so scared, Daddy."

He picked me up and patted my back, saying, "It's okay, shug, you're okay now." I laid my head on his shoulder and relaxed into the comforting, minty fragrance of Aqua Velva.

At home, we met my mom in the kitchen, stirring dinner over the stove. She chuckled as she looked down at me.

"Well, you must've had some adventure," she said. I scowled at her.

"Geez, Christine. You should know she's too young to be riding a city bus alone," Daddy said as he passed through the kitchen.

In the early days, my father was who I could count on—much more than my mother. Although he worked long hours, when he was around, he took a more active part in my life, listening and answering questions and tucking us in at night. He had strict rules and high expectations, but he could be playful and affectionate too.

In the second grade, I couldn't seem to grasp the concept of telling time from a clock. Stern and impatient, my teacher jabbed one of her long, pointy fingernails into the page of my textbook, peeved that I didn't understand. At dawn one school morning, I rose after a fitful night and took my textbook out to the little stoop off the kitchen to study. In a few minutes, my father came out and sat down beside me.

"What's the matter, skeeter?" he said as he put his arm around my shoulder. When I explained my problem, he picked me up and hugged me, saying, "It'll be okay, we'll learn it together," and he set about teaching me.

My mother parented the same way she'd been raised, with little open affection. I don't recall her ever hugging or kissing us, and yet I'm sure she must have, but she lacked the maternal posture I'd carefully observed with my friends' mothers. I knew she loved me, but she was often distracted, impatient, or critical with Jo and me. When we came in crying with a gash or a bump on our heads, she'd give the injury a cursory glance and declare, "You're fine. Go back out and play." A quick hug or kiss to acknowledge our misfortune didn't happen. Even though I loved her intensely, in my young eyes, she had no gift for mothering.

Loretta Young helped me get the attention I craved from my parents, if only for a few minutes. She was an actress and hostess of a popular weekly TV show in the fifties. Decking myself out with scarves and costume jewelry, I became Loretta, creating a glorious grand entrance, imitating her over-dramatized looks, words, and movements, putting on a show for my parents and their friends. I had them in the palm of my hand and basked in the warm glow of approval as laughter, clapping, and calls for an encore rang through the house. "You're one of a kind, Sher," Daddy would comment, laughing.

Looking back, I can see I took on the role of a peacekeeping, smile-making counterweight to the tension and unhappiness in our family, dancing as fast as I could, giving them what they wanted—trying to make our family *normal*.

Like most children, I prized fun and laughter, but my personality leaned toward the intense and overly sensitive. Way too empathetic, I carried the weight of all the underdogs and outsiders on my small shoulders. No one had to tell me to be kind to those less fortunate; they broke my heart. And, unlike my sister Jo, who sloughed off Mother's heavy-shame parenting style, I grew a big tumor of guilt hearing the words, "I'm ashamed of you."

One afternoon when I was six, after overhearing a conversation between the older kids about the reality of Santa Claus, I came in the house and shoved a Bible I'd retrieved from the shelf at my mother.

"If I ask you an important question, will you swear on this Bible to tell the truth?"

Loading clothes in the washing machine, she stopped and said, "What's this all about?"

"But will you promise to tell the truth?" I demanded.

"Oh, for heaven's sake, lighten up, will you? You're too intense. Ask me what you want and stop being ridiculous."

"Is Santa real or is it you and Daddy?" I demanded, staring at her with a stern expression and holding the Bible aloft.

Blowing out a long, slow breath and, pondering two equally unpleasant answers, she said, "Yes, it's me and Daddy. Are you happy now?"

I walked back to the living room and replaced the Bible. Cynical little kid that I was, I'd suspected as much—but at least the truth explained why our Christmas presents were heavy on necessities and light on toys.

When I was seven, a spell of what I called bad thoughts took root in my head and grew more persistent and uncontrollable. The harder I tried *not* to think of them, the more forceful they became. I tossed and turned many nights as disturbing thoughts and images jittered in my brain like trash in a gust of wind. After a few weeks, I broke down in tears to my mother. We sat on the couch and I told her about my bad thoughts—seeing our neighbor in his yard and picturing a hole in his pants that allowed me to see his private parts; how I'd seen the bad word f-u-c-k scratched on the bathroom door at the five-and-dime store and now my mind said it over and over; how I was a bad person destined for hell; how someone would come in and kill us; or how one of us would die of a horrible disease. No matter how hard I tried, I told her, I couldn't stop them. A worried look flickered across her face, but she assured me the thoughts were silly, that thoughts themselves weren't good or bad, and that nothing of the kind would happen. We were safe, healthy, and Daddy would take care of us.

I wiped my eyes and exhaled a deep breath. Her absolution helped me let go; if she called them nonsense, then maybe they were. But later that evening, as I skulked around the corner, I overheard my parents talking as Mother explained to Daddy what I'd told her. She favored taking me to a psychiatrist, but my father shouted, "Are you kidding? That's ludicrous. She doesn't need a psychiatrist, for Christ's sake. It's a phase. Don't make a mountain out of a molehill, Christine."

The problem resolved sometime after, but a pattern of compulsivity and accompanying guilt had made an inroad into my psyche

Daddy's Girl - Sherry O'Neill

DADDY'S GIRL

"I cannot think of any need in childhood
as strong as the need for a father's protection."
—Sigmund Freud

The most handsome movie star couldn't hold a candle to my father with his Superman blue-black, shiny hair; dark eyes that dazzled like polished onyx; sparkling-white, perfect teeth; and a smile that lit up the room. From the earliest days, I was his shadow, clinging to him, walking with him on the top of his shoes, even imitating his mannerisms. I used to say when I grew up that he would be *my* husband. But Daddy also had a dark side and a quick-fire temper.

On one of our frequent rides together, I stood next to him in the seat, arm on the back of his shoulder.

"Do you think it's bad if I love you more than Mother?" I asked.

He laughed and said, "You love your mom, shug. She's a great mom."

"I didn't say I didn't love her; I love her a lot. But I love you more."

He smiled and told me how much he loved me too. Relieved, I laid my head on his shoulder and let the worry drift out the window. We rode along for a while, windows open, listening to the melancholy ballads of country music on the radio. He lit a cigarette with the glowing red end of a cylinder that popped out of a hole in the dashboard and, as he often did, began to tell me a story, a modern Aesop's fable.

"My good friend Bill and I had an argument and we stopped speaking. I made up my mind to call him and put our disagreement to rest. But I got busy and didn't get around to it. Can you imagine how sorry I was when I got the news Bill had been killed in a car accident?" He blew smoke out the window, pursed his lips, and said, "That was a sad day. I've never forgiven myself for not apologizing." He flicked his cigarette out the window and continued. "Always apologize when you've done something wrong. Don't let time go by," he cautioned, "because you never know when the opportunity to say you're sorry will be taken from you."

Wide-eyed, I nodded as I took in this narrative. Daddy was the smartest, wisest person in the world. He could tell a riveting story, and there were many more in his attempt to teach me right from wrong.

Until the age of about eight or nine, most Saturday mornings I accompanied my father to his shop, James Electronics. The olive-green, one-room house that doubled as his business sat at the foot of a bridge and was tucked back from the road under giant, enveloping oaks filled with hundreds of birds. A symphony of chirps and tweets greeted us as we pulled up next to the shop. The trees gave the scene an unnatural darkness, and burst seedpods, fallen acorns, and brown withered leaves piled on the ground, reincarnating as ripe, black soil. I wandered the shadowy outdoors, lost in a make-believe world, imagining mysterious scenarios and eerie characters, stalking for clues like my alter ego, *The Shadow*.

Inside, I played with tiny, colorful parts and snooped in countless boxes of interesting-looking mechanical gadgets that filled Daddy's shop. Saturday mornings meant me and my favorite person in the world, talking and listening to Hank Williams, Patsy Cline, and Dad's favorite, Ernest Tubb, on the radio.

Even at a young age, I was aware of a disparity between the way Daddy treated me and my sister. They didn't seem to share the same warm, comfortable relationship. It was a subtle difference, but it bothered me. Protective of her feelings, I mentioned this to my father, but he brushed off my distress, saying, "You're the baby; the baby always gets all the attention. Jo understands that."

One afternoon not long after, Aunt Corrine and Uncle Leon and our two cousins, Dolores and Ellen, stopped in to visit on their way to Jacksonville. Jo and Dolores were the same age, eleven, and Ellen was three years my junior. My mother's older sister, Corrine, a bitter woman, had an enormous chip on her shoulder. Out of earshot of my parents, she disparaged them to Jo and me, and frequently pulled me aside to whisper, "Are your parents drinking? Tell me right now. To think I had to drop out of school to work and your mother got to graduate. And what's she done with her life? Nothing. Hangs around with her drunken friends and boozes it up." Crossing her arms over her chest, she'd glare at me, waiting for an answer. Her *concern* didn't fool me, and I skittered away; after all, *she* was no powerhouse of ambition—I'd never known her to even have a job. She intentionally passed her animosity to her children, and none of us liked each other, but for my grandmother's sake, we pretended.

The four of us kids went out to the backyard for a game of one potato, two potato. We settled in the grass and put up our fists. As the game went around, without warning, Dolores shot me a haughty look.

"You know Jo isn't your full sister," Dolores said. "She had a different daddy. She's only your *half* sister." We all stopped in midair, and I looked at Jo. Her face flushed and her eyes filled as she jumped up and ran to the back door.

Scrambling up from the grass, I screamed at Dolores, "I hate you!" and ran in the house. I found Jo on her bed, crying into the pillow. "What does that mean?" I asked her. "You're not my full sister?"

She rolled over, wiping her eyes. "It's true. I had a different daddy, but Mama is my mother. That's called a half sister." We hugged, and I told her she was the best sister ever, better than a whole one.

Standing in the living room, I interrupted the adults who were sipping iced tea and talking. "Dolores just told me Jo was my half sister, that she had a different daddy. I don't understand." My mother gasped and put her hand over her mouth and my father's dark eyes flared.

"That's one malicious daughter you've got there Corrine," my mother told her sister.

"Well, Christine, you should have told her and none of this would have happened. It's *your* fault," my aunt countered. Uncle Leon, uncomfortable with confrontation, rushed his family out to the car and they were gone.

No amount of questioning could pry much information from my parents.

"Your mom's first husband died and then we married. End of story," my father said.

Years later, Gram told us Christine had gotten pregnant with Jo at nineteen and had to marry Cecil, a musician and hard drinker who died in his twenties of cirrhosis *after* they were divorced. When my father married my mother, Jo was three years old. He legally changed her last name, and they buried the truth and kept the secret.

I accepted the new knowledge at face value; it had no effect on my love for Jo, and I never considered her anything less than my sister. But the episode left its mark. All of a sudden, I was aware that my parents were capable of keeping secrets and lying. A tiny seed of mistrust lodged in my brain. What else had they hidden? We went on as if it hadn't happened, but after that, I watched my father in a different way, making sure he treated Jo the same as he treated me.

IS THERE A GROWNUP IN THE HOUSE?

"One of the pitfalls of childhood is…by the time the mind
is able to comprehend what has happened,
the wounds of the heart are already too deep."
—Carlos Zafon, *The Shadow of the Wind*

Mother and Daddy had been boozy partiers for as long as I could remember. Even in our first house, some of my earliest memories are colored by the loud, turbulent blowouts that happened on the weekends. I'd climb into bed with Jo, put the pillow over my head, and rub my foot back and forth on the cotton sheet, reciting *Cinderella* or *Snow White* in my head. The wild partying, excessive drinking, and fighting gave me a lingering apprehension, an unquantifiable foreboding. But as harrowing as the weekends were, they had the unquestioned nature of a given, and Jo and I relied on Monday to bring life back to order.

Sunday mornings, groggy and sleep-deprived, my sister and I would tiptoe out to the living room and attempt to restore normalcy. While our parents slept off their hangovers, we'd empty and wash ashtrays, glasses, and dishes, throw away all the beer and liquor bottles, and put the house back together.

After we finished, in an effort to save my soul, Jo would guilt me into taking the bus with her to The First Baptist Church downtown. Sunday school and church were frightening (eternal damnation in the fiery pit) and demeaning to me. One time, after a Bible lesson on creation, I raised my hand and asked the Sunday school teacher the burning question I'd been holding in: "Okay, but who made God?"

The teacher, a plump hen dressed in her too-tight, green taffeta shirtwaist dress and smelling of Coty face powder, jerked me aside and scolded me for asking such a naughty question. "You should be ashamed," she said. "The Lord doesn't like disrespectful children." Even though I squeezed my eyes tight, tears slipped out and I covered my face with both hands.

In another Sunday school class, after a long rant on the evils of alcohol, a different teacher ushered me to a far corner and whispered, "Do your mother and father drink alcohol, even beer? That's a sin, you know. The Bible says the wages of sin is death and damnation to the lake of fire. Do you want your parents to burn in Hell for eternity? If not, you'd better tell me."

How could she know, or was it a lucky guess? Her question, although terrifying, was snoopy and reminded me of Aunt Corrine's interrogations. The teacher stood with her arms crossed over her large bosom, waiting. Defiant, I refused to answer.

"Well, you can stay there until you decide to give me an answer," she huffed and walked away. I stayed in the corner.

For my parents, partying on the weekends came as natural as church on Sunday for most families. If they didn't host the spree at our house, Jo and I found ourselves thrashing around in some stranger's bed, trying to sleep while raucous, drunken noise permeated paper-thin walls. We complained to our parents, but the words banged around in empty air until one evening my mother made the decision to leave us at home alone.

"We'll be home later—you can stay up until nine," she said. Beautiful in her slim-fitting designer dress, she trailed a cloud of Chanel No. 5 as she passed us on the couch. I'd come to associate the scent with dread since she only wore it for parties.

Right behind her, my father gave us a stern look and said, "Don't open the door to anyone, and no fighting."

Staying home alone, although preferable, was scary for me. At seven, I still needed the comfort of an adult at night. Jo checked all the windows and doors to make sure they were locked, closed the blinds, and turned on the TV. At nine o'clock sharp, she switched off the television and ushered us back to our bedrooms.

"I want to sleep with you tonight, please?" I begged. After a sigh and an eye roll, she agreed. We climbed into her bed, and I rolled over, hoping I could fall asleep before my unease turned to pounding fear.

At around 5 a.m., drifting between the half-life of dreams and the reality of the rising sun, I hurtled from bed and dashed into my parents' room. Staring at the uncreased, still-made bed, I screamed, "Jo! Jo! Wake up! Wake up! They never came home last night."

Still sleepy, she walked toward me rubbing her eyes. "Are you sure?"

We walked out to the living room to sit on the couch and wait. "What are we going to do now?" I cried. "What if they never come home? Will we have to go to an orphanage? What will happen?"

She looked out the front window, brows furrowed, and said, "Be quiet and wait. What else can we do? Maybe they got in a car accident, maybe they're in jail, I don't know." We came and went from the couch, looking out the window, bickering, and waiting on pins and needles for the phone to ring or a police car to pull into the driveway. Already a serious nail-biter, I chewed and gnawed my fingers till they bled. A warm rush of relief washed over me in the afternoon when we heard their car pull up.

"Thank God they're home," Jo muttered under her breath as we peered out the window.

"But why is she driving? Daddy always drives," I said.

Mother got out and came around the passenger's side, opened the door, and helped my father out. A large white turban circled his head and he hobbled up the steps. Jo and I scurried to the door, jerked it open, and shrieked in unison, "Where have you been?" Gasping, my sister stared at our father and whispered, "What happened?"

He had black, blue, and red bruises all over his swollen face, and one eye was the size and color of a plum. The turban revealed itself to be a mound of gauzy bandages wrapped all the way around his head, down to his ears. Blood seeped through the gauze and trickled down behind his ear. He limped through the living room with his head turned, holding his side. The bedroom door closed firmly behind him.

Mother's colorful Pucci dress had a rip and blood smeared down the front.

"Mom, what happened?" Jo demanded again.

She sighed, and as if reciting the Pledge of Allegiance, said, "Oh, Daddy got in a fight at the party with a guy who had a gun. The guy pistol-whipped him within an inch of his life. We've been at the hospital getting X-rays and stitches. I'm tired. I'm going to bed. Go out and play." That was it ... business as usual.

Their careless disregard for us had created a "no one cares about me" belief that submerged into my young, tender skull. I went to my bedroom, closed the door, and sat on the edge of the bed, wounded and small. We learned early and often that our feelings didn't matter.

It was Christmas morning and Jo woke me early.

"Let's go look under the tree, but be quiet. Don't wake them up," she cautioned. We'd have hell to pay if we did. I looked at the sparse grouping of wrapped gifts—no doubt underwear, socks, pajamas, and a small toy or two, nothing to raise much interest. Then I spied a shiny blue bicycle standing in the corner with a big red bow on it.

I squeaked, "Look, a bike!" and ran over to inspect it. The tag said, *To: Sherry, From: Santa*, but I recognized it as Jo's bicycle, the one she'd taught me to ride a few months before. I didn't care; wheels meant freedom to travel places I couldn't go on foot. Because the bike had seen little action, it still looked new. Ignoring the offerings under the tree, I zipped back to my bedroom, threw on some clothes, hurried back to the living room, and rolled the bike out the front door and down the steps. Off I went, flying up and down our long street, standing to reach the pedals, going as fast as I could. Cold, sleety wind tossed my hair about, and frigid air filled my lungs, but what I remember most was the feeling of freedom, endlessness, and possibilities. My sister stood at the window watching, and I waved to her as I raced by. She had come through for me, and life would never be the same now that I had mechanized movement.

Later that day, we were leaving for Jacksonville to celebrate with Gramma Elizabeth and Big Pop. The trip was usually the highlight of Christmas, but this year I didn't want to leave my bike. When Daddy woke and ambled into the living room scratching his hairy chest, I ran to him, extolling the thrill of riding my new bike and grumbling it would be a whole week before I could ride it again. He hugged me, saying, "You'll have lots of years to ride it. We'll be back in a week. You always love Christmas in Jacksonville."

I did. There would be no drinking, no wild parties or fights, real gifts instead of necessities, beautiful spreads, and the love and attention of my grandmother. It was one of the few times we were free to act like children because the adults behaved like adults. The luscious aroma of fresh-baked bread, pies, and turkey roasting in the oven and the glittering abundance of shiny decorations created a Christmas wonderland. Lying next to the massive, floor-to-ceiling tree, staring at the baubles and lights dancing and shimmering to the rhythm of the Christmas music, I was swept into a warm, dreamy bliss.

That year at bedtime, when I curled up next to Jo in the antique four-poster bed in the guest room, I dreamed about my new bike and the places I'd ride it. Over the years, I would cycle many miles, from sunup till sundown, an explorer, free and brave under a vast blue sky. In my teen years, it offered escape and yearned-for breathing room.

But the next year, Christmas turned out to be anything but merry. Jo and I stood in our living room by the tree whispering and examining presents, while Mother and Daddy slept off gold-medal hangovers from the bedlam the night before. For some long-forgotten reason, my sister and I began to argue.

My parents' bedroom door opened, and my father stuck his head out. "Pipe down, you two, or I'll come out there and teach you a lesson."

We quieted for a few minutes, but something set us off again, and from nowhere, my father appeared, grabbed us both by the arm, and dragged us down the hall and into Jo's bedroom. He flung us on the bed, snatched the belt he had hanging around his neck, and proceeded to give us a strapping. Whipping the belt from Jo to me, he whaled on us with adrenaline-fueled fury, drawing red and blue welts. We cried and twisted around on the bed attempting to avoid the blows.

"Daddy, please stop! I promise I'll be good. I promise, Daddy, please," I sobbed.

Jo cried and pled with him to stop too, but my father, overcome with animal ferocity, landed one blow after the other, grunting each time the strap met skin and saying, "Take that! You two don't listen and I'm sick of your fighting." Daddy was strong and he wielded the belt with intention. Finally, he backed up, face red and still warped into a gnarled rope of rage. "I bet you'll listen the next time I tell you to quiet down," he said in a satisfied tone. Jo and I lay on the bed sobbing in pain.

I'd had a few spankings in my life, but nothing this violent. My father had taken his hangover out on us, and the thought of that hurt almost as much as the large, swollen welts throbbing with blood and fire. The atmosphere that day retained a chill that no amount of heat could warm, and even though Daddy had extracted his revenge, his mood remained sullen. A deathlike pall hung over the entire day.

My legs stung for a week and sitting down or taking a bath made me wince in agony. Scabs crusted at the edges of the black bruises covering our backsides, but the emotional pain of what he'd done was much slower to heal.

BABIES
1953

"We owe our children, the most vulnerable citizens
in our society, a life free of violence and fear."
—Nelson Mandela

*I*t was Saturday morning and my mom danced around to Glenn Miller on the record player as she bustled from room to room, filling the house with the smell of furniture polish and Windex. Dressed in her old brown pedal pushers, she wore one of Daddy's ragged shirts and a kerchief tied around her head. She wiped out an ashtray and leaned toward me.

"Can you keep a secret?" she whispered.

"Yes, what is it?"

Placing the ashtray back on the table, she said, "Guess what? You're going to have a little sister or brother—would you like that?"

"What? Where will you get it?" I asked, astonished.

She smiled and said, "The stork will bring it, remember?"

Oh yeah, that's right, the stork. I'd forgotten all about him. My mother's excitement spilled over onto me, and I started skipping and dancing around, chanting, "We're getting a ba-by, we're getting a ba-by." A warm smile lit up her face.

A few days later, I overheard Mother talking on the phone to Gram and picked up on the word *pregnant*. What a strange new word. After she hung up, I asked her what it meant.

"It means I'm going to be a mommy again."

That night in the bathtub, I said the word over and over to myself. To seven-year-old ears, it sounded sophisticated, and I couldn't wait to use it.

The next day after school, I went down the street to play with my friend Lynn Williams. Her mom offered us some cookies and milk before we went outside, and we sat at the table enjoying our snack. The new word popped into my head and I blurted out, "Guess what? My mom's *pregnant*."

Scrunching up her nose and looking perplexed, Lynn said, "What's that?"

Before I could answer, Mrs. Williams came charging over to the table, glared at me, and said, "If you were my daughter, I'd wash your mouth out with soap right this minute. Go home now. We don't talk that way in this house. Shame on you. Go home and don't come back."

The cookie fell from my mouth mid-bite, and I scooted out of their house. *Did I get it wrong, or maybe say it wrong?* But no, that was the word my mother had used. I came in our front door crying and told her the story.

"Oh, for god's sake, what the hell is wrong with people around here? And, no, you didn't say anything wrong. What kind of mother is she anyway?" Then she slowly turned and looked at me hard, pointing her finger. "You promised not to tell anyone and that's your punishment." My first brush with karma.

Mother curtailed her drinking during the pregnancy, and the wild parties slowed down. Expectation filled the air, and the four of us had a little bounce in our step. My mother's thin midsection began to expand and soon it looked as if she had a beach ball under her shirt. *A baby, in there?* The questions were endless, but I didn't dare ask them after my run-in with Mrs. Williams. This baby stuff was dicey territory.

A couple of days after school let out for the summer, Daddy woke Jo and me in the middle of the night. He had to take Mother to the hospital—soon we'd have a new brother or sister. I yelped with delight as my mother stood in the doorway with her suitcase.

The next morning, Daddy rushed through the front door and over to the table where Jo and I were eating breakfast. With a big grin, he put his hand on my shoulder and said, "You won't believe it. You girls have a little baby sister and she has red hair."

"Wow!" I leaped from the chair consumed with excitement, slinging myself around in St. Vitus-like movements.

Jo took a bite of toast and told me to sit down and be quiet. Bemused, she looked at Daddy and said, "Red hair? That's weird." Then she looked back at her cereal bowl.

Daddy laughed and replied, "Yeah, isn't it? But she's a beauty. I'll take you two to the hospital tomorrow and your mama can hold her up to the window so you can see her."

"Yippee!" I said with genuine delight. Jo's joyless smile reminded me of the one painted on her doll's face. This obviously wasn't her first rodeo.

CRUMBLING FOUNDATIONS
Panama City
1954–1959

"We do survive every moment, after all, except the last one."
—John Updike

*L*ife took on a new rhythm after the baby came home. I had to move into Jo's room to create space for a nursery, but I didn't mind since I slept with her half the time anyway. But Jo bristled at the idea. A persnickety neatnik, my sister even kept her drawers sorted with military exactness. She made her bed with sharp corners each morning and hung up all her clothes, leaving nothing out of place. On my side of the room, clothes ended up piled on the floor and hanging out of the jammed drawers. Covers were balled to one side or kicked off, homework and books were strewn about, and an empty milk glass on the nightstand vied for room with wadded-up tissues. We shared a closet, too, and you could see where her neat row stopped and my disarray began.

A fight erupted one afternoon when she'd had all she could take of my slovenliness. She came over to my bed where I sat reading and began to slap my arms, telling me how disgusting I was and that she hated me. I grabbed her hair and pulled out a hunk, and she scraped her nails across my shoulder, breaking the skin. I bit down hard on her finger and she let out a howl.

Hearing the ruckus, my mother raced into the room and broke us up.

"Damn it, Sherry! Clean up your side of the room right this minute," my mother bellowed. "For Christ's sake, where is your pride? You're not a pig living in a sty. Your father works hard to give you a nice place to live and clothes on your back. *I'm ashamed of you.*" The shame part acted as a period at the end of all her scoldings.

At 6 p.m. when Daddy arrived home, Mother met him at the door and filled him in on the latest drama.

"Sherry, come out here right this minute," he yelled. I was in trouble, but with Daddy, you could never predict how much trouble, depending on his mood. Would I get a mild reprimand that ended with his arm around my shoulder and the parting words, "Try to do better, okay, shug?" Or would his temper explode all over me?

I took the walk of shame into the living room to find out. He grabbed me by the arm, slammed me onto a seat, put his face close to mine, and, roaring like a cannon firing black gunpowder in my face, said, "Your attitude is going to change or you're going to find yourself in a world of hurt. I've had it with your disgusting behavior and I'm through tolerating it." He concluded with a scary ultimatum. Poking his finger close to my face, he said, "This is going to stop, or else. And you don't want to know what 'or else' is. Do you hear me?"

I was timid in the face of my father's thundering, and the confrontations left me gutted, filled with remorse. But after a week or two, I would relapse. I was a daydreamer by nature, and my eyes didn't see the messiness.

The new baby had a set of lungs that would have made Maria Callas proud. My mother walked the floor with her at night, patting and cooing, but she squalled nonstop. During the day, she calmed down, giving us a goofy, toothless grin and squealing. A beautiful baby, Pam had a pie-shaped face, deep green eyes, and a dusting of orange fuzz on her head.

Once she started crawling around, the nighttime turmoil dwindled, and Jo and I delighted in playing with her. We took her for walks in the afternoon in her little carriage, and someone invariably stopped to remark what a beautiful baby we had. But even before she hit two, she had a will of iron and a defiant nature. The slightest provocation sent her into fits and ear-scalding shrieks.

One Sunday afternoon less than a year later, Jo and I sat in our bedroom listening to the radio with our door open. The muffled sounds of our parents' conversation drifted into the room, and we could make out enough to glean that they were talking about moving. Later that evening, Jo asked Mother what it was all about. They were looking at houses with more room, she said, because there would be another little one joining us.

None of us were ecstatic about the news this time. My sister and I had discovered that babies were a lot of work, and my mother stayed occupied trying to get her bearings around the baby she had. She drank on the weekends through this next pregnancy but didn't let it render her inattentive to Pam. Less jubilant than before, Daddy tried to downplay the fact by claiming he was excited at the prospect of having a boy.

On a wintry day in December, Mother called my father home from work.

"Jim! The baby's coming! We need to get to the hospital now! How long before you can get home?" When they left, Jo and I sat on the couch in the living room, turned on the TV, and waited for the news.

Several hours later, the front door flew open, and Daddy blew in spraying dollar bills into the air. "We had a boy! I got my boy!" he said. Jo and I hopped around scrambling to catch the bills.

The addition of another baby challenged our tenuous stability, but Freddy turned out to be a gift. An imperturbable baby, he was calm, placid, and happy, which was fortunate since Pam demanded most of our attention.

Both of my parents drank to stupidity on the weekends and fought. My father's evil twin always made an appearance after several drinks, and my mother goaded him. Their fights were like train wrecks with mangled and crushed cars lying on their sides hissing with steam, while the injured and dying lay across the tracks moaning. I could feel their anger like a black knot in my stomach as they hurled demeaning accusations, each one ratcheting up the fury. A child suffers a torpedo of destruction hearing or seeing one parent degrade the other—it's a feeling deep enough to sink into the bone marrow.

Neither of them batted an eye that we kids were subjected to this weekend sideshow on a regular basis. Nor did they care that once the shit-faced yelling began, both babies erupted in a vigorous duet of crying, and Jo and I had to drag ourselves out of bed and go in to calm them. I'd rock one and she'd pace and pat the other while our parents, oblivious, ranted on.

This sober-week, drunken-weekend pattern had been a standard in our house, and although Jo and I detested it, over the years we'd come to expect it. By Monday, life slipped back into a normal rhythm, but I could never fully relax; it was only ever four days till Friday.

I can see now that our destruction, even though at times imperceptible, definitely had precipitous downturns. When I was nine, I came in from school on a warm weekday afternoon. Mother sat at the dining room table writing on a notepad. When she looked up and said, "Hello," my heart dropped.

"Why have you been drinking? It's Wednesday. You're only supposed to get drunk on the weekends." She'd never done that before.

"Oh, for god's sake, I'm not drunk or drinking. I'm just tired. Go change your clothes and go out and play."

How much does a nine-year-old know about these things? Clearly, she'd been drinking on a weekday, absent a party, and alone, but I couldn't fathom at the time how that one afternoon would change everything.

My parents splurged and bought a two-year-old house in the upscale Cove section of the city. We were moving up. Grand compared to the little brick box on Fairland, the roomy house was in a prosperous and well-maintained neighborhood. An inside breezeway off the dining room led to a charming sun porch with floor-to-ceiling windows and a back door to the patio and garage. Jo and I danced around with excitement. *They wouldn't buy this beautiful house if things weren't okay … right?*

The move kept them distracted and we drifted in a calm sea for several months. Like a bird feathering her nest, Mother worked to make our home a show place, and Daddy spent his weekends working on projects around the house.

Jo and Mother started taking piano lessons, and the melodic tinkling of keys drifted from the sunroom throughout the house. My mother had the uncanny ability to excel at anything she tried, including playing by ear complete songs she'd heard a few times. She had taught herself to sew years earlier, and her skills were equal to those of a professional seamstress, meticulous in detail. She often drew out her own designs, eschewing store-bought patterns, creating beautiful clothing, drapes, bedspreads, and decorative pillows. No project stymied her, including a small Easter suit for Freddy with a coat, tie, hat, and pants.

A force of nature, she won art awards and blue ribbons for her oil paintings of landscapes and water scenes. Glamorous, in-the-know, with an imaginative fashion sense, Mother could bring a room to laughter with her facile sense of humor, but beneath all that brilliance lay a deeply troubled person, vulnerable and damaged from a childhood of emotional poverty and the pain of never fitting in.

Daddy continued traveling the coast of the Panhandle for business during the week but arrived home on Friday. He built a brick fireplace outside with a chimney for barbecues, and they added a Florida room across the entire length of the house.

The move necessitated a transfer from old, crumbling St. Andrew to the shiny, new, suburban Cherry Street Elementary, within walking distance from home. Marie Farina became my best friend and constant companion through elementary and into junior high. Our third-grade teacher, Mrs. Russell, a tall, thin, ramrod-straight woman with a narrow face, spectacles, and a long, thin nose, wore her hair in a tight bun on top of her head. We nicknamed her "Burnt Rosie," because who's ever heard of *Bertrez* for a first name? Away from school, Marie and I delighted in imitating her peculiar mannerisms and snooty accent.

We played at Marie's house after school most afternoons, but she never came to mine. For obvious reasons, Jo and I didn't bring our friends home to spend the night or hang out watching TV. One afternoon, Marie went to her mom's bedroom to ask if I could stay for dinner.

"Jesus Christ! Doesn't that girl have a home of her own? Why is she always here? Honestly, her parents must not give a damn about her. The answer's no. Tell her to go home."

Dejected, Marie came back to the kitchen, but before she could say anything, I told her I remembered I had to get home to help my mom.

As I pedaled my bike home, those words echoed in my head. The confirmation that no one cared about me landed like a gut-punch, but I did have a habit of inching my way into my friends' families, hanging around, waiting to be invited for dinner or a sleepover, anything to feel safe and avoid going home, where tending two babies in diapers was a full-time job.

Mother did her best to keep things going—cooking, cleaning, and caring for all of us. But with Daddy gone during the week, she began to drink more in secret, stridently denying it while I watched and worried.

One Friday afternoon, after an intense thunderstorm, Daddy came home from traveling and went into the bedroom to change clothes. Dressed in his bathing suit, he came out and said, "Get your suits on and come out to the backyard with me."

We raced to change and took off out the back door. It started to rain again, but the lightning and thunder had passed. We ran around the yard, playing in the rain, chasing each other from tree to tree, shrieking as Daddy grabbed the trunk of a tree, shook it, and showered us with a deluge of rain. I remember that afternoon in sharp detail because he never played with us again like that.

Some months after, a profound change came over my father. Angry and cold, he withdrew from me and began a process of closing all of us out. I looked back for a warning, a prompt, anything to explain why. Could he be angry I was growing up, that I chose to spend Saturdays with my friends instead of going to the shop? He rebuffed my attempts to make up, and when I asked why he was mad at me, or what I had done, he ignored me or answered, "I don't have time for that now." Although he'd always been a formidable mix of fire and charm, this hard, uncaring father scared me the most. Almost overnight, my world turned hostile, untrustworthy. I had to bring Daddy back, right the wrong, but I didn't know how. Except for a brief respite or a rare smile, my one true ally vanished. The answer remained inscrutable, but the cause wasn't as important as the result. Whatever had created this stunning change, it had cost me my father, and losing his love and protection broke something in me.

The Awakening - Sherry O'Neill

A SEA OF TROUBLES

"What fresh hell is this?"
—Dorothy Parker

*M*y mother brought the new, booze-soaked friends into our lives after we moved. I liked *sober* Ann and Marion Harrison well enough, but when the four of them got together, moderation was the last thing on their minds. Classier than my parents' former drinking friends, the Harrisons were tenacious partiers who could go all night. They introduced my parents to several other couples and the drunken revelries began anew.

Saturday afternoon, Daddy hauled an enormous tub of raw oysters into the backyard and covered them with bags of ice. As I watched in dread, he carried case after case of beer and bottles of liquor to the makeshift bar outside. By seven that night, the backyard teemed with people, the grill sizzled with burgers and steaks, and guests sat around downing oysters as fast as they could shuck them. As the booze flowed, happy partiers talked and laughed, but I pictured the evening's ugly progression when tempers flared and arguments led to fights. *If only these people knew when to quit.* Jo and I mingled among the neighbors and friends, and she showed off her new puppy, a luscious, three-month-old little brown nugget.

Later that night, my father and Marion Harrison were having a discussion about the new puppy's breed. The dog was a mutt, but Daddy insisted he was a boxer. He and Marion argued the point for a while, each of them sloppy drunk, trying to justify their opinions. Daddy abruptly staggered over to the puppy and picked him up. Heading toward his shed, puppy in hand, he called for Marion to follow him.

"What the hell are you doing, Jim?" Marion asked Daddy, laughing.

"You'll see," my father slurred, "this boxer needs his tail clipped." He sat the terrified puppy on the worktable, reached for his ax hanging on a pegboard behind him, and with one swift blow, chopped the dog's tail off. Blood spurted and splashed from the wound, and the puppy let out an ear-splitting yelp, dove off the workbench, and took off. The severed tail lay in a puddle of blood on the table. Even though we searched and searched in the following days, the little guy never turned up. Immersed in grief, Jo cried for days but, as usual, the entire repugnant event got locked in a vault, never to be mentioned again.

A brutal current continued eating away the ground on which we stood. Now long, angry silences or nasty rebukes and violent arguments were all my parents had to offer each other. Daddy's traveling left Mother to her own devices during the week, and she drank more and more, losing her grip on sanity, unable to hide the results now, often passed out in bed.

A sickening premonition engulfed me one day as soon as I stepped inside the house from school—even the molecules became deranged in response to my mother's drinking. Their bedroom door sat ajar, and her unconscious body sprawled across the bed. That morning before I'd left for school, she'd promised to finish my Pocahontas costume for the Girl Scout Jamboree that night. I glanced over at the sewing machine. Like a deflated ragdoll, the unfinished costume had been tossed in a heap. After weeks of anticipation, I sat on the porch steps and cried. She'd been sober for at least a month. *Why would she choose this day to get trashed?* It was mean, and I hated her in that moment.

When she sobered up the next afternoon, I asked her why. She looked at me with sad eyes and said, "I wish I knew."

But the cruel, seemingly intentional behaviors stacked up, one after another. I stood on the stage as the curtain came up on our sixth-grade play, *Frankie and Johnnie*. I had the starring role and had struggled with nerves all day. Right before the play started, my mother staggered down the aisle, drunk on her ass, fumbling for a seat. I prayed she wouldn't make a bigger scene.

None of us went unscathed. At Pam's fourth birthday party, Jo and I carried on for Mother while she lay passed out in bed. We told the adults she was ill with a migraine and hoped she wouldn't make an impromptu appearance.

Daddy, a born sailor and exceptional boatman, had joined a boating country club in an effort to build business contacts. He frequently won the sailboat races in which he competed and enjoyed notoriety around the club. The night of the awards banquet, even though she'd been on a sober streak, Mother became so intoxicated that it took several men to pour her into the car. Disgraced and raging, Daddy refused to speak to any of us.

A few weeks later, Jo and I rushed our father at the door when he arrived home.

"Mother is drunk again," we told him.

"Damn it!" he thundered, "I'm going to fix this once and for all." He lit off down the hall with a furious determination.

My sister and I looked at each other, eyes wide. We ran into Jo's bedroom and shut the door. The little kids were in their beds asleep, and Mother was passed out in the bedroom. Daddy stormed into their room cursing, and we heard muffled slamming and banging. Peeking out, we saw our father going down the hall to the bathroom with Mother slung over his shoulder. He threw her in the shower with all her clothes on, turned on the cold water, and roared, "There! That's what you deserve! You're going to stay there till you're sober. You need to straighten up and knock off this shit. I'd better never come home to this again or I can guaran-god-damn-tee-you you'll be sorry. Do you hear me, Christine?"

Daddy had reached the end of his rope, but subjecting my mother to this kind of degradation, tearing away the last shred of her dignity couldn't help. It looked like revenge to me and made me sick.

Not long after, Mother went to a sanatorium in Pensacola. A black-and-white photo of the four of us standing on the steps outside the hospital with bright smiles, dressed to the nines, attests to our joy that she was, at long last, getting fixed.

A month after Mother returned from the hospital, Jo approached me and commanded I come outside and sit with her. "Sit down. I want to talk to you," she said, and she motioned to a spot on the cold, concrete step of the porch stoop. The tone of her voice told me whatever she had to say would be serious. She'd turned fifteen that year and displayed a more mature character than either of our parents.

Putting her hands on my shoulders and turning me to face her, she locked her eyes on mine and said, "Mom has a disease. It's called alcoholism—that's why she drinks the way she does. She can't help it. She's not doing it to be mean. She wants to quit, but she can't." I started crying and Jo put her arms around me and said, "Don't worry. It's going to be okay." She hugged me, patting my back. She had never been that kind to me, and I buried my head in her neck.

Confused and frightened at the word *disease*, I looked up at her through my tears and asked, "Is she going to die?"

"Don't be ridiculous. It's not that kind of disease," she said, exasperated.

"What kind is it?" I asked, wiping my tears and snotty nose on my shirt.

Witnessing this breach of etiquette, Jo jumped up and away from me screaming, "Yuck. You're a pig!" She flounced into the house, slamming the screen door in my face. I could never win with her. I sat on the steps for a while worrying about this new word, *alcoholism*, wondering what it meant and what to do about it.

Determined to create a life of her own, Jo separated herself from the chaos of the family and came and went like a boarder, refusing to be sucked into the daily drama. A lot closer to being on her own, she didn't allow our problems to affect her the way they did me. I envisioned a time when she would be gone and begged her not to leave us when she graduated.

Mother went right back to the bottle soon after arriving home. Naming the condition meant now there was no room for anger; sympathy had to live in that space—after all, she couldn't help it. My parents made a stab at getting along, but acrimony crept back in, and the angry fights and terrible silences began anew.

I had become well aware of the residual effects of my parents' hate for each other and their blindness to anything else. Orphaned, we kids watched the edges crumble and pretended we didn't see and hear things as our parents moved further from us, each rotating in their own orbit.

Retreat was my defense. I spent long days away from home with friends or idling away hours on my bike. The uncertainty and mayhem changed my personality. At home, I was moody, withdrawn, and angry. My father lectured and threatened me on a regular basis about my attitude, but any attempt on my part to change didn't last. Within a few days, I'd be fighting with Jo, teasing Pam to tears, or storming off to my room to pout. We were all trying to survive in a family consumed with pain.

Adding to my anxiety, around this time, almost overnight, my once straight, narrow hips grew curvy, and breasts that before had been flat planes burst into large orbs of flesh. Studying this strange violin-shaped image in the mirror, I saw purple, striated marks on my breasts and hips that hadn't been there before. Alarmed, I called my mother to the bathroom.

"What is this?" I asked. "Do I have a disease?"

As if zapped by an exposed wire, she pulled back, gasped, and proclaimed, "Oh my god! Those are stretch marks! You're too young. Your breasts are ruined!" She crumpled like an accordion and then retreated to her bedroom sobbing.

Wrapping myself in a towel, I followed her. "What does this mean? Am I going to die?"

"Die? No, of course not. But those scars will never go away."

I plodded back down the hallway to the bathroom, dropped the towel, stepped into the tub, and vowed she would be the last person on earth to see me naked.

Jo and I compared notes on the veiled conversations we'd heard about looming problems for Gramma Elizabeth in Jacksonville. Mother later told us that Big Pop, odd to begin with, had become unhinged and no one could control him. He neglected his patients and his dental office and made nonsensical, risky investments; in short, he'd become psychotic. Piece by piece, their fortune was dwindling; their home was in foreclosure, and each day it worsened. Afraid of his violent outbursts, Gramma had no place to turn.

"We're going over to Jacksonville next weekend to move her here," Mother said.

"Where will she live?" I asked.

"We've found a little apartment for her in the projects, and since it's about a mile from here, you two can go over after school and help her get settled."

When my grandmother arrived, submerged in sadness and defeat, she leaned on all of us for support. Mother loved Gramma Elizabeth, but the lengths to which she went in attending her surprised me. She grocery shopped and cooked for her, cleaned her apartment, took her shopping, and accompanied her on job interviews. Mother made sure Gramma stayed with us on the weekends so she wouldn't be alone. The drinking and wild parties took a backseat to caring for my grandmother.

Sometimes I went to her small apartment on Fridays and stayed the weekend with her. Devastated at losing her husband and her life in Jacksonville, she sank into a black hole of depression, weeping all weekend, barely moving or talking. To lift her spirits, I performed my entire repertoire of imitations and skits, but she'd smile, tell me how much she loved me, and descend again into her shadowy place. Her pain affected me in a profound way, and I grieved along with her—my sweet, radiant grandmother, now as dark as midnight.

Gramma went to work as an assistant editor at our local newspaper, but about six months later, she became ill. She had painful bouts of stomach trouble, diarrhea, and constipation. Trips to various doctors turned up nothing.

Mother came into our bedroom one afternoon raging. "I feel like kicking some ass—I'm that angry," she said, pacing around the room. A coworker of Gramma's had left a bottle of mouthwash on her desk at work with a snarky, anonymous note referencing her bad breath. "What a shitty thing to do," Mother went on. "The poor woman is desperately ill, losing weight, and trying her best to function at work. I wish I could get my hands on the bastard that could be that cruel." Never before had I seen my mother feel that deeply or defend anyone with such passion, and I loved her for it.

Over the next weeks, Gramma continued to get worse. There were more doctor visits to no avail. Mother became concerned for her safety and moved her in with us. She doted on Gramma—bathing her, cleaning up her bloody diarrhea, and taking her from one doctor to another with no resolution. At one point, Christine lost it with the doctor and demanded he either find out immediately what was wrong with my grandmother, or she'd make a scene in his waiting room he'd never forget. Sober, my mother's temper couldn't compare to my father's, but she had no problem with confrontation.

Not long after that, one afternoon when Jo and I were in our bedroom listening to the radio and working on homework, Mother flung the door open in a panic.

"Gramma just went to the bathroom and it's nothing but blood and clots," she said. "I'm calling an ambulance." Several days later we received a legitimate diagnosis—advanced colon cancer.

We visited Gramma at the hospital a week later. Once plump, my grandmother was now a gaunt collection of bones covered with paper-thin skin. Her ashy-white pallor accentuated the deep black circles under her eyes. Remembering how callous I'd been when she lived with us, I felt ashamed. At one point I remembered making a flippant, brutish comment to my mother along the lines of, "All she does is complain. She's a real downer. I don't want her to live with us."

In the fifties, death was another verboten topic, especially around children. Too frightened to ask, and unable to process the situation, I fell into a vast well of anxiety. Pictures of my ravaged grandmother played on a steady stream through my mind.

After Gramma's admission to the hospital, my mother went on a roaring bender and berated my father for being a worthless son. He *had* been absent a lot, letting her bear the burden alone, but maybe avoidance gave him an escape from reality. He said he loved his mother more than anything, that she'd been a wonderful mother to him, and he was devastated, but that didn't placate Christine. Her drinking went on unabated in the days that followed, and she continued to deride him. He managed to hold his explosive rage in check, but a pervasive aura of doom settled over our house.

A few weeks later, Daddy called us all together in the living room. "Everybody sit down and be quiet."

The four of us kids pushed in together on the long, green sofa, and Mother sat at the end, legs crossed, elbow on her knee, smoking and tapping her cigarette in the ashtray. Without fanfare, Daddy announced, "We're moving to Jacksonville where there is family that can help us. I can't do this alone anymore."

"What? No! You can't do this to us!" I wailed. "No, no, no!" I jumped up from the couch and ran into our bedroom. Sobbing, I slammed my head into the pillow. Taking us away from the few stable elements we had—friends, school, and a city we loved—was the height of cruelty. I hated the world, and that day, it hated me too.

Jo came into the room crying. "They're going to make me the new girl in school in my senior year," she said. "How can they do this? I hate them! I don't want to leave my friends, and what about David?" Leaving her boyfriend made the reality more painful, and she cried harder.

Mother sat in the living room spinning some fairy tale for Pam and Freddy about how fun the move would be and how maybe they could get a puppy. Jo went out to beg them to reconsider, but she made no headway. Over the following weeks, in an attempt to bring us around, they'd say things like, "You'll be near Gram and Daddy Mac and your cousins, and we'll bring Gramma Elizabeth with us." I would retort, "I hate my cousins and I don't want to live anywhere near them." Tone-deaf to our feelings, they went right on with their plans.

Gramma was hanging on by a thread when we made our last visit. The smell of death and decay filled the room. Although unable to speak, she was conscious and aware. My four-year-old sister wanted to kiss Gramma on the cheek and asked Mom to put her on the bed. Mother gently placed her on the hospital bed and began to speak to my grandmother in a soothing way, sharing their plans to move back to Jacksonville, emphasizing that we were taking her with us. A slight smile crossed Gramma's face.

Pam blurted out, "No, Mama, Sherry doesn't want Gramma to live with us. She said that." Gloating at her own cunning, she'd exacted revenge for all my teasing with those two sentences. My heart knocked hard against my chest and shame poured over me like hot lava. I looked at my grandmother's face praying she hadn't processed this, but within a few seconds, a tear rolled down her cheek. She died the next day.

Regret and guilt filled every cell of my body. *What have I done? How could I have been that heartless?* I asked myself as I sat on my bed and punched my fists against my thighs. The pain my grandmother had endured for all those months and how it must have hurt to hear Pam's words, how unfeeling and oblivious I'd been—the reality of that chewed me up inside. I awoke in the mornings to a pillowcase drenched in tears. There was no one to talk to, no one to help me gain perspective. Seeing how destroyed I was, my parents wouldn't allow me to attend the funeral fearing it would make matters worse.

In the process of grieving, the reality became undeniable—I'd been living in some vague netherworld for the last year, oblivious to everything except my friends, lashing out at home, and leaving my young siblings to the whims of my parents. I vowed to change and prayed, begging for forgiveness. At night before I fell asleep, I spoke to my grandmother, telling her how sorry I was, that I loved her, and I hadn't meant it. A boulder of remorse sat in my chest and sometimes I could hardly breathe.

Months after the funeral, we found out that Big Pop had died some hours after Gramma passed. He left a letter proclaiming his undying love for her and his conviction he would see her in the afterlife. The coroner classified his death as either a heart attack or suicide, but I can't remember which. My father said Big Pop had become homeless before he died, living on the streets as a bum and eating from dumpsters. The fine line between genius and insanity had given way to madness.

BETRAYAL
Panama City/Jacksonville
1960

"Sometimes, the person you'd take a bullet for
is the one holding the gun."
—Anonymous

Once Gramma died, Daddy was eager to move. We had one month of school left, and Jo and I were in a cold, blue funk, already grieving the loss of our beloved village, our schools, our house, enchanting backyard, the bays and the beach, the double features on Sunday, the freedom of a small town … everything. We clammed up around our parents, pouting and ignoring them; you could slice the malice in the air and serve it on a platter.

In that era, children had no say in anything. Your opinions or wishes were neither wanted nor heeded, at least in my family, but Jo and I clung steadfast in our misery and didn't go down without a fight. We cried, begged, wheedled, and argued.

"Why, Daddy, why? We don't want to move. Please don't make us move," I repeated over and over to a silent, sullen father. Daddy had a mutual dislike for my mother's family—he couldn't tolerate their unschooled, backward ways, and they, in turn, read Daddy as snobby and aloof. Why would he want to move closer to them? There had to be something else afoot, but I wouldn't find out for three years.

After loading the last box, we got in the car, settled ourselves and the two little ones, and took one last, longing look at our house and town. Jo and I whispered in the back seat, commiserating with each other and rebuffing our parents.

There were few choices of homes in the area near my grandparents, and my first impression of the new neighborhood confirmed we'd left paradise and landed in a nightmare. The west side of Jacksonville in 1959 was a mean-looking eyesore—dirty, broken-down buildings, weed-infested lots, and old, rusted cars on blocks. Jo and I hated living close to my mother's sister and our cousins who had always looked down their noses at us and made their feelings obvious. I could take my uncle, but my aunt's spiteful animosity and superior attitude toward us depressed me. That any one of them would *help* us, as Daddy had alluded to, was patently ridiculous. At least maybe Gram and Daddy Mac could keep my mom on the straight and narrow, but I doubted it.

A few days after we moved into the crappy little house in the crappy neighborhood, I came in from riding my bike to a scene that left me trembling. My father stood in their bedroom removing his clothes from boxes and placing them in a suitcase.

"Where are you going?" I cried, icy fear nailing me to the floor.

He continued without looking up. "I have to go back to Panama City to wrap up all the loose ends. I'll be back when that's done." His face was hard as concrete.

"How long will that take?" I asked, voice shaking.

He refused to look at me and blew out an impatient sigh. "It'll take what it takes. I don't know … a few months."

My knees went weak, and I sat down on the edge of the bed. *Now I get it—he's not coming back.* What a clever way to execute a clean getaway. He's leaving his wife where he found her, at her mother's doorstep. In a quiet monotone, I said, "I know you're not coming back. You're leaving us here with a mother who can't handle life, hoping Gram and Aunt Corrine will pick up the pieces." My desolation complete, I stood up and said, "You're the meanest person I know." When he didn't come screaming around the corner and berate me for my disrespectful attitude, there was little doubt I was right.

Instead, he called after me, "Yes, I'm coming back. Why are you always so dramatic? Stop imagining things."

Daddy never came back to live in that house, and, despite my nagging, Mother wouldn't tell me why. She wouldn't talk about it at all.

How could everything get this sad and broken?

What boring, gloomy months June, July, and August were. Heat waved and shimmered on the streets. Left naked without the benefit of shade, the asphalt melted into a soft cushion under the blistering sun. All the greenery was shriveled and parched brown except for perky clusters of weeds scattered throughout the neighborhood. The parcel of land on which the subdivision sat had been peeled clean of all trees and foliage by the builder. We had one scrawny, brown three-foot pine in the middle of the front yard that looked as if it'd been fertilized with Roundup. The sad little houses were small, flat, rectangular boxes—assembly-line fabrications of inferior construction. Doors and frames came unhinged and cracked and baseboards fell off. With no insulation, the house was boiling in the summer and freezing in the winter—so cold I kept my coat on in the house.

A kinder person would describe the people around us as country, or less fortunate, but to my snotty thirteen-year-old mind, they were low-life—tattooed motorcycle types with chain-link fences in the front yard and junk-yard dogs that growled and snapped when you came within five feet. Confederate flags and gun racks adorned pickups, and I recoiled in disgust at the first and most prominent casualty in the area—teeth—jumbled, rotted, or missing. The irrefutable conclusion I drew was that very few people in the west side of Jacksonville looked as if they'd ever broken even in life.

My single choice for company that summer was my cousin Ellen, three years younger and as timid as a wren. She refused to come to my house, and if I went to hers, I was subjected to interrogation and judgment by my aunt. One bright spot was a 7-Eleven store about a mile from home. The traffic made it too dangerous to ride my bike, but a walk through the weeds on the side of a busy highway got me there.

I made the trek every few days for gum and candy and to read the comics and movie magazines. Ellen had been strictly forbidden from going there.

"C'mon, Ellen. I won't tell anybody," I promised. "They have candy cigarettes and wax lips and I'll buy you some. It's only a couple of blocks away; we'll be back before your mom knows we're gone." I hounded her until she gave in, and we trotted to the store on the well-worn, weedy path. Delighted I had coerced her into disobeying her parents, I sweetened the pot by suggesting she steal a pack of gum.

"Are you sure it's okay?" she asked in her small, insipid voice, nervous as a mouse.

"Sure, tuck it in there," I said as I pointed to her pocket. She hung her head and obeyed. We started back, and the pained, guilty look on her face told me I'd gotten what I wanted—some hard-earned schadenfreude.

A few days later, a red-hot Corrine came storming into our kitchen where my mother stood cooking dinner. "Go get your thieving, juvenile-delinquent daughter out here 'cause I want a word with her," she yelled at my mother. I heard her and came into the kitchen. Glaring at me, all fiery-eyed, she said, "Ellen told me what you did. Poor Ellie. What is wrong with you? We had to take that pack of gum back and apologize to the clerk. Christine, I'm telling you, you'd better do something about her," she warned as she pointed at me.

Mom put her spoon down and looked from me to Corrine. "What exactly did she do, Corrine?"

"She endangered Ellie's life, and if that wasn't bad enough, she made her steal a pack of gum from the 7-Eleven. *We're* not that kind of people. We don't go around stealing," she huffed, leveling me with radioactive eyes.

My mother looked at me and said, "Why'd you do that?"

Feeling stupid and ashamed, I said, "I don't know. Just bored I guess."

"Well, don't do it again.... Ya happy now, Corrine?" my mother asked in a matter-of-fact way. Mother could be the queen of drama, but this time she took the high road and shut the entire scene down.

Always the one to get the last word, a still furious Corrine turned to leave. "You haven't heard the last of this," she said. Mom went back to her spaghetti sauce, and I retreated to my room.

I started eighth grade that September at Paxon Junior High with about as much energy as a rusted battery. An enormous chasm existed between this school and my old one, and I could see there would be no fitting in. Paxon was located out in the sticks, away from civilization. For the hour it took to get to school, I sat on the bus and stared out the window, mute, while the other students—whom, at thirteen, I referred to as delinquents, hayseeds, and rednecks—screamed back and forth, laughing as they sailed wads of paper at each other. They hung out the windows yelling at passing kids, and I cringed as they butchered the King's English with mangled grammar and country parlance. It was one thing to spend a couple of months in the summer with my grand-parents, but another to live here now as a teenager. Panama City was Paris compared to the west side of Jacksonville, and I grieved for the place that had inscribed its colors, smells, and textures on my mind forever. I missed it all—my friends, riding bikes, spending the night, swimming in the gulf. And each morning when I awoke, an old fear surfaced as I remembered we were without Daddy, our grounding wire.

Mother got a job as a telephone operator at St. Vincent's Hospital and came home exhausted and grouchy, but she stayed sober for a few months. Sometimes I'd ask her about Daddy and why he hadn't come back. She'd reply, "We're working things out," or "Don't ask me that again. It's the same answer it was last time." Maybe I would never see him again.

On the days Mother worked, either Jo or I picked up Pam and Freddy from daycare, walking the mile there and back. Her night-shift work left a vacuum in their supervision, and they logged hours of watching cartoons in front of the TV. At four and five, they were often left to their own care.

None of us had friends in the neighborhood, but I envied the way Jo had acclimated at school. She joined clubs and snagged the starring role in her senior class play. I remained morose and adrift, full of self-pity. I skipped school when my mother was at work and sat at home alone watching old black-and-white movies. Homework or studying didn't interest me, and instead of As, I pulled straight Cs for my non-efforts.

I made one friend that year. I don't even remember her name, but after spending the weekend sleeping on the floor in her dirty, crowded house, I developed impetigo. Appalled, my mother forbade me from going to her house again.

Winter arrived freezing, gray, and hard. I lay in my bed, blankets up to my chin, and watched the spreading shadows of winter branches steal across my wall. Mom had started drinking again, but she held the binges to a minimum. Recovering a day later, she kept her job, and we kept her secret. Each time she slipped, I worried it would get worse. Living close to my grandmother and aunt hadn't kept Mother sober, but it had helped her stay afloat better than she had in Panama City.

A SHINY NEW BEGINNING
Jacksonville
1960

"A second chance doesn't mean anything
if you didn't learn from your first."
—Seneca

To my knowledge, Mother and Daddy hadn't been in communication for months, but one afternoon in late spring, I overheard a phone conversation between them. The words were muffled as I pressed my ear against the bedroom door, but her soft, light tone gave me a reason to be hopeful.

"Mother, was that Daddy? Is he coming back?"

"Who knows?" she answered.

The calls became more frequent, and Mother's mood lightened with each call. A few weeks before school was out, she told us Daddy was coming home soon and we would be moving again. The prospect of leaving the west side and starting over as a family boosted all our spirits. We'd been in the house three weeks short of a year, and Daddy had never even come for a visit.

My parents began house shopping, and within two weeks, we were packing and readying for a move to the more refined Southside of Jacksonville. In the new, upscale development, Love Grove Acres, the large houses sat on expansive lots filled with tall trees. Our spacious ranch had four bedrooms, two bathrooms, a sun porch, dining room, and an oversized eat-in kitchen—the perfect destination for a new beginning.

Jo graduated from Paxon in June and began work as a secretary at

Prudential Insurance Company downtown. I started ninth grade in September, while Pam started first grade, and Freddy went to kindergarten. Daddy bought a small marine electronics business in town, renamed it Southern Electronics, and claimed he would make it the biggest in Jacksonville. Ambitious and hard-working, he would succeed.

A short bus ride delivered me to my new school, Englewood Junior High. Back with my people, I reached out to make friends and met my best friend, Allison, in gym class that year. We formed a tight, lasting friendship that endures to this day. Now that my parents were back together, Mother quit her job and started decorating the house, working in the yard, and getting to know the neighbors. Our fresh start planted a seed of hope that sprouted, making its way up through last year's layers of despair.

I got the news on a wintry day when I came home from Allison's. The kitchen was lit up and warm with the smell of cooking. My mother sat at the big, red-oak kitchen table shelling butter beans. Her eyes were red, and I could see she'd been crying.

"What's wrong?" I asked, as the pinging sound of the beans hit the bottom of the metal pot.

She picked up a Kleenex and blew her nose. "Your sister eloped."

"What? Why would she do that?" She had only dated her boyfriend, Gene, for about six months, and half of that time he was on a naval carrier at sea. Why would she sacrifice the beautiful, lavish wedding she'd been dreaming of and planning since we were young girls for a relationship like that? It didn't make sense. Most Saturday afternoons, I'd find her stretched across her bed gazing starry-eyed at oversized, glossy bridal magazines and talking about her fairy-tale day. And her hope chest was filled with, well, so much *hope* … what had happened?

Jo didn't get in trouble with our parents like I did. She never sassed, did her chores on time, and yessed my parents into the ground. She was dainty and ladylike, and way better at kissing ass than I would ever be. Graceless and gawky, I questioned and argued, often disagreeing, and daring on occasion to talk back. Jo had been known to pick up her plate and glass and move from the dinner table with her nose in the air, announcing with an imperious look, "I refuse to eat with Sherry; she has the table manners of a pig."

Years later, I discovered that under that halo, my sister was doing things that would've curled our parents' hair. She confided some of her secrets when we were older—the most shocking that she'd begun having regular sex at fourteen. I never would have guessed, but then again, we were all accomplished at keeping secrets.

My mother let out a loud, operatic sob and wailed, "She's disgraced herself and this family."

"Oh please, Mother. It's not a scandal to elope."

"She's pregnant!" she cried, wiping her eyes. "I'm furious with her—how could she do this to us? I just don't understand. I'm beyond disappointed. I wanted something better for her."

You're disappointed? That's ironic since you're probably the reason she's leaving. Anxious to talk to Jo, I ran down the hall and knocked on her door. She opened the door looking shaken, but flushed with defiance, and turned her back on me to continue packing.

"You're leaving? You can't leave me here. How will I manage without you? I'll be all alone now. And Mom said you disgraced the family. Why'd you do that? I hate you." Jo looked at me and opened her mouth to speak, but I ran crying from the room, screaming, "You're a traitor." I didn't give her a chance to say a word. She left without speaking to anyone, and I stood at the front window, tears streaking down my face as I watched her load suitcases and boxes into her new husband's car. Jo had escaped one of the few ways a girl could in 1960—latching onto the first guy who came along.

My sister and her husband moved to Key West and we didn't hear from her often. After a few months, I wrote to her, and she responded with an invitation to come down in the summer and spend a month or two with her. Thrilled, I told Mother of my plans over breakfast the next morning.

"Please, Mother, you *have* to stay sober for the month I'm gone," I said, pouring cereal in a bowl. She had begun drinking again after Jo left but was clinging, white-knuckled, to whatever sober days she could string together. "I can't have a good time if I think Pam and Freddy aren't taken care of," I continued.

Looking at me with pained eyes, she took a drink of coffee. "I know, I know," she said. "Don't worry about it, and I wish you would stop monitoring my every move." *Ah, if only I didn't have to.*

I marked the remaining days of school off the calendar with a red pen and dreamed of the ten-hour Greyhound bus ride to Key West. Two weeks after ninth grade ended for the summer, Mother dropped me off at the bus station. Sitting alone in the big, blue seat and watching the miles go by, I gloried in the independence and imagined myself much older and disentangled from my parents, a career girl on vacation.

Unlike the tourist destination it is today, the Key West of 1960, undiscovered by the world, was a quiet, empty fishing village and naval base. Lack of traffic left me free to explore the city on a bike, winding my way in and out of nooks and crannies. Gorgeous, iridescent sunsets graced the incoming fishing boats in the evenings, and we stood at the docks watching in fascination as fishermen unloaded their catches.

Jo and I talked for hours in their tiny apartment, just the two of us, since Gene was at sea on a tour of duty. All those years before she left, she had taken care of me and the two little ones. She'd been my hero and I missed her in so many ways.

"How are things at home?" she asked one afternoon as we lay across her bed.

"Even worse than when you left," I said. "Something terrible is going to happen, I know it." She nodded as she rubbed the huge mound on her stomach.

"Hey, what's it like to be pregnant?" I asked, patting her belly.

"I still can't believe I have a life growing inside me. It's weird what my body does now without my permission. Here, feel right here." She took my hand and placed it on the left side of her belly. A tiny flap of bird wings touched my hand.

"Oh my god. Is that a kick?" I pulled my hand away, squealing.

Jo laughed and said, "See what I mean?"

"That is amazing."

"I'm excited, but also kind of scared. I know one thing, though. I'll be a better parent than either of ours, that's for sure."

"No doubt about it, but that bar is pretty low," I said, and both of us laughed.

I had no desire to have kids. With only negative role models, I thought the job would be impossible. And being trapped like my mother and now Jo was a fate I could live without. Many years later, explaining why she never had any children, my sister Pam commented, "I was a cute kid, but my parents threw me away like trash. I learned as a child that kids were dispensable." Good point.

The days in Key West went by in a quick, hazy dream. I wanted to stay all summer, but I had to get home to my mother and siblings. Jo and I hugged before I got on the bus and promised to keep in touch. She assured me she would call when the baby arrived. In less than two months, with Gene still at sea, she'd face that birth alone. I couldn't imagine being that brave.

As the bus pulled out and I waved to her through the window, my heart clenched and my eyes welled up. Tiny except for the big, round belly, at eighteen, my sister was more girl than woman. But, in many ways, Jo had come into the world an old soul, her strength bequeathed to her by Gram.

Back home, I breathed a sigh of relief—my mother had managed to stay away from the booze in my absence. Two days later, she went on a two-week jag.

Without my sister, tending to Mother was my responsibility. Down the drain went full bottles of vodka I'd find in toilet tanks, between folded blankets, and in shoeboxes. The car keys had to be hidden at the first sign of trouble, and I couldn't leave the house if she were drunk. My friends wearied of the last-minute cancellations and my social life dwindled. Her sober times weren't to be trusted either. Whether they lasted three months or one day, the inevitable first drink sent us into a precipitous dive. Dread kept me in a heightened state of awareness, and I watched her like a hawk, checking for the fail-proof indication she'd had even one drink—a barely perceptible, slow eye-blink.

"You've been drinking! Don't try to tell me you haven't," I'd say, confronting her.

She'd laugh and say, "You are such a neurotic kid. I haven't been drinking," or "Don't be ridiculous. I'm not drunk." But I was never wrong about the eye-blink, and once she'd taken that first drink, there was no question of the outcome.

Seeing my mother stagger around, incoherent and slurring was scary and repulsive. When at last she lurched to her bedroom and collapsed in bed, I stood at the blackened doorway listening for the slow, steady breathing of the unconscious, and eased the door shut. Time to hide the car keys.

After a few hours, still drunk and sizzling with dark energy, she often arose to fight an invisible foe, ranting at the injustice of her life, swearing, crying, and slamming and flinging dishes. Depending on how well I'd hidden the keys, the next sound we'd hear was the Olds screeching out of the driveway—four in the afternoon or four in the morning.

Her drunken nocturnal roaming was obvious in the morning from the leftover burnt popcorn, dirty pots, and black stove burners still raging red. A trail of once-burning cigarettes dangled off the sides of ashtrays, some with ashes nearly as long as the cigarettes. Pam, Freddy, and I faced this mayhem alone since Daddy traveled during the week and only put in an appearance on weekends when they would drink together and fight.

My siblings and I attempted to get dressed and escape the house early during her bouts—it didn't matter where—to play with friends or rove parks and playgrounds. One Saturday morning before we'd had time to leave, I stood at the kitchen table pouring Lucky Charms into three bowls. The kids were still half asleep and grumpy.

"No! The blue bowl is mine, give it here," Pam screamed at Freddy.

"Hush! Do you want to wake Mother? For heaven's sake, take the red one," I said, sliding it in front of her.

Mother had been passed out in her bedroom for a few days, but when I turned to put the cereal away, bam! There she stood, bleary-eyed, disoriented, wearing a ratty housecoat, alcohol fumes radiating from her like an invisible, shimmering heat shield.

I screamed. "Go back to bed! Why can't you get your shit together?"

Grabbing a plate from the counter, she hurled it at my head, and as it crashed to the floor, I ran down the hall for my bedroom with her in pursuit. Once inside, I slammed and locked the door. She crashed the heavy bathroom scale into my door over and over until I heard the crunching sound of wood giving way.

"Why do you always treat me this way?" she said, weeping and howling. "After all I've done for you. No one appreciates me. No one cares what happens to me."

When quiet was all that I could hear, it meant she'd retreated to her inky-black bedroom and I could come out.

A mighty gush of compassion would sweep through me when she showered, got dressed, and presented herself, bloated and the color of dishwater, shaky, and humiliated, but clearheaded. She'd redouble her efforts at sobriety for a while, and during that time, a shadow of her former self—capable and funny—surfaced. Even though her absti-nence couldn't erase the past, at least without alcohol she wasn't crazy or abusive. Watching her pull it together after each of these collapses heightened my empathy, and today I think of the determination and will that it must have taken to lift herself back into the real world and try again. I was convinced she did it for us.

GLASS
1960

"How can I keep my soul in me so that it doesn't touch your soul? How can I raise it high enough, past you, to other things?
—Rainer Maria Rilke

I rolled over in bed, kicked at the tangled sheets around my legs, and threw the pillow on the floor. I'd been tossing and turning for hours, trying to block out the shouting in the living room as my parents' voices fell and rose, dwindled, and churned up again. Their night of drinking had culminated in a predictable way.

"Damn it!" I whispered in my dark room. "Shut the hell up and go to bed." I punched my fist into the mattress and jumped out of bed. As if driven by some hidden force, I walked down the hall and into the kitchen. Reaching into the upper cabinet, I removed six large glass mugs and sat them on the counter. Standing at the end of the long hallway next to the kitchen, I heaved them, one by one, at the far wall, about fifteen feet away. Like a string of lit firecrackers, they made an explosive crash as they hit and shattered into daggers of glass. At the sound of the fourth glass exploding, my parents stopped fighting and Daddy flew into the doorway from the living room.

"What the hell are you doing?" he screamed. "Have you lost your mind?"

I wanted to answer, "Yes, haven't you?" But instead, I ran down the hall, avoiding the broken glass, careened into my room, power-slammed the door, and locked it. *Ha! Maybe that'll distract them for a while.*

"You'd better get out here right now and clean up this mess!" Daddy yelled as he banged on my door. "You're grounded till further notice. Don't even think of going anywhere. You're not too old to get the crap beat out of you either." I heard Freddy crying in the background.

Let me get this straight … I'm the bad guy here? That's laughable. My hands wound into tight balls and my stomach churned. How much more could we endure? Our home life had taken an alarming toll on my nervous system. Sometimes my head threatened to explode and send me swirling in space, a fiery ball disintegrating piece by piece. I worried how it was affecting Pam and Freddy in unseen ways. Those poor kids had experienced few peaceful days in their lives.

Attempting to soothe myself, I lay in bed and began to form a mantra, something to counteract the devastation of my parents. A normal world existed out there, and I was determined to have it. *Hang on … they won't have all the power forever, and when I'm on my own, I will have a wonderful life and make good decisions.* At least they'd shown me who I didn't want to be.

The next morning, as I swept the broken glass into a dustpan, Daddy walked past me, stiff and spilling leftover fury in his wake. Stopping at the end of the hall, he turned and walked back.

"Tell your mother I'm not going to put up with much more of her shit," he said through gritted teeth. He stomped out the house, and I stood staring after him. *Why couldn't at least one of them be caring and grounded? Was it asking too much to have one sane, reliable parent?*

As the broken glass slid into the garbage can, a tsunami of sadness came over me. The close relationship my father and I had shared when I was young was gone, as were his love and care. He had emotionally abandoned all of us, and nothing I said or did would bring him back. The question of what would happen to us if he left had plagued me for years, but now the weight of it grew more ominous as our mother hung on by the skin of her teeth.

BREAKING
Jacksonville
1960–1962

*"Memories are bullets. Some whiz by and only spook you.
Others tear you open and leave you in pieces."*
—Richard Kadrey, *Kill the Dead*

*I*n the early sixties, mothers were wholesome stalwarts of the family, and even though I found the behavior of both of my parents disgusting, somehow my mother embarrassed me more. I didn't have to be taught to keep the turmoil and drinking a secret. From an early age I knew it was shameful and did my best to hide it. But as my parents began to spiral out of control, long-kept secrets had a way of slipping out.

My friend Tippy and her uber-cool parents were building a house in our neighborhood, directly behind our house. "I can't wait till we move into the new house—it'll be great—no more worries about getting a ride. All we'll have to do is make a short trip through the woods," Tippy said as we talked on the bus together.

"I know, I can't wait either," I agreed, but a small prick of apprehension poked at me. *What if she decides to take a walk over when my mom is on a bender?*

After they moved in, I went to her house several times a week, sometimes for dinner, but I had yet to have her over to my house. I couldn't put it off much longer.

Standing on her driveway as fluffy clouds moved around the weightless blue sky one afternoon, we talked about friends, boys, and school with the angst of typical teenagers. They'd been in the new house for several months and I stared at it in awe. The split-level was terraced up the uneven, woodsy lot like it had grown from the earth, and the rough-sawn wood and massive glass windows gave it a forest-primeval feel.

Tippy spoke about a girl in her class who'd been caught cheating, but I was half-listening, contemplating instead my incredible luck that Tippy Anderson, one of the most popular girls in school, had chosen me as a friend.

"Are you going to the Y-Teen dance Friday night?" I asked. "We can go together."

She looked at me with her round, dazzling blue eyes and said, "Yeah, I'm hoping Billy will be there." *If anyone could entice our ninth-grade heartthrob, Billy White, it was Tippy.* I watched the sun bounce off her black, soft curls and luminous skin; if only I could be Tippy—happy, popular, and pretty, with a great family.

She broke eye contact and looked down, beginning to nudge the sand at the edge of the driveway with the toe of her buttery-yellow Capezio. When she looked back up at me, her eyes were sad and apologetic. "I can't be friends with you anymore. My parents won't allow it. I'm sorry."

Heat flared my cheeks and rushed down my neck as if I'd been slapped. There was no point in asking why. A month before this, the police had been called to our house over a drunken fight between my father and a neighbor. I suddenly felt shabby and leprous, and my voice dropped to a whisper as I said, "I understand."

I hurried down her driveway, my insides trembling as a parade of thoughts marched through my mind: *Now everyone knows our dirty laundry. How many of our friends has she told? No doubt about it, we're definitely white trash now.* I hated myself and my life.

At school, as the clock wound down toward the sound of the 3:15 dismissal bell, I bit down on my pencil over and over until it looked like a termite-infested stick. I had no way of knowing what I'd encounter at home or if I'd ever be able to relax again. My hands trembled as I opened the front door and yelled, "Mom! I'm home. Where are you?"

In the last few months, I had discovered that eating gave me comfort and a release from the constant anxiety, an escape from the phantom of tragedy stalking our family. And eating rich, calorie-laden sweets gave me even more comfort and flight. The more I ate, the more I was able to disassociate from time, place, and the pain of existence for a short while. But the more I ate, the more weight I gained. Before this, I'd been blissfully unaware of my body and had taken my slimness for granted, but now I fixated on each additional pound. At night, looking in the mirror, I pinched and grabbed fat, imagining I could cut it off with a knife. My confidence eroded with each additional pound, but bingeing gave me a way to cope, to calm myself. How fitting that the one thing that made me feel better made my life worse.

In the following weeks, I added about twenty extra pounds and grew out of my clothes. Mortified, I hid in my father's loose-fitting shirts. Junior high was a lawless and cruel society, and few things were worse than being a fat girl. Since Sandra Dee had burst onto the screen as Gidget in the fifties, thinness was the essence of class, grace, beauty, and self-control. I'd seen the way heavy girls were treated, how they were made friendless and ostracized and were whispered about and labeled with cruel names behind their backs. Back then, before 40 percent of the country was obese, fat people were considered lazy, dirty, or even stupid.

I devised a plan of action to help disguise the extra weight—a five-inch-wide stiff belt that I wore over my clothes cinched at the waist as tight as I could pull it. I took it off as soon as I got home from school, but lying in bed at night, I could still feel the indentations of the hard, unforgiving belt on my skin. "Hey, you might want to take your girdle off now 'cause your lips are blue," or, "Hey, you know you walk like a penguin in a corset," were two of the comments and jokes

I remember. A few days later, the belt came off for good, and I inhaled the deepest breath I'd had in days. There had to be another solution, but the more chaos at home, the more anesthesia I needed, and the more I binged, the bigger I got. What had started as a way to bludgeon my senses had become a powerful compulsion. My parents, locked in their private agonies, paid little attention to any of us; I'd have to figure this out on my own.

A conversation in gym class about diets gave me an idea. I bought a small calorie book and began to severely restrict my food intake. Each day, I ate the same thing—one boiled egg for breakfast, an apple for lunch, and a tiny piece of meat with a handful of vegetables at night. For four months, I didn't deviate from this regimen except to add some sugar-free Jell-O once a week. I exercised endlessly thanks to a booklet I'd found called "The Canadian Air Force Fitness Challenge." I did squats, jumping jacks, and push-ups till I was exhausted. My stomach clawed at me day and night, but the illusion of control boosted my spirits. Calorie counters were scattered around the house, and I noted anything that went into my mouth. *Two pieces of gum—ten calories; one-quarter cup of green beans—fifteen calories.* I tried to keep the count around three or four hundred a day. My friends and family had no idea of the severity of my self-imposed starvation.

Rigidity equaled security and shades of gray no longer existed. My mindset became black or white, good or bad. Doing my best wouldn't suffice; I had to be perfect. I had unknowingly replaced one compulsion with another.

In the beginning, starving gave me boundless energy and made me feel strong, and I celebrated as the pounds disappeared. There was gratification in hunger, in needing little, and the body I was creating gave me a sense of power. When I lost the extra pounds, still not thin enough and caught up in the dizzy rapture of starvation, I restricted my food even further, fasting on Tuesdays and Thursdays. Weighing myself or standing naked in front of the mirror made me gasp in delight. I ran fingers over jutting hip bones, ribs I could count, and a bony clavicle, all gifts of deprivation.

Friends marveled at my willpower and envied my tiny frame. For a girl who craved approval and attention, the compliments were the next best thing to love. Meanwhile, my hair began coming out in a molting frenzy, while strange, baby-fine hair started to appear on my arms and chest. I was weak and lightheaded, near fainting with spots before my eyes. My legs and feet seized up with painful cramps, and I dreamed of food, often awaking in a panic believing I'd eaten a slice of pizza or a burger. Yet I wanted to lose more. Unaware I had begun to unravel, I had no exit plan.

"You look wonderful. Now don't gain it back," my mother cautioned. "Remember, nothing tastes as good as thin feels."

Setting a good example, urging us to study and make good grades, and teaching us morals had never been her strong suits. Looking good trumped *being* good. Perfect the exterior and the world was your oyster. "Never, ever go out of this house without your hair and makeup done. You never know who you'll run into," she was fond of repeating. My father's comments, although more subtle, alluded to the value of women based on their looks and thinness. As a result, Jo and I lived for the outside, our self-worth dependent on how others perceived us. Unintentional as it may have been, my mother and father packed my bags early for a long, painful journey with food, weight, and appearance.

The knowledge that I was starving and unhealthy butted up against the elation of having ultimate power over something. Adding a few extra pieces of fruit or a piece of bread to my diet caused me to fall into binge mode again. The slightest deviation set me off. *Two bananas? What the hell, I might as well eat this whole coffee cake.* The starve-binge cycle took over, and for the next few years, I would starve myself for weeks on end and then binge for days. Then I'd go back to starving and weighing, obsessive, completely immersed in a powerful eddy from which I could not extricate myself.

Toward the end of my sophomore year, we were all circling in a downward spiral as the move that had promised to be a shiny new beginning evolved into hard times.

GIVING IN TO DARKNESS
May 1962

"Suffering feeds like a brutal fiend inside her."
Antony Basone

*I*sat on my bed curled over a science book, making notes for a test the next day. A commotion in the hallway caused me to stare at the closed door. I heard my father shouting, and then the sound of his station wagon peeling out of the driveway, tires squealing. *The Flintstones* resounded from the TV in the living room where Pam and Freddy sat, engrossed, and I went out to investigate.

"What just happened, Pam?"

"Daddy took Mother somewhere, but they'll be home soon," Pam responded, turning away from the TV only long enough to answer.

Experience whispered, *this isn't good*, and my stomach began its slow churn. By this time, my mother had become powerless over her drinking after years of dancing at the edge of losing control. Now the sober days were few, and the progressive nature of addiction was undeniable.

On the weekends when my parents drank together, long-buried injuries surfaced, and the fights escalated to slobbery yelling, pushing, and shoving. Pam, Freddy, and I cowered in my room, silently agonizing over the scene going on beyond the door.

A couple of hours later, the familiar engine-tapping sound of my father's car snapped me to attention. Daddy stomped down the hall and threw open my bedroom door, "I was at the hospital. They had to pump your mother's stomach. She took a bunch of pills and they're going to keep her in the psychiatric ward for sixty days. Maybe they can fix her once and for all," he said with a face full of disgust.

"But, Daddy, wait. What about Pam and Freddy? They get home from school before me—where will they go?"

He wheeled around, his eyes as black as obsidian. "Goddamn it! Now what?" He'd forgotten about them. I went next door to ask our neighbor, Mrs. Kajawa, if she could watch Pam and Freddy for a couple of hours until I got home from school, and she graciously agreed.

By this time, Daddy wanted to be anywhere but with us. Maybe this latest turn of events would be the last straw for him. Openly fed up with my mother, he railed about her weakness and lack of self-respect. He roundly rejected the idea of alcoholism as a disease, preferring to think of it as simply a failure of will. Finding her drunk or passed out, he'd explode, "You could quit if you wanted to. I've had a gutful of your shit!"

But my mother wasn't weak, and she wanted more than anything to quit. Sometimes her binges looked vain and self-indulgent, even purposeful, but when I witnessed the deep remorse and her struggle to stay sober, it was obvious something else was going on. Daddy didn't have a problem with alcohol like she did, yet he was unwilling to change his behavior to help her, compounding the misery by joining her on the weekends, knowing full well how the night would play out.

The placid days in June and July while Mother recuperated in the hospital were the first we'd had in years. Daddy left early for work and came home after we were in bed. Without my parents around, the madness they created disappeared. Even my little sister, Pam, relaxed, finding no reason for her rage and outsized temper fits. I understood all that rage, though—I wanted to lose it too, throw myself on the floor, thrash around, cry, and scream with fury at my parents.

Daddy took advantage of Mother's absence to stay away even on the weekends, checking in once or twice to see if we were okay. Allison came over every day, often spending the night. We hung around the house watching the kids and talking on the phone. Alli's cry, "Pick up the phone, it's Charlene," sent me flying to the extension in my parents' bedroom, hoping to get an update on the latest gossip.

We climbed the TV antenna ladder attached to my house, spread out blankets on the roof, and slathered baby oil on each other. Lying in the sun, blasting Top 40 hits on my transistor radio, we laughed and talked about boys, our friends, and school. A budding awareness of sex led us into speculation and wonder as we attempted to put the pieces together from gossip and misinformation. Being with Allison that summer was a transcendent distraction, our laughter a soothing balm.

A sad, silent weight hung over Mother when she came home from the hospital, her fragility all too obvious. I breathed in her sadness and throbbed with sympathy, vowing to stay by her side, protecting and supporting her, expressing how much we loved and needed her.

"Why did you take the pills, Mother?" We were sitting on the couch in the living room when I broached the subject.

A smoldering ashtray by her side, she sat with her arms wrapped around her chest, cradling her vulnerability, and stared off into the middle distance, detached. Speaking barely above a whisper, she said, "I didn't want to live any more as the person I'd become."

Over the next three months, I took on the mantle of Mother's sole friend, confidante, and cheerleader as she unveiled stories of her life with Daddy. She leaned on me, telling me things a fifteen-year-old shouldn't have to hear.

"Your father and I were madly in love when we married, but I couldn't handle his jealousy and blind rage when he drank," she told me as we sat at the kitchen table. She tapped her cigarette in the crystal ashtray, and I admired her long, slender fingers, nails ablaze with shiny-red polish. She blew a gray cloud into the room and recounted an evening not long after their wedding. They'd been out to a club and Daddy had become insanely jealous, getting into a fight with one of their friends.

"After we got home, he continued to rage, and I couldn't say or do anything to calm him. He went into the living room and smashed all of our wedding gifts."

Daddy was a cheater almost from the beginning, she said, and indulged in many dalliances through the years. Growing up, I'd chosen to deny the way he flirted and charmed attractive women, eyes lighting up in their presence as he seductively lit their cigarettes. The revelation infuriated me.

Recounting one of his flings, my mother stopped abruptly between tears, blew her nose on a tissue, and said, "Can you imagine … a carhop … a floozy! Certainly he could've done better than that."

Her hand shook as she poured another cup of coffee. "I couldn't take his cheating anymore and I made up my mind to do something about it. I decided to get pregnant," she said as she stirred milk into her coffee, looking at me for validation I couldn't give. Even at my age, I was floored by the lunacy of that idea. She reminded me that despite a partial hysterectomy that left one quarter of one ovary, she had conceived and given birth to Pam nine months later. My brother, Freddy, was born a year and a half after.

"When he left us on the west side for a year, that's where he was, back together with the carhop." Just as I'd suspected, he *had* lied to me that afternoon in the bedroom when he spoke about "some loose ends to tie up in Panama City."

My mother had always had a problem with boundaries. In fourth grade, I was summoned to the office in the middle of class. Through the glass doors, I could see her, dressed in pretty, bright-green pedal pushers and a sleeveless print shirt knotted at the waist, matching scarf fashionably tied under her chin, and sunglasses on. Seeing me, she raced out and grabbed my hand.

"What happened? Where are we going?" I cried.

"Don't worry, nothing's wrong," she said with a smile. "I've got the best surprise for you. We're going to Jimmy's Drive-In. I can't wait for you to taste your first bite of something called pizza pie. You're going to love it!"

She often invited me to skip school so we could go to the beach or shopping, and she even drove the getaway car when Allison and I toilet-papered a yard. But, as much as I loved her, I needed and longed for something she couldn't be, even without alcohol—a mother who fit under the heading of *parent*. Years later, I stumbled across a quote by the brilliant Dave Eggers that said it best: "Did children want sports cars for parents? No. They wanted Hondas. They wanted to know that car would start in all seasons."

And now, she remained oblivious to how her stories affected me and planted me firmly in the middle. She viewed me solely through the lens of her own wants and needs. Naïveté, plus a strong pull of protectiveness and compassion, blinded me to the manipulative nature of our conversations and how destructive they were to me. Forced to take sides, I sympathized as she eviscerated my father, describing a man I didn't know.

Daddy's malevolent glare when he passed us in the kitchen convinced me he now viewed me as her pawn and co-conspirator. But my mission was to be there for my mother, to help her stay sober and regain her life. Since he wasn't willing to do those things, someone had to.

"I need our talks. Thank God you're here for me," she said as she patted my hand.

"I'm here for you, Mother. I'd do anything to make you happy. You can count on me."

She stood abruptly and tightened the sash around her lime-green, silk robe, picked up her cigarettes and lighter, and said, "Look what time it is, and I'm not even dressed. This won't do." On her way from the kitchen, she stopped and turned to me, "Don't worry about me—I have no desire to drink again after what I've been through. That part of my life is over."

If only I could trust you. I'd heard her renounce alcohol many times and didn't put much faith in this latest pledge. But a small part of me still held on to the most fickle emotion: hope. How I longed to believe she could get better.

PART III

Aftermath - Sherry O'Neill

THE AFTERMATH
Jacksonville
August 22, 1962

"Justice without force is powerless;
force without justice is tyrannical."
Blaise Pascal

The evening of my mother's suicide attempt with the razor, I came home from the hospital, put the kids to bed, and collapsed on the couch to wait for my father. Was it only two years ago that we had moved into this house? I remembered the joy and excitement of a new beginning, how we'd all trusted possibility.

The ghosts of those early days haunted me now—the day I came in from school to find my mother in a jubilant decorating frenzy, goggles on and sledgehammer swinging, knocking down a four-foot brick wall that separated the living room from the dining room. "Here, put these goggles on and grab that hammer. This wall's gotta go," she said. I didn't know smashing bricks could be that satisfying. I remembered the afternoon she picked me up from school, ripping her Oldsmobile up to the curb with a screeching metal sound. "Hop in and brace yourself. My brakes went out, but we'll make it home without a problem." At an oncoming red light or stop sign, she jerked the emergency brake and a loud, grinding sound stopped the car as we skidded, plumes of smoke from burnt rubber billowing behind us. We laughed till we cried. Sober memories, now gut-wrenching in the face of this day.

Eleven slow, crystal dings from the antique clock brought me out of my reverie and a sob rose in my chest. Her first suicide attempt had been traumatizing, but *this* day? This day had chiseled a hole in me, the magnitude of its impact resounding as broken promises and lost faith lay in shambles. Nothing would ever be the same.

Daddy's car pulled into the driveway, and I bolted up straight, heart pounding. Coming in the front door, he shot me a look of annoyance.

"What are you doing sitting there?" he said. "It's long past your bedtime. Go."

"Mom's in the hospital again, Daddy."

He let out a loud, angry sigh as he walked over and sat down on the couch. Before I could finish, he started yelling and punching his fists into the cushions. I jumped in terror.

"Jesus Christ! I've done all I can for that woman. Goddamn her! She's on her own now. I'll be damned if I'll put up with any more of this—she's not going to pull me down too!" Filled with white-hot fury, he stormed from the room.

There was no measure of my devastation as tears streaked down my face. As usual, his first and abiding concern was for himself. Unbelievable. I had hoped he would put his arms around me like a father should and say, "Don't worry. It's going to be all right. I'm here and I'll take care of you." *What an idiot I am. Wake up and admit that no one is going to take care of us.*

After a time, he came back into the living room, his face unreadable. In a steely voice, he said, "Pack your clothes tonight and pack for your sister and brother in the morning. You're all going out to Gram and Daddy Mac's to live." He turned to walk back down the hall. He intended to blow our world apart.

I ran after him and begged, "But, Daddy, please, I don't want to go to Gram's. I'll have to change schools and I'm starting eleventh grade. And what about Mother—what will happen to her? Why can't we all stay here with you? I'll take care of everything. I'll babysit Pam and Freddy. It will be like last time. I'll make it work. Please, please, Daddy. Please don't leave us."

It was too late. His mind was made up. He was not only getting rid of her; he was getting rid of us too. Looking away, he said in an icy voice, "It's for the best."

I glared at him. *Yeah, the best for you.* Running into my room, I flung the door shut and crumpled onto the bed.

Awake most of the night, I paced around the room quaking with rage, crying and talking to myself. *Were there no limits to my father's cruelty?* He didn't care if I had to change schools or abandon my friends to live in the middle of nowhere with my elderly grandparents. I loved them dearly, but they lived in a turn-of-century setting and hung onto old-world beliefs. How could a father dump his two young, rambunctious children on an aged, infirm octogenarian and his wife who had no energy to raise them? No matter what, I wouldn't forgive him for this.

What awaited us at Gram and Daddy Mac's was an austere regime: Sunday school, Sunday church services, and Sunday night training union, followed by Tuesday night visitation of the sick and Wednesday night prayer meeting. Every single week. I felt sick thinking about it.

The sights and sounds of Gram's church filled me with dread— the feel of the hard, fold-down seats; the musty smell of wet cinder block mixed with body odor; the preacher yelling and condemning his parishioners to the burning flames of Hell; the rapt expressions of compliant sheep as they nodded, calling out, "Amen, brother"; and grown men and women with their naked emotions on display making their way to the front of the church in tears and sobs. It was appalling, all of it.

Even as a small child, without understanding my feelings, church and everything associated with it made me miserable. I watched in amazement as other kids embraced the rituals with open faces and spouted Bible verses with zeal. Some molecular instruction that had been passed to me during conception wouldn't let me accept the indoctrination. Now that I was older, my animosity had grown with the awareness of hypocrisy—the instant gratification and short-lived commitment of spiritual passion, and the evil done in the name of religion. I wouldn't last long with that barrage of phony, self-righteous sermonizing. But, as I was well aware, church attendance was not optional at Gram's.

I wore myself out that night raging and crying for what I'd lost and what I'd never had. *Oh God, what will I do without Allison?* She had kept me sane through everything. I needed her; I needed our friendship. And did my father even care what happened to my mother—his wife with whom he'd shared a life for sixteen years? Where would she go and what would she do? Unlike him, I couldn't give up on her and our family. *How could he do this to us?*

As I woke the next morning, I was hit with the undeniable fact that our family no longer existed. My eyes didn't want to open, so swollen from all the crying, and my body felt heavy, lethargic. Dreading what lay ahead, I began to pack. At about seven, Mrs. Johnson called.

"Sherry, how are you holding up?"

I mumbled, "Okay," but she could hear my distress.

"What's wrong? Talk to me."

I related my father's plans as tears rolled down my face. She said in a calm, business-like manner, "Sherry, put your father on the phone please…."

Later that morning, we loaded our suitcases into the car. Daddy had never met or even spoken to Mrs. Johnson before, but without a second's hesitation, he accepted her generous offer to take me in for two years so I could finish high school. As I comforted my sister and brother, I asked myself, *How selfish are you?* They would have no father, mother, or family now. Maybe they felt like I did when Jo left—afraid and abandoned. I understood my sister's need to save herself, but these kids were too young to comprehend that. Although they would be taken care of and have the stability they urgently needed, my siblings would miss me and our life together. Smoldering in silence in the back seat, I incinerated my father with my eyes and cursed him for forcing me to choose. *Are you satisfied now, Daddy? You got what you wanted.*

I will never speak to you again. From this day forward, I have no father.

When we arrived at Allison's, my siblings and I gave each other tearful hugs. Unaware of the impact of Daddy's actions, they nonetheless sensed the calamity surrounding this sudden decision.

"Don't worry," I told them. "You're just going to stay with Gram for a while till Mom gets out of the hospital, and I'll see you soon." Retrieving my things from the trunk, I waved to the kids through the window and turned toward the house.

THE JOHNSONS
September 1962

"As the sun's shadow shifts, so there is no permanence on earth."
—Rumi

"**S**herry, you belong with us. At least as long as it takes for your mother to get on her feet. You and Alli are like sisters, and we have plenty of room and love for you," Mrs. Johnson said as she hugged me. Why did this woman love me when my own father didn't?

Vivian Johnson, a kind, sensible woman, had a career working for a large insurance company as an underwriter. Unlike most women of her era, she left for the office each morning in her sharp, tailored career clothes. With a tall, willowy model's grace, she projected an imposing visage. In a strange twist, her face bore an uncanny resemblance to Christine, my own mother.

At a young age, for financial reasons, Vivian had been forced by her family into marriage with a much older man. They had five children, but when life with him became untenable, she divorced him, took her children, and began a new life, providing a stable, loving home for her kids without a man or husband in sight—not a small feat in the fifties.

After the divorce, the six of them were a merry band for several years. Finances were always an issue, but they were happy and healthy. Eventually, Vivian met and married her second husband, Jake Johnson. At over six feet tall, he was a large, imposing man with a full head of silver hair, a handsome face, and a Santa Claus stomach. When they were dating, Jake was charming and chivalrous, exhibiting a take-charge attitude that gave Vivian a feeling of security for the first time in years. But after they were married, his bold persona began to

119

take on an air of control and arrogance, and his words were often harsh and insensitive. Allison and her brother Pete embraced him as their stepfather, but the first time I met him, the dark cloud of antagonism and constant negativity that surrounded him repelled me.

Before I moved in with the Johnsons, I'd gone home with Allison most days, often for dinner. "Well, I see the little *dago*[1] is having dinner with us again tonight," Jake said with a chuckle as I sat at the table with Allison. I had explained to him I was of Irish and English descent, but he'd scoffed and said, "Well, then, there must've been a *nigger* in the wood pile," referring to my dark hair and skin.

Jake sat at the head of the table, elbows propped up with his nine thick, square digits entwined in a lopsided prayer pose, ruling over us with sarcasm and critical commentary geared to display his superiority. I don't remember how he lost the second finger on his left hand, but in my mind, it added a sinister shadow to his persona.

"I'm not eating this. It's overdone. How hard can it be to cook a steak medium rare?" he said, his words dripping with scorn. Like a brat throwing a temper tantrum, Jake slammed his knife and fork on top of the plate and shoved it away. A protective urge swelled in me when his barbs pierced Vivian, and I had to bite my tongue. On the weekends, she helped with his paperwork, and I'd heard him often rebuke her in a loud voice, "This contract doesn't go in that file. What's wrong with you? How many times do I have to tell you?" *Someone should tell him he doesn't deserve a wife like Vivian*, but we were all too afraid to speak up.

Alli and I shared a secret code and lived in our own bubble, often laughing at inside jokes and annoying those around us. In looks, we were at opposite ends of the spectrum. Tall with long arms and legs like her mom, Allison had peaches and cream skin and big, green-

---

1 Insulting term for a person of Italian or Spanish birth origin.

ish-brown eyes framed by short, sandy-blond hair. She had a delicious, full-bodied laugh that made me want to be funny, and even though gossip held a particularly high value to a teenage girl, my best friend never divulged what she'd witnessed at my house.

Back and forth from her house to mine on our bikes, we were inseparable, mocking each other and everyone else in that way teenage girls do, cackling to the point of tears. But our intentions were benign; we weren't mean girls.

After I'd been living with the Johnsons for a month or two, Mrs. Johnson offered to take me out to Gram's for a visit with my siblings. From appearances, they were adjusting well, but who could say what far-reaching effects all this would have on them? My grandparents provided security and stability, but they were emotionally detached. Love didn't mean hugs, warmth, or overt affection, not even any positive reinforcement. It was the same environment my mother had experienced. Gram (and most people of her era) held the belief that tenderness spoiled children and made them weak. Pam had grown into a feisty little girl who was independent, tough, and smart as a whip. Maybe she'd be okay, but Freddy reminded me of myself, sensitive and thoughtful, and my heart went out to him.

Daddy lost no time divorcing Mother after he'd disposed of his children. In one stroke, he destroyed our broken family forever and absolved himself of accountability. He didn't reach out to me once during the time I lived at Allison's—not even a call on my birthday or Christmas. Disappearing into his new bachelor life, he occasionally visited Pam and Freddy for fifteen minutes, driving them to the 7-Eleven for an Icee. Living in that confined, remote location with nothing but church for entertainment, they counted on his visits. But sometimes he left them sitting on the porch in their Sunday best in tears, a no-show without even the benefit of a call.

Gram, never a fan of Daddy's, said he was too busy buying Cadillacs and keeping company with "bimbos" to bother with his kids. I chuckled at her use of the word, but she had reached the end of her tolerance for my father's mistreatment of his children. She had no use for Jim Knoche.

It was not possible to reconcile this heartless father with the one I remembered from childhood. *Where is his conscience? How can he rationalize his behavior?* He'd done nothing to atone for his callous decisions, oblivious of the turmoil he'd caused. I couldn't believe how totally Daddy had abandoned us.

As much as I appreciated the Johnsons' sacrifice in taking me in, sometimes I longed for my family and home, a place I could be myself, warts and all. Vivian had saved my mother's life and opened her home to me, and that was a debt I could never repay. I couldn't disappoint her; I had to be above reproach.

One Saturday morning, Allison was at her babysitting job and Pete was out with his friend Roy. It was a beautiful, unseasonably warm day for late fall, and all the windows were open. Sun spilled into the living room, creating a golden spangled pattern on the blue carpet, and as I listened to the ambient sounds of kids playing outside, an unexpected warmth and sense of well-being touched me. But in an instant, the roiling internal conflict I faced daily replaced it, reminding me why I was there. The placid environment wasn't enough to heal what I had been through. Concern about my mother and siblings stomped in and out of my head on a minute-to-minute basis, and a universe of loss shadowed me.

Mrs. Johnson and I were home alone, and I was folding clothes, sitting on the love seat. She sat across from me on the tan, brocade couch in the living room, her glasses perched on the end of her nose, studying a paper she'd removed from the briefcase next to her. Looking up at me, she closed the briefcase and patted the cushion on the other side. "Come sit with me and tell me how things are going. I don't need to work on this right now."

I moved over and answered, "I'm doing great. I love being here with all of you."

She removed her glasses and said, "I know this is a tough thing to get through. You can always talk to me, you know."

A lump formed in my throat, and I swallowed hard. "I'm okay, thanks." Complaining about something that no one could fix seemed ungrateful in light of what they had done for me. Mrs. Johnson couldn't alleviate the guilt I felt for deserting my siblings or the fear I carried for my mother's welfare. Our family had lived by the credo, "Snap out of it. Life goes on. You're too dramatic, too sensitive." Maybe my feelings weren't even legitimate.

Afraid to rock the boat, and not trusting my own perceptions, I hugged her and said, "I'm great. Don't worry about me."

Days were manageable but, as with most anguish, the nights were the worst. Fearsome dreams of the bloody scene invaded my sleep, and I thrashed about, talking and crying, fighting enemies, and finally awakening with wracking sobs. Alli wrapped her long arms around me and moved me to her bed. As I wept, she held me tight and told me it would be all right. We slept in her twin bed together most nights as I clung to her for safety, while across the room, my twin bed sat empty. Allison and Vivian pulled me through those dark, first weeks, and my gratitude for that will last a lifetime.

Sometime in September I went to visit my mother in the hospital. Although hoping for the best, I trembled as I made my way through the front doors. She had been there since late August and I hadn't spoken to her in that time.

I stepped off the elevator onto the psychiatric unit and the odor of chemicals, stale air, and the unmistakable smell of sick people accosted me. St. Vincent's was an old hospital, but it was clean and bright, and the floors were polished to a high sheen. The lady at the front desk directed me to a large day room down the hall. Reaching the doors, I glanced through the glass at the top. My mother sat alone at a table, smoking. Before I could search for someone to let me in, I heard the squeaking of rubber shoes and keys jangling as a nurse approached.

"Are you family?" she asked in a curt manner.

"Yes, my mother, Christine Knoche, is a patient."

She nodded and unlocked the door. I stepped into the room and, seeing the other patients, I drew in a sharp breath and braced myself. Four or five patients were sitting in chairs, vacant faces staring at nothing, hair matted, and hospital gowns stained. Locked in an unnamed prison, most had an empty, neglected look, but one woman was moving in a frenetic fashion, mumbling and flinging her arms around. It looked like a casting call from Hell, and the aura of hopelessness was something I would never forget.

Mom sat alone in a molded plastic chair at a small, round table nervously tapping her unfiltered Kool in the overflowing ashtray. Both wrists were wrapped in small casts. She had her back to me, and I walked over and put my hand on her shoulder.

Turning toward me with a look on her face like a soldier left behind on the battlefield, she said, "Thank God you're here." Befuddled and crying, smoking one cigarette after another, she repeatedly asked where Pam and Freddy were, and each time I explained they were with Gram and Daddy Mac. She begged me to take her home. I promised it would be soon, but even as I said that, tears gathered in my eyes. Where would she go now that Daddy had wiped out any notion of home?

The next week at our visit, she looked more together and self-possessed, but she erupted as soon as I sat down. "I will never forgive you for putting me in here. If you know what's good for you, you'll get me out this instant! You can see I don't belong here."

I explained that we took her to the hospital to save her life, and I wasn't keeping her there—the law required a sixty-day hospitalization.

She discounted anything I said and screamed, "I hate all of you. You'll be sorry for abusing me. I'll show you!" Hearing the outburst, the nurse came over to suggest Christine's visit had ended and I should go.

Mother's attitude didn't bode well for her future. Maybe the medication had addled her mind, but this blame game made no sense. To move forward, she had to face reality and let go of her victim mentality. I didn't feel the tenderness I had toward her at the first visit. *I hope they keep her for a year*, I thought as I pressed the elevator button for the ground floor.

Over the next months, I settled in at the Johnsons' and embraced the peacefulness, but a lost, out-of-place sensation lingered. When I mentioned it to Allison one night as we were washing and drying dishes, she stopped, turned to me, and said, "No one's making you stay here. If you don't want to be here, maybe you should go find your own family." Then she stomped out of the kitchen. I stood trying to understand her reaction. A frantic search of my memory to uncover what I'd said or done to cause it left me blank. Whatever the reason, her piercing remarks hurt to the core and added to my alienation.

Not long after, the familiar unnamed hunger and the gaping hole where my family should have been drove me into secret bingeing, eating unconsciously and compulsively. I began hiding food in my dresser drawers to be eaten in the middle of the night. I ate candy and cookies behind locked doors, in the closet, anywhere out of sight. My weight began to climb again as control slipped away. One evening, after bingeing all afternoon and eating a huge evening meal, rivers of shame and panic rushed through me. An idea popped into my head. Get rid of the food! I'd never heard of anyone doing this, but it made sense— too much in, take some out. I walked into the bathroom, locked the door, ran the water in the sink, jammed two fingers down my throat, and vomited in the toilet until my stomach was empty. Relief and a sense of cleansing followed—a forgiveness for my sins. Disgusted, I swore to myself it was a one-off. I'd never do that again.

I sat at the tiny desk in our room working on homework, trying to concentrate as undulations of misery rolled through me. Remembering the candy I'd hidden in my boots in the closet, I felt better. As soon as Allison left the room, I jumped up, retrieved the chocolate bars, stuffed them in my shirt, and went into the bathroom to eat. Sweet escape. I finished the candy and wandered into the kitchen. Making sure I was alone, I reached into the pantry like a thief, sneaking open a large bag of chocolate chips. Standing hidden behind the pantry door, I poured out one fistful after another, cramming them into my mouth until the bag was empty. I hoped no one would notice the empty bag at the bottom of the garbage. After dinner, a trip to the bathroom, and with the door locked and water running, I vomited until the last taste of sweet chocolate bile devolved into empty, dry gagging.

The shame of this secret planted a seed of self-loathing that took hold and grew. Each time I finished vomiting, I brushed my teeth, washed my face, and stared at my reflection in the mirror: *That's the last time! Never again!* But the more I did it, the more urgent the desire. Terrified at the velocity and force of this new compulsion, I lived in dread that someone would find out. *Why can't I stop? What is happening to me?*

Years later, I recognized the unexpressed rage—the fuck-the-world attitude at the core of my emotions—but at the time, I only saw it as a way to have my cake and eat it too. I feared I might be insane or defective, and it was a secret I guarded with my life. In my family, where negative emotions were either brushed off or ridiculed, anger and rage didn't have a place. Mother and Daddy were the only ones allowed to rant.

At Christmas that year, the Johnsons gave Allison and me equal gifts: bathrobes (mine blue, hers pink), two outfits in opposing colors, books, perfume, records, and more. Touched by their sensitive and loving gesture, I hugged them both and told them how much it meant to me. By contrast, my own mother and father ignored me over the holidays. *What kind of parent doesn't even call their kid to wish her a Merry Christmas?* I didn't know if they loved me. Maybe they did, but I was sure they loved themselves more.

Gram told me that Mother had been released from St. Vincent's, but no one had heard where she'd landed. *Please don't call me. Please leave me alone.* I wanted to cauterize my brain of all of them.

"Well, hello, stranger. How are you?" my mother said.

At the sound of her voice, my stomach dropped and I clutched the telephone receiver.

"Oh, hi, Mom. I'm fine. How are you?"

"Well, I'm doing great. I feel better than I have in a looong time. I'm getting back on my feet and things are going to be better than ever."

"I'm glad."

"How is it going over there at Allison's?"

"Okay, I guess." "Fine" would have meant I didn't miss her, but I couldn't say I was having problems either—that might instigate a plan of action.

She exhaled smoke and said, "Pam and Freddy were happy to see me. We had a wonderful homecoming. And the big news is Gram agreed to help me buy a house so we can all be back together—one big, happy family, minus your bastard father. What kind of son of a bitch divorces his wife while she's in the hospital? He never even came to see me or told me about the divorce. I had no idea until I got the papers. Can you imagine how blindsided I was?"

"I know, I know," I said, sympathizing. I couldn't imagine how painful it would be to have your husband pull a fast one and divorce you while you were recovering in a psychiatric hospital. What a cold, spiteful move.

"Mom, sorry but I have to get off the phone. Mr. Johnson is expecting a call," I lied. I couldn't take any more.

"Oh, okay. Write my number down and give me a call tomorrow."

I reached for the pad and pen and jotted down her number. After I hung up, I sat at the table. *Oh my god, it's starting again.* All I could hear in the kitchen was the sound of panting. My safe place had been invaded, and the knowledge of where this would end was lodged in the deep recesses of my brain. I grabbed the phone and dialed my grandmother's number.

"Did you say you'd help Mother buy a house?" I demanded. "How could you?"

Shifting the snuff in her mouth, she said, "Well … we'll see."

"No, we won't see. I don't want to go live with her. I'm telling you in advance. I don't trust her. At least Daddy kept a roof over our heads and made sure we had food and money for school."

"We'll see what time will tell," my grandmother said, ignoring my comments.

And what about the money? I didn't want my grandparents to be duped out of what little they had. Gram was naïve as to the extent of my mother's deterioration. She wanted to help, but she didn't understand Christine's brand of self-destruction. True, we came from a long line of alcoholics and narcissists, "eat up by the drink," Gram would say, but they'd never crashed and burned in the spectacular way my mother had. According to Gram, my grandfather had been a rounder and drinker, some said an alcoholic, when he was young, but she'd saved him with an ultimatum. He found Jesus and never took another drink in his life. Maybe in Gram's eyes, her daughter was like that, but Mother was in a different league. She was too far gone for Gram or Jesus.

UNRAVELING
Jacksonville
February 1963

"Half of the people lie with their lips;
the other half with their tears."
—Nassim Taleb

Mother called often, using her persuasive skills to convince me she had changed and that moving us all back in together was in our best interests. I fought the urge to trust her again. Leaving the safety of the Johnsons' was way too risky, but she was still my mother. How could I turn my back on her now? The desperate neediness in her voice twisted me in knots.

A few weeks later, she called again. "Guess what?" she said. "I think I've bought a house. It's not finalized yet, but it's looking good."

My heart sank. "Where is it?"

"It's in Riverside, in a beautiful neighborhood."

There is no damn way I'm going to go live with her. Riverside was on the other side of town, an hour away, too far to commute. I fidgeted with the curly, olive-green phone cord, winding and unwinding it on my finger. The idea of going through the trauma of another change, trying to make friends and all the rest, was too much.

"It's going to be great, all of us together again. You'll love this little house, and getting around will be easy since we're right on the bus line."

Using any excuse to hang up, I said, "Well, it sounds interesting, but I have to go help with dinner now. Sorry, I'll talk to you later." I slammed the phone down, ran to the bedroom, closed the door, and flung myself onto the bed. "Leave me alone! Everyone leave me alone!" I screamed into the pillow. The walls were closing in. "I hate you, I hate you, I hate you."

If she cared about me, she'd leave me where I am. That thought circled through my mind in the coming days as I tried to avoid the obvious—my mother lived in a world where reality was altered and skewed in her favor. Lost in denials and delusions, she acted on her own needs, much like a child, demanding what she wanted. The more she called, the more I ate to forget, and the heavier I got.

Mother bought the house and moved in two weeks later. On her calls now, she regaled me with the beauty of Riverside and the perfection of her new house, pressing me to tell the Johnsons my decision. "The house has a darling front porch with a swing, and you'll have your own bedroom. You won't have to share." I said I didn't know if I could trust her sobriety. Our lives were littered with her broken promises.

"I haven't had a drink in six months. I'm attending AA meetings religiously and feeling great, steady on my feet. I have a job, and soon I'm going to bring Pam and Freddy over as well."

I listened with a sharp ear to see if I could detect the minute change in her speech pattern after a drink, but there was nothing suspicious. I tried to reason with her, insisting that changing schools in my last year of high school would wreck me. I was on such shaky ground as it was; I didn't need another challenge.

"Oh, come on, you'll be fine, and we'll have a wonderful life together."

In the past, I had given her my loyalty even when it put me at risk. I wanted to change that pattern, but my mother's childlike optimism and vulnerability evoked potent feelings that grew more difficult to ignore. The little girl in me would still do anything to make her happy.

I stalled for two more weeks, but by March, she'd become relentless and even Gram called to say she expected me to do the right thing and go live with my mother. I pleaded with Mother one night on the phone and asked why, why couldn't I just stay with the Johnsons? Her reply landed the the kill shot.

"*That* is not your home. *This* is your home. We'll have Pam and Freddy here and the four of us will be a family again. Isn't that what you want? You know this isn't my fault. Your father divorced me at my lowest, ripping us apart. How can you desert me when I need you the most? I have no one else in the world to turn to. Don't you care about me anymore? What point is there to my sobriety or any of this if we're not going to be a family?"

I wanted to scream, "Leave me the hell alone!" But a part of me wanted to hug her and tell her I'd be there for her. Against my will, I gave in.

Vivian took an adamant stance against the move, saying it would be an enormous mistake to live with my mother now. "Give her some time to see if she can make it on her own. She's trying to take on too much responsibility too soon. You have only her word she's not drinking."

Jake interrupted and said, "Trusting that woman is a stupid mistake. She's no good. She's setting you up. Your father was right to leave her."

Oh really, Jake, and was he right to leave us too?

"Jake, those comments aren't helpful. This is not Sherry's fault," Vivian reminded him. It was wise advice, but none of their words addressed the pathetic, twisted sense of responsibility I felt for my mother's well-being.

In the weeks leading up to the move, I ate with abandon, sometimes throwing up, but often having no opportunity to purge. I grew bigger, as did the shame of letting my surrogate family down. Taking a chance that any one of them might discover what I was doing presented too great a risk. In the end, the one person I deserved *was* my mother.

When I told Vivian I was moving to my mom's, she frowned, looked at me with sharp eyes, and said with an angry sigh, "Well, that's your decision." Her reaction told me that if they were right, coming back wouldn't be an option. I had sealed my fate.

PART IV

Cricket - Sherry O'Neill

MOTHER
April 1963

"Alone, all alone, nobody, but nobody
can make it out here alone."
—Maya Angelou, *Alone*

On a bright, crisp Saturday in the middle of April, Allison and I loaded my clothes and a few miscellaneous items into Jake's car for the ride to Forbes Street in Riverside. Inside the intimate interior of the car, the air hung heavy with unspoken words. Allison and I sat in the back together, but she kept her head turned away from me, angry I had disregarded her family's advice. Another chapter of my life was closing, and as I stared at the passing scenery, a shroud of sad resignation settled over me.

In the end, it had become clear that moving was the best way to protect myself from the humiliation, shame, and ultimate rejection when the Johnsons discovered my secret. And I couldn't face the judgment and whisperings of my friends when I got fatter and fatter, when they had boyfriends and dates and I didn't.

We pulled up in front of the house on Forbes Street. A craftsman bungalow built in the thirties, it sat on a quiet, tree-lined street. The scene called to mind days gone by as elderly neighbors, long-time residents, puttered in their yards and strolled the sidewalks. Mother had decorated the house nicely, but there were only two bedrooms.

"Where will Pam and Freddy sleep?" I asked her.

"Well, open that door right there," she said, pointing to a corner inside my intended bedroom. A small room, not much bigger than a closet, had been added by previous owners. "That will be Freddy's room, and Pam can either be in my room or yours." That wasn't even remotely a room of my own, but at least she was sober, and we could work out those details.

A walk around the neighborhood late in the afternoon brought me face to face with the new school. My first thoughts were, *big ... too big.* It was twice the size of my current school, and the old, beautiful architecture looked nothing like the other schools I'd attended—one-story, concrete structures in the suburbs without a trace of aesthetics.

Ivy climbed up the walls and down into the flower beds, and fifty-foot live oaks webbed with moss provided deep shade. Damp mold in streaks of black and gray stained the building and lichen cast an eerie green tincture. The setting reminded me of *The Mystery at the Moss-Covered Mansion*, a Nancy Drew book I'd read as a child.

My parents had graduated from this high school in 1938, and even back then, Robert E. Lee High had been an upper-crust school, but now it was considered one of the most prestigious in the city. How could I possibly thread myself into this tableau, this beautiful but sinister-looking school with all these elite students?

Wandering aimlessly, I admired the old, mammoth oaks; green lawns; views of the river; and the dignified, once grand, rambling Tudor, Mediterranean, and Colonial-revival homes of the nineteenth century. Had the families who'd occupied them through the years been happy? Had they loved their children? The quiet, understated grace of this side of Jacksonville couldn't be denied.

Over dinner, Mother spoke about her job at Purcell's, an upscale ladies' dress store downtown, and mentioned casually I would have to take the city bus and transfer to the school bus at Beach Boulevard to finish my junior year at Englewood. Riding city buses still made me anxious, probably a holdover from my disastrous solo ride when I was five, but Mother smiled and told me not to be silly. "Everyone takes the bus around here and you'll get used to it in no time." Maybe I'd get used to it, but the additional hardship of getting across the city on two different buses was a burden I didn't need, and one that could have been avoided, absent my mother's demands that I move two months before school ended.

Monday morning, I rode the city bus for an hour, getting off in front of Smokey Joe's Bar-B-Que Joint, where I waited for the school bus. We bounced around for another forty-five minutes on that bus, slamming into potholes and stopping to pick up students. At long last, I arrived at school feeling as if I'd put in a day's work. It amounted to almost four hours to and from school every day compared to twenty minutes from the Johnsons'. The anger I should have felt never made it to my consciousness.

Most nights, Mother arrived home at ten or eleven, and within a couple of weeks, my life became filled with loneliness and alienation. Walking down the breezeway at school on our way to the bus one afternoon, Allison abruptly stopped talking, turned to face me, and said, "What's wrong? You can tell me." But our lives had diverged drastically, and I didn't think she could understand. Allison was blossoming before my eyes—becoming more confident and beautiful with each passing day as I slid helplessly in the other direction. No one could help me, and I didn't want her pity. I said she should forget about me; I would only bring her down. We hadn't spoken since. I withdrew from my other friends as well, so that even at school, I was alone.

When night fell, every creak and groan from the eerie, old house terrified me. My imagination ran wild with the idea of what an easy prey I'd become. Streetlights, benign in the daytime, cast weird shadows on the dark, empty street, and the unfamiliar sounds and sights became magnified in the dark. More than once, I was certain I heard someone rattling the front doorknob. Internal conversations about my past went on ad nauseam, and the long, brutal nights echoed with regret for the life I'd left forever.

Now solitary and forgotten, a tiny speck in a vast, uncaring emptiness, I escaped into the comfort of food. On the bus in the afternoon, I gobbled down five or six ice cream sandwiches from Smokey Joe's. Alighting three blocks from home at the city stop, I went in the donut shop and bought a dozen day-olds, finishing half of them on the walk home. Lumbering down the sidewalk, I could feel the fat splurging up on my body, enveloping me in a capsule of blubber. But the hollowness inside was bottomless. Sometimes drunk with food, stumbling around and foggy-headed, I collapsed into bed to sleep it off.

On one of her rare Saturdays off work, Mother and I were cleaning the yard together. Standing on the porch smoking a cigarette and drinking her fifth cup of coffee, she watched me rake leaves as the morning sun fell in warm patches on my arms. The sounds of neighbors greeting each other on the sidewalk could be heard over the low hum of lawn mowers.

"My god," Mother called. "You've gained a lot of weight. You must be sitting around here eating all evening."

"No, I'm not!" I lied as a shot of red infused my cheeks.

"Well, this has to stop. You'll be starting a new school and you can't go there looking like this. We have to do something."

Later that day, sitting in the swing on the porch drinking lemonade, Mother said, "I'm taking you to the doctor next week. Obviously, something is wrong with your thyroid. You must be miserable with all that weight." And right on cue, my side of the swing came crashing down from its bolt in the ceiling and we both slid to the floor.

The following week at the doctor's office, I braced myself for a degrading experience. After the nurse had recorded my vitals, the doctor came in, introduced himself, and studied my chart. He declared me fifty pounds overweight and gave me a strict diet to follow—eight hundred calories a day. I could expect to lose about ten to twelve pounds by the time of my follow-up visit.

A month later, the nurse weighed me again. She looked perplexed as she adjusted and readjusted the sliding square on the scale and finally recorded my new weight. I had *gained* twelve pounds since our last visit.

The doctor stared at the chart and demanded, "How do you expect to lose weight if you won't even try? I'm not interested in patients who don't follow my directions. There's no point in coming back if this is your attitude." He slammed his pen down on the desk.

A churning fire lit up my face and a drop of sweat rolled down into my breasts. The rest of his words reached me through a long tunnel, distorted and meaningless. On the bus home, my mother took up where he'd left off … disappointed in me … my future … willpower and pride in my appearance. I listened silently, hating the weak, gluttonous person I'd become. It would take me many years to fully grasp the connection between bingeing and the emotional despair and anguish my parents had created for all of us.

With only a few weeks until the end of school, I dreaded the long summer days alone, never uttering a word to anyone. Distraction came in the form of food; I ate and ate, not bothering to purge. My grandmother called on occasion to check on me, but I didn't tell her what I suspected. Christine's old behaviors had resurfaced—breaking promises and disappearing at night, offering one flimsy excuse after the other, toying with my sanity. She had never again mentioned bringing Pam and Freddy over to live with us and I was relieved. They were safe with my grandparents. I wouldn't allow them to be brought into this mess.

A niggling worry prompted me to call Purcell's one afternoon to verify her employment. I was told she'd been dismissed a month earlier. Stunned, I hung up and yelled to the empty house, *Where have you been going every day?*

"How dare you check up on me!" Mother shouted, taking the offensive when I confronted her.

"Where have you *been*?" I repeated, ignoring the phony indignation.

"I'm sure I told you, Sherry. I've been working at the drugstore a couple of blocks from here. They hired me as store cashier even before I left Purcell's."

"And you didn't bother to tell me?"

"Don't be so touchy. What difference does it make to you where I work? I have a job—that's what matters." Her head games were dazzling in their audacity. I asked if she was still attending AA meetings. "Well, I've been working long hours lately, but I'm starting back this week," she replied.

She was lying, but I didn't have the determination to argue. Fighting with her was like trying to walk on ice; it took too much energy and left me battered and bruised. In a desperate state the next day, I called the number listed in the phone book for Alcoholics Anonymous. Could someone from their group come over and convince my mother to go back to AA? The woman on the phone explained that my mother had to *want* to change, that no one could make anyone get sober. She discussed Al-Anon, a program for the family members of alcoholics, and suggested I attend a meeting.

The following week, I went to my first Al-Anon meeting. Over the ensuing weeks, in Al-Anon meetings as well as open AA meetings, I shared my grief and learned about the disease, the progressive nature of it, and what lay ahead if my mother didn't get sober. I developed a kinship with the others in Al-Anon, but after several months, as the lone teenager, I stopped going.

I no longer begged Mother why she had demanded I live with her when she didn't bother to come home, why she left me all alone for nights on end, or if she simply enjoyed torturing me. Instead, I told her how miserable and alone I was. She deflected by suggesting I go out and meet people and do things; it wasn't her fault if I elected to sit around all day and wallow in self-pity.

The nights ravaged my spirit—hour after hour, time stretched out into silent infinity and the house filled with a flood of cold darkness.

The habitual isolation left me hungering for human contact. Being alive was meaningless in the days and long nights of solitude and exile. Without anyone to talk to, each passing day I lost a little more of myself.

Night after night, crying at the front window, I asked out loud, *Where are you?* A cesspool of emotions swirled inside me as I cursed her, hated her, felt sorry for her, and felt sorry for me. *If I ever have children, I swear to God, I'll never treat them like this. I will never, ever be like her. Please God, don't let me be like her.* When the roaring in my head became too much, I had to leave the house, walk the streets late at night, and attempt to calm down.

One night, an urge for oblivion tore through me with a savage hunger. I walked into the bathroom, opened the medicine cabinet where I'd seen a prescription bottle of sleeping pills, and poured them out on the counter. *Good, there are at least forty pills here. That should do it.* Sweet escape, whatever the cost. If I died, all the better. I washed down a handful of pills with water and went to bed. A cloud of calm descended and I relaxed, letting myself be erased. As the world slipped away, I knew I didn't want to return.

Days later, I awoke disoriented and unsteady. Had my mother come home at all while I'd been unconscious? I gulped down another handful of sleeping pills and lay in bed anticipating the dark curtain that would fall. Several days later, I opened my eyes, surprised I was still breathing. Somehow in the groggy, spaced-out fog, it occurred to me: *I've missed too much school. As long as I'm still alive, I can't let anything interfere with my promotion to twelfth grade.* I fumbled to get dressed and wobbled to the bus stop on autopilot, still fuzzy and confused.

Memories of that day and those of the following two weeks wax and wane in a frustrating way. They're there but are too soft and blurry at the edges to grab. I recall being asked by other students if I was okay. What had I been doing? Falling in my plate at lunch, scuffling through the halls, or maybe passed out in a corner.

Toward the end of the day, my psychology teacher came to my desk and inquired in a whisper if I was ill. I nodded and she suggested I see the school nurse. The memory ends there, but I know I made it home because I recall standing in the bathroom, looking at my reflection in the mirror, and taking the last handful of pills.

Again, days later, I roused from my coma to a quiet house that held no indication my mother had been home. Trance-like, I went into the bathroom, opened the medicine cabinet, and removed a razor blade. I sliced across my left wrist, surprised at the lack of pain, and then cut the right one. For good measure, I cut horizontally and then slid the razor down my wrists vertically. Red ribbons poured down my arms, and big, bloody teardrops splattered onto the blue ceramic tile floor. As I moved the razor to my left hand to go deeper, the phone rang. In a robotic state, I walked to my mother's bedroom and answered it.

"Hello."

"Hi. How are you?" my mother asked.

"Fine," I said, my voice a monotone.

"Glad to see you're finally awake," she said, as if I'd just roused from a long nap. No mention of the pills.

In a flat voice, I said, "I've sliced my wrists."

"Oh my god! I'll have a coworker bring me home. Put the razor down. I'll be there soon."

I hung up, laid the razor on the nightstand, and wandered back to bed.

"Wake up, wake up!" Mother said as she shook me. "You're fine. I'll bandage your wrists and they'll be as good as new. You don't need stitches, and we do not need any nosy social workers around here."

I tried to open my eyes but couldn't. She propped me up and began to wrap gauze around my wrists as I slept. Through the haze, I heard something about the bloody bedding and the need to soak it before the stains set. At one point, I opened my eyes long enough to see the man who had brought my mother home.

Several more days elapsed as I slept around the clock. The gaping wounds bled through the dressing each time it was changed, but I slumbered on. I could have used stitches, but the price for that might have been a mental hospital or a foster home—even worse fates.

After I regained consciousness, I asked my mother about the man who'd brought her home. Even in a drugged state, I had noted something unsavory about him.

"Oh. That's Doc Simon. He's the pharmacist at the drugstore. We're just friends, not dating or anything like that. I called him when I needed a ride home."

Lie. That's where she stayed when she didn't come home, and that's where she'd gotten the sleeping pills.

Mother came and went during my recuperation, but we never had the talk about why I did it or what had driven me to hurt myself. She downplayed the incident and floated the fairy tale that the pills weren't strong enough to kill me anyway. (The bottle had contained Seconal, a powerful barbiturate prescribed in the sixties and well known to cause overdoses.) She added that she hoped I'd gotten whatever rebellion I had out of my system.

Contemplating a return to school, I asked Mother, "What will I say about these?" I held out my wrists.

She replied, "Oh, make up a story. I know, say you were locked out of your house and had to break a window to get in. Voilà, simple."

At school the next day, when asked, I repeated the obvious lie, unable to look anyone in the eye. A concerned teacher took me out in the hall and asked if I was okay or if there was anything she could do. As tears threatened to spill, I looked down and mumbled, "I'm fine. Just an accident with a broken window."

School provided a six-hour distraction, and with summer approaching, I questioned my chances of survival over three long, wretched months with no one to talk to, nowhere to go, and nothing to do but eat all day *and* night. I had to get a job, any job, a waitress job maybe. The money I made would go toward new school clothes to fit my ever-expanding body. I picked up a paper on the way to school to search the classifieds.

"Hi. Guess what?" My mother stood in my bedroom doorway as I lay on the bed reading. I hadn't seen her for over a week, but she had dropped in, she said, to give me the good news. "I've found a wonderful doctor who can guarantee you success in losing weight. I made an appointment on Friday and I'll meet you at the bus stop after school."

"Mother, please. I can't stick to those starvation diets; you know that. What's the point?"

"The point? Well, we have to keep trying, don't we? I know three different women who've lost weight with him. Let's see what he's all about."

I hated the person I'd become—a miserable loner who lived in the shadows, ashamed of the way I looked, afraid all the time. Over the months, my physical appearance had morphed into someone I didn't recognize. My once normal walk, now a "waddle-walk," was accompanied by an embarrassing noise as my thighs rubbed together with each step, chaffing the inside of my legs bloody. My heart-shaped face had ballooned to the point of nearly squeezing off my vision, and my breasts had grown enormous and heavy, overtaking my top half and spilling from my bra. I would take any help I could get.

The doctor's waiting room was a revolving door of patients coming and going. We followed the nurse back to an office where she left us without weighing or examining me. Within minutes, a jaunty doctor popped into the office. He said he was a weight-loss specialist and assured us his foolproof plan worked like a charm. Scribbling on a pad, he handed me a prescription.

"No strict diets or deprivation and no mandatory exercise," he said. "Take one of these pills in the morning and the weight will melt away."

"You mean it burns up the fat?" my mother asked.

"Better than that. She won't want to eat at all. Drink plenty of water. Come back next month and we'll see how you're doing," he said, and he breezed from the room.

What? Was this a joke? I told my mother it probably wouldn't work, but I'd try.

Twenty minutes after I swallowed the first pill the next day, a surge of energy and a gentle but perceptible sense of well-being stirred. I had no urge to binge or even eat. Each day, I took a pill, drank lots of water, and forced myself to eat a few nibbles. The feeling of control, energy, and mental acuity lifted my spirits. I tackled the cleaning, did extra-credit homework, hauled laundry to and from the laundromat, and stacked clean, folded clothes in our drawers. Then I started on the yard. I even took the bus to the library downtown, checked out a fifteen-pound typewriter for my final term paper, and lugged it home. At the end of the month, I could button my ladies' size-XXL shirts.

Mother and I rode the bus to my next appointment, but as we stepped off the elevator, an official sign attached to the doctor's office door screamed in large black letters, "THIS OFFICE IS CLOSED."

"Hells Bells! What is this?" my mother shrieked. She stomped into the office next door and returned after a minute. "Can you believe it? They shut him down. She said he didn't have a license to practice or some stupid thing. We'll have to find another one."

My mind raced. *What if she can't find another doctor with the magic pills?* I would be right back where I'd been: teetering at the edge of an abyss. She didn't find another doctor, and that's exactly what happened.

Riding the buses home on the last day of school, a sense of free fall engulfed me. I'd been scouring the want ads for jobs, but the prospects were dim. No matter how menial the position, the employers I spoke to required a high school diploma.

Without school, I fell into depression, holding myself together precariously, one day indistinguishable from the last. I ate, watched TV, and slept. Some days I didn't get out of bed.

Since Doc Simon had come on the scene, Mother rarely came home. Food in the house was in short supply, but I used her drug store account to order ice cream, chips, cakes, cookies, and candy for delivery. The few times I did see her, she reeked of alcohol and had that familiar, stomach-turning countenance—slurred words, exaggerated movements, and eyelids half-mast. I assumed she'd be jobless soon. Staring out the window at the black night, I watched the insects swirl around the street lamp. *How did I end up here?*

SUMMER JOBS
Jacksonville
June 1963

"If you want the control of someone, all you have to do
is to make them feel afraid."
—Paulo Coelho

Mother lost the charge account at the drugstore for non-payment but somehow retained her job. If she dropped by and left me money, I ate junk food from Burger King, but when there was no money, I stole candy bars, cupcakes, and pastries from the grocery store or made fried concoctions of flour, sugar, water, and oil.

Two weeks into summer break, Mr. Bernstein, the proprietor of a small deli, hired me over the phone after I lied about my age, education, and experience. The deli, about thirty miles away, required two buses (a city bus downtown and a Trailways bus to the beach). With hours from 10 a.m. to 9 p.m., I'd be lucky to get home by 11 p.m. or midnight—a daunting prospect. But I needed to work, so I wrote down the name and address of the uniform store that sold the white nylon dress and clunky white shoes required for work.

My reflection in the mirror the next morning made me cringe. *Dear God, I hope I don't see anyone I know in this hideous getup.* I looked like a big, white blimp. Grabbing my purse and lunch, I dashed out the door to the bus stop.

Mr. Bernstein turned out to be a sour, distrustful sort, hovering over me like a vulture with a dead carcass, demanding I work faster, and criticizing my ineptness. He and his wife skulked around, watching and whispering. Sitting down for a break or even for lunch wasn't allowed, and by the end of my shift, I ached all over. To spite them, I sneaked pastries from the glass-domed counter displays, wrapped them in napkins, and hid them in my purse.

Within a month, between my paltry paycheck and tips, I'd amassed about sixty dollars (a princely sum in a time when a gallon of gas sold for a quarter). I stored the stash in a locked drawer at home and kept the key on a chain around my neck.

At ten or eleven at night, I caught the Trailways bus from the beach to the station downtown. Defenseless and exposed, I stepped from the bus into a squalid mélange of shady characters and derelicts looking for a handout, leering, and making comments. Moving through that gauntlet, I walked several blocks on dark, empty Jacksonville streets to the city bus stop. A fear I'd never known gripped me when I was out alone late at night with only my instincts to guide me. How was it possible that a few months ago I'd had people who cared about me and an eleven o'clock curfew?

Each night I come home from work, the scene is the same: Stepping off the city bus at midnight, blocks from home, almost safe, I take a studied look around the street to make sure no one is lurking. The trees block the streetlights, and in the black of night, there are no warm, welcoming porch lights, no flickering TVs or glow of a reading lamp in the windows. There's no one but me and the dark, death-like silence. Reaching my front porch, I try to calm my pounding heart, but a flash of panic hits as I unlock the door and step into the shadowy, silent house. My hand curls around the large two-by-four I keep by the front door. Moving on cats' paws, I check each room for intruders, leaving lights blazing in my wake. Something about a house lit like a stadium makes me feel safer and less alone.

After I complete the routine, I collapse on the couch, remove the ugly white clogs, and rub my achy, burning feet. Ankles swollen, feet throbbing, buttons popping, an unfathomed gulf of sorrow beckons.

One night during the ride from the beach to town, I considered finding a job closer to home, unsure if I could tolerate Mr. Bernstein and his bitter wife much longer. But the chances of getting another job were close to nil, and any job was better than none.

When the bus pulled into the greenish-yellow neon of the Trailways station, I climbed down and walked into the nearly empty café inside the station. Choosing a stool at the counter, I sat and smiled at the pleasant waitress waiting to take my order. She returned, placing a piece of coconut cream pie and a Coke in front of me.

"How are you tonight? My name's Diane, by the way," she said, pointing to her name badge. "It's been crazy tonight, overrun with customers, but I've made some great tips. Best waitressing job I've ever had." Noticing my uniform, she asked, "Where do you work?" I gave her the name of the deli and spoke about not going back since I'd been paid for the week.

"Hey, they're looking for a waitress here," she said. "You should check with the manager. He's here somewhere." She craned her neck to look for him. "They're strapped. One of the girls walked off tonight." Her eyes locked on a tall, heavyset man and she called out, "Hey, Tom, this young lady is looking for a waitress job." Giving me a wink, she said, "She's experienced and ready to go."

He took a cursory look at me, turned, and headed for an office door, saying over his shoulder, "Follow me." Once inside, he handed me an application and pointed to a chair and table in the corner. "Fill this out. When can you start?"

Surprised, I looked at him and answered, "Tomorrow?"

This could work—one bus ride home and better tips than I'm making.

149

I filled in the one-page application and handed it to the manager. He took it, mumbled something unintelligible, and stepped into a walk-in closet, returning with a large white uniform trimmed in red that sported a sleek, silver-and-red bus logo over the chest pocket.

"This is your uniform. Start tomorrow at ten o'clock. Diane will tell you the rest," he said without making eye contact.

Diane looked older than her twenty years. The uniform hung on her thin, waif-like frame, and a barrette held back stringy, dishwater-brown hair from her face. Splotchy, gray skin and the dark shadows under her eyes gave her a haggard look, but her smile was engaging, and she had a warm, welcoming manner. Diane mentioned she'd dropped out of school at fifteen and had been waitressing for five years. She zipped around like a drop of water on a fiery skillet, full of energy and able to juggle five customers at a time with ease. Without her help, I would have been fired the first day; she taught me the ropes and jumped in if I got swamped. Over the following weeks, we chatted when the counter was slow, getting to know each other and striking up a friendship.

One evening Diane approached me and said, "You have to come home with me and meet my baby. She's beautiful. How about tonight?"

I agreed—anything that delayed going home was a plus. Walking to the bus stop after our shift, Diane stopped to light a cigarette.

"You want one?" she asked, offering me the pack.

"Oh, no thanks," I replied. Her offer made me recoil internally. Who was I now? Working in a sleazy bus station, walking dark streets downtown alone late at night, and now I was going home with a woman that by most definitions would be called a stranger to me. Torn from the life of a middle-class teenager and navigating this coarse under-world, I stood outside myself and saw a lost, abandoned girl trying to survive the only way she knew how.

"My old man will be home, but it won't be a problem. He'll be happy to meet you," Diane said with a smile.

We talked on the bus and I looked out the window as old, decaying tenements and sketchy-looking people came into view. *What have I gotten myself into? This might be a bad idea.* Each succeeding street took us deeper into skid row until finally Diane pulled the buzzer. Walking toward her place, I tried to disguise my fear, smiling and nodding as she spoke. After a couple of blocks, she stopped in front of a grubby, broken-down tenement.

"Well, this is it," she said sheepishly, as if seeing it through my eyes. "Home sweet home." The small yard was overgrown with weeds as tall as shrubs and littered with trash, rusted toys, and garbage. Upon entering, a greasy cloud of rot, mildew, and urine smacked me in the face as we started up the tattered stairs. I huffed and puffed my way up four flights, taking in the graffiti-laden walls, chunks of peeling paint, and black, blooming mold while Diane chattered about her baby.

Arriving at her door, she struggled to find her keys in a junk-laden purse. *There is no way in hell I'm eating or drinking anything here.* My mind darted around for an excuse, any excuse to leave … stomachache, fever, forgot something I had to do. The door flew open and I jumped. A tall, menacing man glared down at me.

"Oh, hi, hon," Diane said, smiling. "That's Dwayne, my old man," she said as he turned and walked over to a small table in the corner of the room. "This here's Sherry, my friend from work I been telling you about? I brought her home to meet Bunny and have dinner with us. Did you bring some of them burgers home from work?" Diane rattled on as she hung her purse on a nail in the wall.

I eased a few steps into the room and avoided looking at Diane's husband. The apartment was sparse but tidy with a battered, threadbare couch facing a small, flickering TV on a metal stand. A furtive glance in the man's direction revealed a guy with long, greasy black hair and a skeletal frame wearing a yellowed, wife-beater T-shirt. A bottle of brown liquor and a glass were on the table. He slumped down in the chair, tapped a cigarette in the overflowing plate, and reached a tattooed arm up to smooth back his locks. Turning his chair in my direction, he looked me up and down with disdain and mumbled a hello. Without taking his eyes off me, he lifted the glass to his lips. I blanched and took a step back when I saw what else was on the table. His black, flinty eyes bored a hole in me, and a smirk curled his lips.

"Ain't you ever seen a gun before, girl?" He picked it up, twirled it on his finger and laughed. "Ha! You look like you seen a ghost. It ain't gonna hurt you unless I pull the trigger," he taunted.

Diane's demeanor suggested nothing out of the ordinary as she smiled and said, "Oh stop it, Dwayne, put that damn thing away." He poured another drink and glared at me with defiance as he rubbed his hand over the gun.

I'm over my head here. "Oh my gosh, I just remembered. This is Wednesday, isn't it?" I asked Diane with as much sincerity as I could muster.

"Yeah, why?" she replied.

"My mom's AA meeting is at eight and I told her I'd meet her." Before Diane could say anything, I rushed to the door, pulled it open, and apologized. "I'm sorry, Diane, but I've got to go."

"But you ain't even met Bunny yet. She's next door with my neighbor. Come on, just a quick minute." As she shut the door behind us, I heard Dwayne making the sound of a clucking chicken and laughing.

The baby was all rosy-cheeked and cuddly, but I didn't trust my trembling hands to hold her. "Aww, she is gorgeous, look at those blue eyes and all that hair. Wish I could stay and play with her, but I have to hustle. We'll do this another time, Diane. Sorry again."

"Okay, sweetie, see you tomorrow, and be careful going home," she said as she shifted the baby from one hip to the other. I sensed a hint of sadness and resignation in her voice.

As I scurried to the bus stop, dusk was on the verge of turning to night, and I prayed the bus would come soon—hanging around this area after dark was risky. Wiping clammy hands on my uniform, I moved away from a couple of rowdy, drunk sailors who were trying to engage me in a vulgar conversation. Keeping my eyes averted, I lifted my shoulders back and jutted out my chin in a no-nonsense posture. *Leave me alone.*

The bus chugged to a stop and I got on, taking a seat in the front. I relaxed as a flood of relief washed over me. But, despite a near-empty bus, the sailors stumbled on and collapsed in the seat behind me. My heart started racing … If they followed me, I'd be at their mercy, alone without even a neighbor to call (still no 9-1-1). Willing myself to remain calm, I tamped down the panic. The sailors leaned forward, slurring, speaking in a rude, boisterous fashion, and slapping the top of my seat.

"What would you do with a piece of ass that big?" one of them said to the other.

"Ha! I never fucked a fat girl, but tonight might be the night," the other one answered.

A shaft of terror pierced my spine. The men were smoking and flicking their ashes in the aisle, and a second later, a searing pain on the top of my shoulder made me jerk forward. Stifling a scream, I repressed the urge to reach behind me and coldcock one of them. They continued to taunt me, but I played brain-dead. After an agonizing ride, the bus approached my stop, and I stepped down, grabbed a pole for balance, and faced the bus driver.

"This is my stop, Post and Forbes Street," I said.

He glanced at me and began the process of stopping and pulling back on the lever to open the door. If they followed me and raped or killed me, maybe the bus driver would have the presence of mind to remember me, my street, and those two sailors.

The bus door swooshed open, and, despite my size, I rocketed off the bus and bolted toward home, looking over my shoulder the whole way, heart pounding like a jackhammer. When I reached Forbes Street, convinced they hadn't followed me, I stopped, put my hands on my knees, and bent over to catch my breath. I was safe!

Finally in the house, and with the ritual of the two-by-four and the lights completed, I came into the living room and sat on the couch. I reached up and touched my wet cheeks, unaware that tears had pushed their way out, and screamed into the empty room, *I'm only sixteen! Why are you letting all these horrible things happen to me?* The God I'd prayed to as a child no longer existed, and it would take many years before I considered believing in anything.

I inched a trembling hand around to examine my shoulder in the bathroom mirror. A large, brown-rimmed hole in my uniform framed a deep, angry burn. Judging from the size of the hole, the synthetic fabric had incinerated as soon as the cigarette touched it. I dabbed the fiery wound with peroxide and dressed it with bandages.

Had he meant to hurt me, or had it been an accident? I'll never know ... *I'm lucky the uniform didn't catch fire and melt to my body.*

After my visit to her apartment, Diane remained helpful and kind, though somewhat guarded. I sympathized with her and her situation, but I couldn't afford to take chances, and Diane's husband was a chance I had no desire to encounter again.

One evening, toward the end of August, Diane and I were working the late shift with another waitress. Snowball was thin as a razor with a personality to match. She had shiny, dark-chocolate skin and a street-tough, intimidating manner. Her snide remarks about my size, weight, and lack of skill were constant, and in a voice soaked in sarcasm, she pointed out my supposed errors in front of customers.

Snowball thought nothing of making comments like, "It's hard to move around in here girl. Your fat white ass takes up all the room," or "That uniform don't fit you. Next time you need to go to Omar the Tent Maker to get it." Diane told me that behind my back she referred to me as honkey girl.

When I worked the early shift with her, I'd heard her call out, "Well, good morning, Mr. Tom. How are you? How about a cup of coffee? Made fresh," she sang to the manager. "I really like that blue shirt on you. Brings out the blue in your eyes." She poured it on thick, flattering and fawning, but behind his back, with her cronies at the bus station, she made brutal fun of Tom, mocking his walk and laughing about what a dumbass he was, a real "reee-tard." Afraid to open my mouth around her, I ignored the comments and did my job.

Although better than working at the deli, waitressing at a bus station was tricky. Buses arrived in multiples and impatient passengers stood at the counter, sometimes three deep, waiting to take a seat. We each had assigned stations, and speed was critical; the departing bus waited for no one. This particular night had been frantic with three of us trying to move customers in and out as fast as possible.

Toward the end of the shift, a well-dressed gentleman sat down on a barstool in my station, smiled, and ordered a cup of black coffee and a piece of lemon meringue pie. Unlike most of the beleaguered humanity that traveled by bus, he appeared prosperous, dressed in a well-fitting, navy sport jacket and creased beige trousers. I brought his order and we spoke for a few minutes. Snowball interrupted our conversation with a "tsk, tsk" and pointed out that I hadn't given the gentleman a glass of water.

"She don't know nothing," she said, placing his water in front of him and sneering at me. My face flushed, but I let it go. Life hadn't prepared me for dealing with someone like Snowball.

Finished with his pie and coffee, the customer walked to the cashier to pay. He returned to the counter to leave a tip, smiled, and waved to me as he left. I was busy with another patron, but my heart did a little flip when I saw him place a crisp, ten-dollar bill next to his cup. That's about eighty dollars today—imagine, an eighty-dollar tip for pie and coffee! I left the counter to place an order with the cook, and when I returned to remove the tipper's dishes, the ten-dollar bill was gone. I stared for a second trying to take it in. Tears filled my eyes as I looked around the station, assuming another customer had taken it.

Diane came up to me and whispered, "Meet me in the back room." I made sure no one needed me and followed her to the office. She grabbed my arm and pulled me into the room. "Snowball took your ten right outta your station. I seen her with my own eyes. She swiped it off the counter and put it in her pocket, pretty as you please."

That did it. Fortifying my courage, I walked over to where Snowball stood stacking glasses on the shelf. "Give me back my damn ten dollars right now," I demanded. "I know you took it and I want it back."

She continued wiping and stacking glasses as if she hadn't heard me. Then, in a guttural tone, she glanced over and said, "Prove it." Before I could say another word, she took a step toward me and reached in the pocket of her apron. Black eyes burning into mine, she opened her palm to expose a large, silver-and-black switchblade. "Y'all want some of this, honkey?"

That night, I kissed my ten-spot goodbye and walked out of the Trailways bus station for the last time. All in all, the jobs had been a demoralizing experience. I had saved a healthy amount of money, but I was grateful to hang up my apron. The summer of waitressing had given me a new appreciation of just how sheltered I'd been growing up in Panama City.

L. Christine McCord (Mom) "Cricket" 1948 (age 27) Middle: Jim Knoche (Daddy)
Circa 1948 (age 27) R. Me and Jo Circa 1949 (2 yrs and 6 yrs old)
(This photo pretty much sums up our personalities from the beginning)

Me Circa 1950 (3 yrs old   *Jo Circa 1947 (4 yrs old)*

Jo and me, circa 1950

157

Daddy's first shop where I spent many happy Saturdays

Me (Second grade, 6 yrs old)

Me posing in front of our new house in Panama City (1953)

The new house in the Cove (the only day it ever snowed) Panama City, circa 1953–1959

Jo's 5th grade picture

Freddy (at 7 yrs. old)

Pam (at 5 yrs. old)

Daddy grilling in the backyard in the Cove, 1957

L to R: Freddy, 3; Pam, 4; me, 11; Jo, 15; 1958

159

L to R: Pam, Mother, Freddy, Jo, and me on the patio at our house in The Cove, (Shortly before we moved back to Jacksonville)

Mother in Love Grove Acres before it all fell apart (She made the outfit, including hat and matching fabric covered shoes) 1960

Pam and Freddy (7 and 8 yrs. old) in front of the fig tree at Gram's, 1962

Me and my mom (I had just started 9th grade at Englewood JH)

SCHOOL DAZE
Jacksonville
August 1963

"I keep thinking this tragedy of ours is going to be over.
But it just keeps going, doesn't it?"
—J. R. Ward, *Lover Awakened*

Going back to school hung over me like an upcoming jail sentence. Confronting the registration process alone would be scary, but finding my way around the vast, unknown school without a single friendly face was far worse. The movie I played endlessly in my mind featured me lost and scrambling in a panic, heart pounding, tears cresting, a spectacle arriving late to class. Where would I find the courage to get through this? Being a poor, fat girl who lived with a broken-down mother wouldn't enhance my likelihood of acceptance either.

Two weeks before the start of school, I gathered thirty dollars from my summer stash and took the bus downtown to Penney's. In the Women's section, I grabbed several shirtwaist dresses, a couple of blouses, and two skirts to take into the dressing room. After ensuring that I could button them, get the zippers up and the belts around me, I didn't dawdle in the mirror to see how I looked. Nothing looked good on me, and mirrors only confirmed the fact. I paid for my purchases and rushed out of the store before I ran into someone from my old life.

My mother seldom put in an appearance now, but when she did, the sour smell of alcohol seeped from her pores. She raved about Doc, saying he was kind and generous, and judging from the prescription bottles rolling around in her purse, he kept her well supplied. I'd discovered Doc was the store manager as well as the pharmacist, which explained why she still had her job. Though my waitress money provided a safety net for the time being, there was no Plan B, and I was well aware that the powder keg on which we sat could blow up at any moment.

The long, ugly days often drove me outside on extended, pointless walks to escape the silence. I passed windows of unknown families, people gathered around tables eating, playing, and laughing, and a heavy ache filled my chest.

One evening as I sat on a stool at the counter in the drugstore where Christine worked, my eyes locked on a guy sitting in a booth sideways, long legs stretched out on the seat, his back resting against the booth divider. Reading a paperback folded over in the middle, he smoked and nursed a cup of coffee. I caught his eye and smiled. He looked surprised but smiled back. He had a handsome, intelligent face, and something about him intrigued me. The next time I talked to Mother, I asked her if she'd seen him around the drugstore.

"Yeah, I know who you mean. His name is Charley and he's in here all the time, sitting for hours, drinking coffee and reading his books. I've chatted with him a little and I think he must be some kind of brain. He reads high-brow literature by authors I've never heard of. He's nice, but I bet he's got a backstory, sitting there all day reading and drinking coffee. He never orders anything else."

I made it a habit to go in more often, and he was always in the same booth, reading. I sat at the counter sipping an iced tea or Coke, hoping he'd say hello or acknowledge me in some way. Smart guys were sexy, but I lacked the confidence to initiate an exchange. Obesity had stolen my moves.

Working all summer, mingling with people, and staying distracted made the empty hours now seem even worse. Images of my friends and the fun they'd had over the summer bedeviled me, but not nearly as much as the mounting dread of school.

The third of September—7 a.m. The alarm clock's shrill ring. I climbed out of bed shaking with nerves, got dressed, and pounded down a few Twinkies for fortitude. Arriving at school and standing out front, I tried to will myself to go inside. Kids gathered in groups on the grass, laughing and talking, some rushing through the doors. *Well, here goes nothing.* I took a deep breath and walked toward the front door.

Chaos reigned inside as students raced around squealing, hugging, and yelling hellos to each other. The smell of floor wax and pencil shavings filled the air, and I shuddered as I looked around the cavernous interior.

"Excuse me. Do you know where I go to register?" I asked a girl standing behind me.

Pointing ahead of us, she said, "Over there, I think."

I kept walking toward three adults bent over tables filled with papers. "Can you tell me where registration is?"

A woman looked up and said, "I can do better than that. Come with me. I'll take you."

She began a fast walk into a labyrinth of halls and turns. Jostling the crowds to keep up, I rounded the last corner and there she stood, posed in front of a door with her arm out as if introducing the latest Amana refrigerator. "Here it is—registration. Go right in."

I walked in and took my spot behind a mother and daughter standing at the counter. A low hum of excitement filled the room as students and teachers came and went. The buzzing, bright fluorescent lights lit the place up like a prison yard.

At my turn, I stepped up to the counter and a serious, bespectacled woman looked at me with sharp eyes. "Yes, may I help you?"

"I'd like to register for twelfth grade, please."

She left and returned with a clipboard and a sheaf of attached papers.

"Okay. Fill these out. Do you have your transcripts and transfer forms from your former school? We'll also need your Achievement Test scores for the last three years, doctor's notice, and proof of residence. Where is your parent?" the registrar asked, looking around me.

I swallowed, feeling my face flush. "She's working and couldn't be here."

She studied me over her glasses a second too long, sighed, and said, "Well, what about your father? He can sign for you as well."

Neither of my parents gives a shit about me. They don't care if I live or die. How do you expect me to get either of them here? I cleared my throat and lied, saying, "My father lives in another state and my mother works during the week till six o'clock."

Without a word, she stepped away to a nearby desk and whispered with another woman. Back at the counter, she removed the last three sheets from the pile, stapled them together, and handed them to me. "Have your mother sign these before a notary public and bring them back tomorrow." Looking around me, she called out, "Next in line."

I sat in the plastic chair and began filling out the forms as the sound of classroom bells announced the beginning of school. Tears gathered in my eyes and I looked up to make sure no one had noticed me, placed the clipboard and pencil on the chair next to me, and exited the office.

Outside, the air was touched with transitory morning coolness and the sky was a clear, cobalt blue. I walked toward Willowbranch Park, a shaded haven I'd seen on my way to school. Passing a small pastry shop, I wiped my tears, went in, and bought a bag of comfort.

The dark, woodsy park had a hushed, Zen-like quality. Tall weeping willow trees swayed in the breeze, their tips grazing a glassy pond where ducks paddled in an aimless curve. Parks, or "God's temples" (a description I had picked up from a poem), helped me feel less alone. The squirrels and birds and their curious pursuits captivated me. I'd read about squirrels once, how they lived solitary lives except for brief mating periods. They were loners and, like me, no one would miss them when they were gone. Lucky squirrels—they were happy in their solitude.

Nature's endless cycle and perfect symmetry often comforted me, but nothing worked as well to soothe me as fresh, sugary sweets. I walked over and sat on a bench, took out my pastries, and ate and cried as lusciousness ushered me across the brink into mindlessness. As soon as the first bite went down, a warm disassociation came over me and I could escape.

But arriving back at home, the impossible nature of the latest hurdle brought on a new wave of despair. My mother would be no help, and no one else cared. I climbed into bed, pulled the covers over my head, and slept, awakening in the late afternoon. Unable to spend another minute in the house, I left, walking toward one of my favorite places, the meditation garden of St. Paul's Episcopal Church. A beautiful architectural landmark surrounded by tall, indomitable trees, the church reminded me of antiquity and old European cathedrals. The St. Francis sculpture in the center of the garden and the birds darting from tree to tree were welcome distractions for a churning mind.

Rounding the corner of hedges in front of the garden, I stopped short. Someone sitting on *my* bench? The man looked up from his book and nodded to me. Oh, it was Charley, the guy I'd seen in the drugstore.

Before I could think, I walked over and said, "Hey, you found my favorite place to sit. Mind if I join you?"

He uncrossed his legs and moved to the side of the bench. "Please do," he said, and he folded his book closed. *Is he as lonely and lost as I am?*

"What are you reading?" I asked.

Smiling, he turned the book over and looked at me with shy, dark-brown eyes. "*On the Road*, by Jack Kerouac."

"Is it good?"

"Yes, it's very good. I like the way he writes, and the story is wild."

165

"Tell me about it."

And that's how we met and began to get acquainted. Charley, twenty-six and even worldlier than I'd fantasized, had gone to college part-time in California where tuition was free. But when his number came up, he was drafted and spent three years in Germany with the Army. After his recent release, he had returned home to stay with his mom and siblings until he figured out what he wanted to do.

Both avid readers, we talked past dark about books and authors. Despite an expansive knowledge and love of literature and philosophy, he had a humble, self-deprecating quality. The conversation lacked the awkward beginnings of most exchanges and was more like that of old friends catching up.

At a fitting pause, he turned to me and said, "Well, I'd better be getting home for dinner."

"Oh, yes, me too. It was nice getting to know you."

He nodded and said, "Likewise. Maybe I'll see you around."

We turned in different directions and I called, "Have a great evening."

"Thanks. You do the same."

The pain I'd brought to the church had lessened and I felt brighter. Our conversation was the first I'd had with someone interesting and intelligent since leaving the Johnsons' six months before.

CHARLEY
August 1963

"That it will never come again is what makes first love so sweet."
Emily Dickinson

A week later, as I sat in a booth at the drugstore having dinner, Charley came in and walked over to me.

"Hi, I remember you," he said, smiling.

My heart fluttered and I smiled up at him. "Hi to you. Want to sit down? I pushed the plate of food aside, too nervous to eat. This time, he had a different book, *The Collected Poems of Ezra Pound*, and I asked him to tell me about it.

He fanned the pages, nodding, and said, "Sure."

Ezra Pound was a poet, but also a controversial expat disenchanted with American capitalism. Learning about Pound and his anti-Americanism prompted me to ask Charley to tell me about Communism. In school we'd learned to live in fear of the bomb, but I knew very little about the actual form of government.

He chuckled and said, "I promise I can put you to sleep in less than fifteen minutes."

"No way—I want to hear all you know."

We left the drugstore and strolled on the sidewalk for a while. He was a fount of knowledge and could speak with skill on any subject. But he listened more than he talked, and his playful sense of humor made me remember again how enjoyable a good conversation could be. We sat on my porch swing, talking and laughing for another two hours, our faces open to each other, our banter deepening my attraction.

Alone that night, I recalled the evening and my new friend. An intense observer of people, I had made certain inferences about Charley. Under his glib comments and charming, witty repartee, there existed a deep melancholia, an injured soul at some critical impasse. His appearance leaned toward scruffy, like he needed a haircut or a shave, and his clothes, while always clean and pressed, consisted of two or three outfits that were beginning to fray around the edges. There was no question of his Spartan existence, and he was alone, lost in his head, much like me. Rather than dispiriting, I found these facts compelling and attractive. He had a slight swagger and a way of listening, taking in each word I spoke as if hearing some new, revolutionary information. The twinkle in his eye and sardonic wit told me he viewed life as I did—one big, cruel joke. Charley was the coolest guy I'd ever met.

Each time we were together after that night, the conversation took on a life of its own. He recommended books that I checked out at the library and read. We had discussions of plot lines, hidden stories, and the authors' intentions that lead to revelations about ourselves and our views of the world. Eager to learn, I relished my cram course in literature.

At dusk one evening, sitting on the porch, admiring the peach glow of sunset, we spoke about personal matters—where we were born, our families, our school experiences—and he asked me in a gentle voice, "Why aren't you in school, working toward graduation?" I took a slow, deep breath and explained the ordeal I'd gone through trying to register and how I had no one to help me.

He stopped the swing and turned to face me. "That's it? That's the reason?" I nodded. He eased his arm around my shoulder and said, "I can help you. We'll go together and get you registered. I know how to maneuver around that kind of red tape." I think I fell in love with him that minute.

The next morning at seven, he stood on my porch ready to deliver on his promise. At the registration counter, Charley explained to the woman that he was my brother and we needed to get me enrolled and in class ASAP. She handed us the sheaf of papers and we sat down to fill them out. Completing as much as I could, we went back to the counter.

"Would it be possible for the school to request the necessary forms they need from my sister's previous school since it's in the same city and time is of the essence? It's October now and she is already a month behind," Charley said.

"I'll confer with the registrar. Wait here." A few minutes later she returned. "Since you are her brother, please fill out and sign the admittance forms right here." She tapped the line with her pen. Directing her words to me, she said, "Sign these authorizations and we will request your previous records. Then you need to go to the counselor right away to set up your curriculum for this year. You'll need to be in class tomorrow. In the meantime, we'll work on getting all your transfer documents in order. Come with me. I'll take you to her office." I smiled at Charley and he winked at me.

The next morning, I arrived before school started to familiarize myself with the building. These first days would be baffling amid unfamiliar surroundings on three floors and little time between classes.

I'd always craved the reassuring pattern of school, the validation I received in test scores and grades, and the sheer thrill of learning. Charley got me back in school, and now he encouraged me to excel. No one had taken interest in my schoolwork since Daddy taught me to tell time in second grade, and I drank in the inspiration.

The social aspect of school was awkward and lonely. Most of the kids had been together since freshman year and were in one clique or another. My size kept me from reaching out. Unless spoken to, I remained silent and hidden, watching the fun and teasing as if it were a movie. Within a few weeks, the teacher moved me into an accelerated English class where we studied the classics and wrote poetry, essays, short stories, and plays. I was called on often to read my writing and received regular praise from the teacher. Shy and self-conscious, I stood and let my words define me, realizing that this class was the lone time in school my voice would be heard.

Joney Williams, another big girl as disenfranchised as I was, sat next to me in our Americanism vs. Communism class. Our outcast status created a quick friendship, and we bonded over envy of the beautiful, thin, rich girls with their expensive designer clothes and shoes and their shiny, new, mostly foreign cars, agreeing those girls were beyond our reach. Having a friend made school days more bearable.

I'd never been the *most* popular girl before, but I'd always hung with the alpha crowd and accepted that as my rightful place. Now I was *persona non grata*, a label that gave me a deeper empathy for girls like me who went unnoticed and friendless. Sometimes, I wanted to yell at the snobby kids, *Hey, there's more to me than meets the eye. In my other life, I was one of you—slim and popular and outgoing.* But that was then. Besides, I had Charley, and with him, none of that mattered.

We met most days either on my porch, at the kitchen table, or at the drugstore. I confided about my mother's drinking and abandonment and how perilous the future was. He shared feelings of failure and anxiety about his prospects. He longed to finish his college degree, but his mom had no money left after paying the rent. Life had been turbulent with a mentally ill, physically abusive father who'd never made enough to support the nine of them. Charley left home after high school and struck out for California. Working a day job, he went to college at night until he got his draft notice. He'd come back home after the Army because his father had been permanently placed in an asylum somewhere downstate.

Even though we were no more than friends, Charley was a lodestar, a lighthouse beacon for me and someone I could count on. Then, as sudden as a slap, he disappeared. I searched our usual haunts, but no one had seen him. Maybe I'd had more invested in the relationship, but how could he have left without at least saying goodbye? Devastated, I reminded myself, *This is what people do—they disappoint you, hurt you, and leave you....* I ate to fill the space he'd left.

Then, a week later, he stood knocking on my front screen door. "Hey, kid," he said, smiling.

Drowning in a flood of emotions, I opened the door. "Oh, hi, Charley. How've you been? Come on in. Haven't seen you around for a while," I said, as cool as a cucumber.

"Yeah, I had to go down to Sanford to take care of my father. We all trade off and it was my turn."

"Oh," I replied, nodding and smiling. New to the game of playing hard-to-get, I nonetheless wanted him to try and win me over and to show equal—if not more—commitment than I did. On some unconscious level, I sensed the necessity of this.

A couple of weeks later, sitting at home alone at night watching TV, a soft knock on the door startled me. With a grip on my trusty two-by-four, I tiptoed into my mother's room and peeked through the curtain. Charley! Rushing to the door, I swung it open and looked up into his roguish smile.

"Hi. What are you doing here?" I said, beaming.

He smirked and said, "So much for a nice welcome."

"No, come in. I love seeing you at my door at night."

"Here's the book I wanted you to read," he said, and he handed me F. Scott Fitzgerald's *The Great Gatsby*, a book we'd discussed that was one of Charley's favorites. *He'd thought of me!* I smiled and thanked him, reaching to turn off the TV.

"Sit down," I said "Let's talk. Want something to drink?"

"No, thanks."

He sat on the small couch next to me and tapped out a cigarette from his Winston pack, lighting it and blowing the smoke over his shoulder. Comfortable together, we talked and flirted playfully for about an hour as electricity danced between us. His nearness was seductive as we sat inches apart, brown eyes gazing into brown eyes. On an impulse, I reached over and kissed him. He kissed me back, but then pulled away, rubbed his hands on his thighs, and looked toward the ceiling. I thought he would get up and leave, but he turned toward me, caressed my neck, and kissed me with an intense longing.

We sat on the couch making out for an hour until my lips were on fire and my body quivered. Even though I'd kissed a few boys before, this was different—consuming, overpowering, and carnal. I had stepped into a crackling hot tornado of sensations.

When we came up for air, he broke away and, holding my hands in his, said in a gentle voice, "This isn't right, I've got to go. You're only sixteen." He put his cigarettes back in his pocket.

I put my hand on his knee and said, "Please don't go, I don't care about the age difference."

A tender look crossed his face. "I know you don't, but I'm too old for you in this way," he said. "I shouldn't have done that." He stood up to go and joked, "I think it might be against the law anyway." I grabbed his hand and kissed it, and he touched my cheek and walked out into the night.

I lay in bed that night, my insides thrumming, unable to resist revisiting the encounter in my fevered mind, playing it again and again, holding his hand, caressing his face, kissing his lips. Nothing would ever be the same. I was different and our relationship had changed— there was no going back. I hoped more than anything it wasn't over. *This must be what all the books and movies are about.* I drifted at the edge of sleep, tickling the memory again.

When not preoccupied by school, the thought, smell, and essence of Charley was all there was. It had been two days since our encounter on the couch, and I yearned to see him again. I couldn't accept the idea that maybe he didn't feel the same.

The next afternoon, I spread my books and homework out on the dining room table and began reading as a mild breeze from the open front door ruffled the corners of pages. The sound of footsteps across the wooden porch caused me to turn and see Charley standing at the screen door. I walked out to greet him, and we sat on the swing together. He took my hand in his and looked down at our entwined fingers.

"I wanted to see you again and tell you how much these last weeks have meant to me. You're an amazing girl and I wish …"

"What? That I was older? Is that honestly what it is? Because it doesn't make a whit's difference to me."

"You're young, and I don't want to feel like I'm taking advantage of you. Anyway, you don't want to mess around with me. I'm not in a good place right now, not ready to commit to anything like a love relationship. And most of all, I don't want to hurt you."

"I'm not in a good place either, but that's even more reason we should be together. I may not look it, but I've lived several lifetimes in these sixteen years." In my mind, we fit together like hand and glove. We shared a deep empathetic connection, and I could tell that he, like me, had been a different person before his life landed on the skids.

This may be the last time I'll ever see him. I rested my head on his shoulder as tears slipped from my eyes. He reached under my chin and pulled my face to his for a long, passionate kiss.

"Then you think this could work?" he whispered, looking down at me.

"I know it will work," I replied and kissed him. That night our friendship became a love affair.

I had no qualms about my feelings for Charley, and he cared for me, but having a high school girl as a sweetheart rattled him. Oblivious to the impact that would have on our relationship, I disregarded his words. But, I must admit, he did warn me.

Before Charley, sometimes when I couldn't sleep and the hopelessness of my situation reached an apex, I would wander the streets in the middle of the night, often a mile or two from home, daring anyone to confront me. Rage bubbled quietly beneath my sorrow and misery.

One morning around 2 a.m., as I walked through the darkened neighborhood crying and muttering to myself, a police car cruised by and stopped. One of the policemen got out, walked up to me, and asked what was wrong. I mumbled something about a fight with my parents, and he put his hand on my back.

"Let us take you home," he said. "It's not safe for a young lady to be out this late alone."

Before Charley, life was a wrenching endurance of meaningless days. But now life meant something. My desire to live had been restored. If only my mother could keep the electricity on and the mortgage paid till graduation …

As the weeks went by, Charley and I became closer, both emotionally and sexually, and I walked around in the fiery, ardent hunger of first love. An utter novice when it came to sex, I explained to him I wasn't prepared to go all the way, afraid of getting pregnant like my sister Jo. I could barely take care of myself. This was a year or two before the pill, and the available birth control was hit or miss. Kissing my neck, he raised his head and said with a mischievous grin, "I get it. That's okay. There are other ways to love each other, and I'll teach you."

My house became our retreat, and with Mother absent, we had ultimate privacy. Charley never asked me to do anything I didn't want to, nor did he pressure me in any way. Tender and thoughtful when he touched me, a lover who put my needs and wants above his own, he was a man, not a boy, and he understood what was at stake for me.

After we'd been together for several months, we were sitting on the swing outside on a cool evening, kissing, holding hands. Without thinking, I said, "I love you, you know." We hadn't said the "L" word yet and it was a gamble.

He smiled and touched my face. "I didn't think I'd ever say that to anyone, but I love you too." We kissed and my mind emptied of all concerns as slow-building warmth filled my body, sweeping me into an overwhelming peak of pleasure.

Charley never overcame his reticence about my age, and I could tell sometimes it troubled him. He would go incommunicado for a couple of days, leaving me anxious and desperate. When he resurfaced, I'd warn him, "You can't do that to me. I've spent my life surrounded by unreliable people. It's the one thing I can't deal with."

"I'm sorry, baby. I needed a day or two alone to sort some things out." He didn't want to discuss it but promised he'd let me know when he needed downtime.

"The 'downtime' isn't the problem. It's the not knowing. Please, please don't leave me in the lurch like that." His disappearing acts stirred up painful memories—stability and security meant everything, and I had no idea how to move past my crushing need for them.

Charley invited me to dinner with his family, but I was reticent to accept, fearing his mother might reject me because of the age difference.

"My mother is the sweetest woman you'll ever meet," he said, laughing. "She knows how old you are and hasn't voiced any objections about it."

As he'd described, Lottie Wright was funny, kind, and crusty with wisdom. As we got to know each other, I discovered her life had been difficult. Dr. Wright, her husband and father of the children, had been violent with her and the kids and was inconsistent in providing for the family. A brilliant man, he'd been a writer and university professor at one time, but he struggled with anger issues, mental illness, and alcohol. I wasn't given the name of his illness, but it must have been severe to land him in permanent lockup.

A hard worker, Lottie put in long hours in the ladies' wear section of a department store downtown. Maybe fifty-five, she looked exhausted and much older than her age. But as the sole supporter of her two daughters—Emmalou, a year younger than me, and Susie, twelve—she had to keep going. Charley also had an older sister, Jane Ann, who lived a few blocks from me and was married with three little ones. His three older brothers lived on their own in Jacksonville.

By late October, I hadn't seen my mother for some time. I assumed she was still carousing with Doc from the drugstore, and even though I'd become proficient at taking care of myself, I agonized over the knowledge that sooner or later things would collapse. When she did show up, she would give me a wad of ones and fives from what appeared to be an endless supply of cash. As a result, I'd spent little of my summer job money.

I was sitting on my bed reading our English assignment, *An American Tragedy*, when the phone rang. I picked it up and the voice at the other end sent a shock wave through me.

"This is Sheriff Davis with the Duval County Sheriff's Department. Are you the daughter of Christine Knoche?"

"Yes, is there a problem?"

"Have you heard from your mother recently?"

Pulse racing ... *Was she dead?* "No, I haven't," I said.

"We'd like to come over and speak to you about a situation. Are you going to be home in half an hour?"

I hung up as my mind scrambled around like roaches when the light comes on. *Was she in jail, in the hospital, dead? And what would it mean for me?*

In less than an hour, two officers arrived at the door. After ushering them in, I sat on the couch, not trusting my shaky legs. They both stood in front of the fireplace facing me, and one of them asked again when I had last heard from my mother.

"What's happened … is she dead or something?"

The taller one held his hat in his hands and turned it around and around as he rocked back on his heels. "No, no, nothing like that," he said.

"Well, then, what? What has she done?" I said, more anxious with each word.

"We're trying to locate Bernard Simon, the pharmacist at the Riverside pharmacy, and we believe your mother may be with him."

"Oh. You mean Doc Simon?"

"Yeah, that's the one. He absconded with a lot of money from the pharmacy, along with a ton of pills and other drugs. We were told by employees at the store that your mother was his girlfriend?"

Oh boy, this is serious … this is where it ends. "No, officer, I'm sorry, I don't have any information about that," I said. "She has been dating Doc Simon for several months, but that's all I know."

"Have you ever met Simon?"

For some reason, I lied and said no. I'd seen him for a second when my mother got a ride home the day of my razor incident. I stood up and assured the policemen I would have my mother contact them as soon as I heard from her.

"Well, please tell her to call us right away—this is an urgent matter," one said, handing me his card.

Moving to the door and opening it, I replied, "Oh, yes, I will. Thank you." I ushered them out before they could start asking how old I was and why I was living alone. The soft swish of the closing door and the clunk of the lock echoed in the silent room.

Another week went by before Mother called. I'd been on my way out the door for school and had to make it quick. "Where in the hell are you?" I demanded.

"Sorry, I didn't get a chance to let you know, but Doc and I have been down in Sarasota for a little vacation."

"Vacation? Is that what you call it? You'd better get your ass back home pronto because the police are looking for you two. I have to go now," I said and hung up.

She came home a few days later stinking of alcohol and wove a bullshit story about how Doc hadn't done anything wrong. He was taking his scheduled two-week vacation, and someone had robbed the drugstore in his absence. She claimed it was a big misunderstanding that would be resolved in no time.

I shook my head in disgust and said, "This is serious, and it just might be resolved by the police hauling you off to jail with your boyfriend."

Doc Simon did go to jail, and we never heard from him again, but my smooth-talking mother wasn't charged with anything. She did lose her job, and from that point on, things got worse real fast. Without a paycheck, she couldn't pay the mortgage or the utility bill. Drinking or drunk during the day, she hung out at the bars at night, sometimes coming home, but often not returning for days. Gram gave her enough money to cover the bills for a couple of months, but when I spoke to my grandmother, I lied and said Mother would get a job soon and that she should keep her money. I didn't mention how dire the situation was—we were hurtling toward the brink, and Gram's money wasn't going to save us.

CROSSING THE RUBICON
October 1963

"The wound is the place where the light enters you."
—Rumi

One evening a couple of weeks later, Charley and I strolled toward my house after seeing a movie in Five Points, a quaint area nearby with a theater, small shops, and restaurants. A solitary car parked at the curb in front of my house caught my attention, but I assumed it was someone visiting a neighbor. We lingered on the porch, kissing and saying good night. Charley liked to walk his mom home from the bus stop when she worked late, and after one long, last kiss, I watched him disappear into the shadows and I stepped into the house.

Grabbing the two-by-four, I started to check the rooms but stopped in front of my mother's door. *Had I closed it before I left?* I couldn't be sure. Easing the door open and peeking in the room, I gasped. The shades were open, and a full moon illuminated the room. My naked mother gyrated on top of a bald, heavyset man who was also nude. The two-by-four dropped from my hand and clattered onto the floor, but they were too drunk to notice. Dashing for the front door, I scuttled down the steps onto the sidewalk and ran, the image of my mother and the man burned on the back of my eyelids. *This is it. I can't take any more. I'm never going back to live in that house.*

Two hours later, after walking in circles, crying, and wiping tears on my sleeve, I ended up in front of Charley's house. He brought me in and held me while I cried. We lay on the couch together in a bed he made for me and talked about what I would do next. Six more months of school and I was homeless.

Jane Ann, my favorite of Charley's sisters, came over the next afternoon with her three stairstep kids who were still in diapers. One, if not all three, was usually crying, hungry, or wet. But Jane Ann was amazing—blessed with the "happy gene" and always ready with a droll comment or a snappy zinger. Her wide smile and effortless laugh never failed to lighten the mood.

"How do you manage with three babies this close in age?" I asked her.

"Most days I feel like I live in a blender on full blast without a lid, but it helps to be crazy and medicated," she teased. Tiny—under a hundred pounds, I'm sure—Jane Ann moved like a whirling dervish with a cigarette in one hand and a cup of coffee in the other. Her head of long blonde, cork-screw curly hair was bigger than she was.

As I changed the youngest baby on the couch, Charley challenged my diapering skills.

"Hey, I'm sure I'm better than you are," I said, and I held the baby up for inspection.

"You know, you'd make a great nanny. Jane Ann, are you in the market for a nanny? All you need to do is provide room and board for this young lady and she's yours," he said as he swept his arm over toward me. For a split second, his words hung in the air, but then the light went on. Charley continued in earnest, "She could be an extra pair of hands around the house."

I chimed in, saying, "I'm good at laundry and cleaning, and I need a place to stay until I finish school." I held my breath waiting for an answer.

Jane Ann's eyes got wide and she said, "Hell, yeah! I think that would be dandy. We can set up a bed for you in the boys' room. Sounds like a plan. I could sure use a little help."

"Oh, thank you, Jane Ann," I said, hugging her. "You won't regret this, I promise." I loved her for not prying into why I needed a place to stay. My boyfriend's sister's crowded apartment would be my new home.

Later that afternoon, after I'd gone home to grab some of my things, Jane Ann ushered me into the apartment. Stunned, I stood in the doorway with my bags hanging at my sides.

"Come in, come in," she said. "I know it's a mess right now. I haven't had time to tidy up." *Tidy up? This place needs a bulldozer.* My eyes tried to take in the jumble of confusion and mess: newspapers and mail stacked on surfaces, clothes piled and strewn in corners, toys scattered two and three deep, dirty dishes growing mold in the sink and on the table, garbage overflowing in the kitchen, and ashtrays spilling butts and ashes. *How did people live like this?*

I couldn't survive in that squalor for six months—there was nothing left to do but whip it into shape. After I returned from school the next day, I started the laundry and cleaned up the kitchen. It took me two weeks of hard labor, but at last the apartment was clean and tidy. Once we had cleanliness and order, Jane Ann and I organized the kitchen, laundry room, and all the toys, making it much easier to keep some kind of control. She thanked me over and over, saying this was her new beginning.

"After the third baby, I gave up. I didn't know where to start and I had no time. You are a miracle worker," she said. I beamed with a sense of accomplishment, grateful I could pay back her kindness. Over the weeks, we became close friends, and I shared my circumstances with her.

November 22, 1963: An announcement came over the PA system during algebra class. President Kennedy had been shot and was hovering between life and death. The classroom erupted in screams and tears thirty minutes later when the intercom crackled with the news that he had died and school would close. A general malaise fell over all of us at Jane Ann's. We couldn't remove our attention from the TV, and even the babies were more subdued than usual.

Each day I lived with Charley's sister, her husband Chet, and the kids, I gave thanks for a safe place to lay my head at night and for people who were willing to offer me a soft landing when I needed it most. I grew to love the children, and with more attention, they calmed down a bit. Jane Ann got her mojo back and with my help, she kept the apartment clean and organized.

The day before Thanksgiving that year, I lied when I called Gram and explained I was too sick with a stomach virus to come for dinner. The tradition was to celebrate at her house with extended family, but this year I would be with Charley. She didn't know I'd moved out, and I doubted my mother would show up without me.

A large crowd gathered at Lottie's for Thanksgiving, including all the siblings and their spouses, as well as a few of Charley's Army buddies. Their warm, authentic clan pulled me in, and my cheeks flushed with happiness amid the laughs and good-natured teasing. That day, I experienced a connectedness I hadn't known, and I squeezed Charley's hand under the table. He bent down and kissed me while his brothers hooted and clapped.

In December, Jane Ann came home from her errands and told me she had heard scuttlebutt in the drugstore that my mother was looking for me. It had been over a month since I'd left. *Please leave me alone and let me finish school in peace.* But within a few days, she called, hopping mad.

"I want you home now," she said. "I won't stand for you running away. I've made a nice home for you and you're too young to be living anywhere else."

I laughed at the absurdity. "You fooled me once, but not again. Don't hold your breath waiting for me to come back. I'm staying here till I finish school." Furious, she slammed the phone down, and I remembered too late the peril of making my mother that mad.

The following week, I'd come in from school and started a load of laundry when the doorbell rang. Looking out, I gave a little yelp and dashed to the kitchen.

"Jane Ann, there are two policemen at the door and I'm sure they're here for me. What do we do?" I whispered.

She stared at me, trying to gather her thoughts, then grabbed the dishtowel, dried her hands, and went to the door.

"Hello, officers, how may I help you?" she said.

I stood behind her and one of the cops looked around at me. "Are you Sherry?" he asked. I nodded, and he said, "Okay, get your stuff. We're here to take you home."

Jane Ann and I looked at each other, and she turned back to the policemen. "She can't go back there. It's an unfit place for a young girl."

I found my voice and said, "I'm not going back there. You don't understand what my mother did." I explained in brief what had happened the night I left.

"Look, let's all just go talk to your mother," one of them said in a sympathetic tone. "She seems like a nice person and a worried mom. Let's see if we can work this out. Come with us."

I had no choice. I'd go with them, talk to her, and explain I wanted to stay with Jane Ann till school ended. If she didn't let me, then I'd take off again when she disappeared. In either event, I'd be back soon. I left my things and got in the police car.

After we arrived at Forbes Street, all pretense of kindness or concern was replaced with hostility as the cops joined us in the living room.

"We know troublemakers like you—runaways who break their parents' hearts and get into all kinds of trouble, land in jail," the older cop boomed. "You're headed down a road of misery, young lady, and we're trying to stop you."

"You've caused your mother enough grief," the other officer said. "You need to straighten up right now. You know where runaways end up? In juvenile detention, that's where. Do you want to go to detention?"

Eyes wide, I looked at him.

"No?" he continued. "Well, then shape up. Stop causing your mother pain and worry and be a good daughter."

The room spun like a Tilt-A-Whirl at the county fair. I stood and shouted, "You've got it all wrong here. I'm the victim. My mother's the troublemaker. Do you think it's safe for me to come home at midnight and find my drunken mother in bed with some big, drunk, hulking stranger? Naked? I'm afraid to live here. I'm trying to finish school, and I need a stable environment to do that." Sensing their animosity toward me, I stopped. *I need to proceed with caution. They have my fate in their hands.*

My mother, who was sitting in the chair across from me and had yet to speak, moved to the edge of her seat. "I was chloroformed, Sherry," she said in a calm, confident manner. "I was raped. He put a cloth over my mouth and attacked me."

My head swiveled toward her in astonishment. "Huh? You've got to be kidding. Do you think I'll fall for that, Mother?" I gave a derisive snort and said, "That's a good one, Mom. You must be watching too much TV."

The cop threw his hand up as if stopping traffic. "Stop. Stop right now," he barked. "Your mother has explained what happened to her, and you could have the decency to respect that. She's been through a trauma, and you've chosen to be a delinquent. Do you know how many kids would give their right arm to have a loving mother and a home? Now calm down and try to listen to your mother's side of things."

How could grown men, policemen no less, get sucked into my mother's lies? I crossed my arms over my chest and glared at her with contempt. She looked past me and stood up.

"Thank you, officers," she said to the cops. "I'll take it from here, but thank you for bringing her home."

"Oh, you're welcome, ma'am," the policeman said, giving a smarmy bow. "Call us again if you have any more trouble with her." Turning to me, he made his voice stern and pointed his finger in my face, "As for you, if your mother tells us you've run away again, we'll be back and take you to juvenile. You've been warned."

They left and I looked at my mother, stupefied.

"Why do you want me here? You're never here, you're drunk when you are, and there's no money for food or the mortgage. Can't you see what you're doing to me? I don't get it. Why can't I stay with Jane Ann until I graduate?"

She put her head in her hands and started crying. "Why did you do this? Why did you run away? I've been trying to keep a roof over our heads, and you don't realize how difficult this is on me. I have no one to turn to, no one to help. You wouldn't come home when I asked. I had no choice but to call the police. You're *my* responsibility."

I did a double take. "Your responsibility?" I screamed. "Since when? I've been living alone in this house for *eight months*. I never know where you are, and I'm scared every night living here alone. I *cannot* stay here anymore. I'm going back to Jane Ann's." I stood up to go get some things from my bedroom.

Angry, my mother jumped up and grabbed me by the shoulders. "You're not going one damn place. Don't even think about it, because if you do, I'll call the police again and you'll be off to jail." She grabbed her purse and left out the front door.

Trying to rationalize my mother's behavior hurt my head. As angry as I was, my heart still ached for her and what she'd become, but what could I do? She had no intention of getting clean or being responsible, and it had taken her over a month to miss me. Maybe she had shown up at my grandmother's for Thanksgiving and this was the result. Or maybe it was another of her mind games. I'd lived with them my entire life and I was through. Someone had to change, and it would be me. I gathered up the rest of my things, put them in bags, and left for the last time.

A month later, when the police came to Jane Ann's a second time, they told me I had a choice—either go back home with my mother or call my father.

"We'll give you three days to decide, and we'll be back," one said.

Defeated, I had nothing left to do. But who brought my father into the picture ... my mother? No way. She hated him and would rather die than admit failure. I never found out.

The next morning, I called Gram to get Daddy's number. He had sold our house, remarried, and bought a new house. We hadn't spoken in nearly two years, but after hearing my voice, he said, "Well, what do *you* want?"

I gave him the abridged version of my life for the last eight months, including Mother's behavior and my determination not to return to her. His reply is etched in my memory.

"Shit! What do you expect me to do about it?" he said. "You wanted to live with that goddamned woman, now go live with her."

Boom! A firecracker exploded in my chest. I stifled the urge to scream, *I'm your daughter, take care of me. How can a father be this heartless?* Or the simple, *You owe me.*

Instead, I said, "Okay, but the police are involved now, and they know you're my father and I'm your responsibility. I'll give them your phone number and you can explain why you don't want to help me."

In a low, intimidating timbre, he said, "Don't you dare threaten me with that snotty tone. That's right, I *am* your father, and you will respect me." Click. The line went dead.

This should be interesting. What now? I raced out the door for school. When I got home at four, Jane Ann said my father had called back and would call again at six. A couple of hours later, I picked up the ringing phone and a cold voice on the other end said, "I'll be there tomorrow in the morning. Have all your things packed and ready. I don't want to be kept waiting. You're going to live with Norman and Viola" (my mother's brother and sister-in-law).

How had they been dragged into this mess? We'd shared a few holidays and summer get-togethers, but I didn't know them well. I had visited their house once in my life. Uncle Norman was the one in-law Daddy tolerated, but why would he think it appropriate to dump his daughter on them? The lengths my father would go to be rid of me still hurt more than I expected.

My aunt and uncle lived close to the bus line so at least I would be able to finish school and still see Charley. I packed my possessions in two cardboard boxes and one garbage bag as Jane Ann stood by crying and dabbing her eyes. Charley and I sat on the couch holding each other, and he assured me nothing would change. He would meet me after school, and on the weekends, we'd be together like always.

"I need you," I whispered. "You're the one good and sane thing in my life."

"I won't leave you. I'll always be here for you. We'll make it work."

Winter had come on strong that year, and the morning of my move, the sky was bleak and smeared gray, lending a gloomy backdrop for the leafless trees as they bent in the wind. My father pulled up in his long, shiny Cadillac, his scowl visible through the window. Next to him sat his new wife, Joy, a young, twenty-four-year-old delicate flower wearing a mink hat and coat, appearing every bit as high-maintenance as Gram had described. It was hard to believe she had a five-year-old daughter—she looked even younger than her numerical age. They stayed in the car while Charley loaded my two boxes and bag in the trunk. I squeezed his hand and he hugged me.

"You're going to be okay," he said. "It's five months. You can do that with your eyes closed. I'll call you tonight." He shut the car door, waving as we pulled into the street.

Once on the road, my father demanded, "Who was that?"

Defiant, I answered, "My boyfriend, Charley."

"Your boyfriend," he repeated, his tone incredulous. "How old is he?"

"Twenty-seven."

He turned around and glowered at me. "Twenty-seven is way too old for you," he said. "As of today, he's no longer your boyfriend. That's final. I forbid you to see or talk to him again."

Gazing out the window as dirty specks of rain spit on the car, I watched the scenery fly by and smiled in my mind. *If you think you're going to step in now and tell me what to do, you'd better think again, buddy. I'll see who I want, when I want, and you'll never know.* I ground my teeth and fired mental daggers at him.

THE MCCORDS
January 1964

"Our most basic instinct is not for survival, but for family."
Blaise Pascal

*T*he atmosphere in the car crackled with hostility as we drove across town. Daddy didn't introduce me to Joy, and she sat as silent as a figurine, not even acknowledging my presence. *Fine with me. I'm not planning on having anything to do with a woman who would marry my father. I'm sure they deserve each other.*

We pulled into the dirt driveway on Shen Avenue, and I stared at the tiny house where my aunt and uncle lived with their four kids. *Maybe I'll be sleeping outside in a tent.* Uncle Norman met us at the door and gave me a lukewarm welcome.

"Take your stuff into Judy Ann's room," he said. "She'll be sleeping in the Florida room."

Judy Ann, the sole girl in the family, had relinquished her room for me, and as touched as I was by the gesture, I didn't feel it was fair.

"Judy shouldn't have to sleep in the Florida room. I'll be happy to sleep there," I told my uncle. He mumbled something about my aunt and cousin being in charge of that and said I should talk to them.

I listened from the bedroom as Daddy instructed my uncle about Charley. Under no circumstances was I to see him or have anything to do with him. *What an ass. It'll make things a little more challenging, but it's nothing I can't sneak my way around.* Daddy had been a great role model for that.

In the new living arrangement, I kept a low profile, again trying to blend in. Sharing one small bathroom with six other people presented

189

a contest of wills. Morning fire drills started with, "You're taking forever. Get out now or I'm going to be late!" "Mother! Get Judy out of the bathroom." "No, I'm next! It's my turn." We stood bunched up in the small hallway, grumpy and impatient.

My aunt cooked tasty, well-balanced meals, and over the weeks I adjusted to eating dinner at 4:30 p.m. when Uncle Norman arrived home from his civil service job. Tall and lanky, he had a sardonic, antagonistic air about him, but he also had a great sense of humor and could be charming, funny, and quick to laugh at my quips. Uncle Norman and Aunt Viola were good people, but at the time, I questioned their motives in taking me in. I came to believe they did it out of loyalty to family and a higher calling of kindness and empathy.

In the beginning, Uncle Norman studied my comings and goings and questioned me every day in an effort to enforce the no Charley directive. He and I played a cat-and-mouse game for five months, but in the end, my capacity for lying and secrecy won out, and while he came close, he never caught me red-handed.

Charley and I were together as much and maybe more than before. I devised an elaborate plan for sleepover ruses with Joney, my friend from school. It worked like this. I gave Uncle Norman her phone number, and if he called, she answered as her mother and had a ready excuse: "They've gone for a walk," or "She's in the bathroom." Then she'd make a quick call to me at Charley's and I would return his call. Uncle Norman called one time and the plan worked like a charm. But one evening, he secretly followed the bus I rode to Charley's. When I arrived, Charley's sister Susie opened the door. Not long after, the doorbell rang. We peeked out the window and I saw my uncle's Peugeot parked across the street.

"Play along with me," I whispered to Emmalou, grabbing her by the arm. We answered the door and I said, "Uncle Norman! What are you doing here? Is everything okay?" He looked from me to Emmalou and back again, and I pointed to her and said, "This is Joney."

She smiled and said, "Hi."

"Oh, hello. Checking to make sure you made it," he said, and he turned to leave.

"Okay ... bye," I said as I closed the door. "Whew! That was a close call." After that incident, he eased off on the reconnaissance, no doubt pleased to have his home to himself on the weekends.

Many evenings after dinner, my uncle plopped down in his chair in front of the TV and knocked back several tall boys, one after the other until, florid and bleary-eyed, he took himself to bed. No one mentioned this, but I recalled a line from the book *Walden* by Thoreau that we were reading in class. Something about how the mass of men led lives of quiet desperation. Was that what I saw in his eyes sometimes?

Aunt Viola, a second-generation Italian who was soft-spoken and petite, was the glue that kept all the pieces together. She ran a tight ship and could be formidable, barking orders and issuing corrections to her kids in a nasal, high-pitched Rhode Island accent that begged to be imitated. With me, she was kind and considerate and never raised her voice. Dedicated to her job as a salesclerk at Atlantic Mills, a discount department store, she worked long hours with the energy of ten people, and my cousin Normie and I joked the store should be renamed "Viola Mills."

My cousin Norman, Normie to us, was a year younger than me, and we formed an allegiance, shared secrets, and broke the rules together. Judy Ann, a few years younger and a virtuous mini-me of my aunt, was fond of repeating, "I'm going to tell Mother," if anyone got out of line while my aunt was at work. Craig and Martin, two years apart, were younger cousins, and we had little-to-no interaction. I remember them as shy, awkward adolescents, out playing in the afternoon until called to dinner.

I settled into a routine at the McCords', but I never lost the feeling of a perpetual, one-night guest. A sensation of standing out of camera range and watching the action lingered. But the peace of mind in knowing I could finish school gave me the impetus and opportunity to crank out term papers and homework by the pound and earn all As. After signing my report card, Aunt Viola chastised my cousins, "If Sherry can do that, you can too. Now work harder. Bring home As instead of Cs."

Charley received a cash settlement from an accident he'd been involved in two years prior, and he used the money to buy me a small solitaire diamond ring.

"Are we engaged?" I asked in a timid voice.

"Would you like to be?"

"Yes, wouldn't you? It would be blissful, and I know we'll be happy together. I can't wait." I'd slip the ring on in the morning at the bus stop and remove it before I got home. We spoke about getting married and what it would be like, but it remained on the periphery.

My mother had begun calling me, curious about her brother's life, but the conversations sent me into a tailspin of depression. I started attending Al-Anon meetings again to help me deal with it.

One evening, drunk on her ass, she asked me, "Where will you go when you graduate?"

"I'm not sure yet," I answered, but it wouldn't be with her, no matter how much she begged or cried.

Bingeing while living with my aunt and uncle was impossible. Aunt Viola kept an inventory of every crumb of food in the house, but for the first time in years, I didn't feel the compulsion. As a result, I'd lost a few pounds, and I asked my aunt if it would be possible to have more fruits and veggies in the house.

"Sure. Tell me what you want. And by the way, there are several girls at work who've lost weight with the help of a special doctor. If you want, I'll get his name and you can explore it. Let me know if you decide to go and I'll give you the money."

Dr. Roach, a legitimate physician, specialized in weight management. An anal, prickly man, he lectured me about the hazards of obesity. Checking my weight on the chart he was holding, he sniffed at an invisible stench and looked in my direction over his glasses.

"This is unacceptable. You're a pretty young girl and this weight has got to go." (Was that a compliment? It felt more like an insult, i.e., *you'd be pretty if you lost weight,* and it never failed to humiliate me.)

Sitting behind his large desk, he went over the diet, giving me detailed handouts and explaining that the secret was grapefruit. One had to eat three a day, combined with copious servings of fruits and vegetables and a limited amount of protein. No fats or carbohydrates. Deflated, I knew I couldn't maintain a program that austere for long. But then he whipped out his prescription pad and began to scribble, his pen racing across the pad as he ripped each page from the tablet with a dramatic flair. He prescribed four medications: vitamins, calcium, a diuretic, and, yes, a little green magic pill. Recalling my experience with the little blue pill, I nodded at his directions, eager to get started.

Within a week, the weight began to drop off and my clothes weren't straining at the seams as much. The pills deadened my appetite and aided in keeping a focus on eating less. By the end of May, I was down to 117 pounds. I'd lost over sixty pounds in five months and a lightness had returned to my mind and body. *Is that me?* My silhouette in a glass window at school startled me. Charley told me often how proud he was of my accomplishment and that I looked fantastic, but added, "I loved you before and I'd love you at any size."

With a few weeks remaining until graduation, the troubling question of where I would live mounted. My father's court-mandated support checks to my aunt and uncle would end at graduation, and while I didn't think they would kick me out, they also weren't inviting me to stay. It would be best for all involved if I moved on.

Charley's job with JCPenney cut into our time together, but we spoke on the phone every day. Graduation reminded him of our age difference, and he balked at taking part in any of the festivities. I insisted we go on what became a disastrous double date with my cousin and his girlfriend. Turns out, a twenty-seven-year-old man has little in common with two sixteen-year-olds, and the artless conversation stood as a stark reminder of the gulf in our ages. As the clock ticked, the awkwardness rose, hitting the red zone when Charley lit one of his Winston's at the table. My cousin, a sixteen-year-old preppy wannabe, glared, clearly disgusted. *What had I been thinking?*

That experience left Charley reeling and ushered him into a mental space that he alone could occupy. I questioned if he would come around this time. As graduation neared, the days were filled with finals, term papers, and shopping for a white formal. Instead of caps and gowns, the girls would wear long white dresses and carry a dozen red roses, and the boys would be in tuxedos. I was disappointed and found it pretentious. Anyone could wear a formal, but only graduates wore caps and gowns. With sarcasm, I reminded myself we were, after all, an *elite* school.

With my weight loss, the dressing room no longer loomed as a destination of dread, and as I zipped one gown after another, the image in the mirror gave me goose bumps. *I'm me again; I won't ever go back. I'll never be that other girl again.*

But wait, did I think I could stay on the pills for the rest of my life? The truth is, I didn't *think* at all. For a girl who labored under the concept that her value depended on her looks, escaping the shame and self-loathing was as far as I could see. In the following years, I would discover that both past and self are synonymous, and that life-long trauma doesn't magically disappear, but on this day, I floated in a fog of oblivion.

Out on the street, walking toward the bus stop with my purchases, the air smelled sweet, overflowing with promise. I smiled, glancing at my reflection in the store windows as a rush of happy anticipation hit me without warning.

A few days before graduation, Daddy Mac collapsed and died. He'd been diagnosed with an inoperable abdominal aneurysm two years ago and it had burst. He died at home, gripping his abdomen, doubled over in pain with Gram by his side. Three days later, Uncle Norman took me to the funeral home for the viewing. The rest of the family had gone earlier in the day.

It was a tiny room with somber lighting. The large casket took up almost all the space and no one else was in the room. A massive building collapsed on top of me as I stared at the waxy figure of my grandfather, dressed as I'd never seen him, in a suit and tie, with his leathery hands folded over his chest. My first dead body. The reality of death, its brutal finality and ruthless inevitability, took the wind out of me. The small room began to telescope, narrowing my vision, and my knees went weak. Transfixed, unable to move, I was sinking under the weight of it. How could this be? I'd seen my grandfather a week ago and he'd been fine. Uncle Norman took my arm and led me from the room and out to the car. We were silent as we rode home, the image of Daddy Mac in the coffin clear as a photo in my mind.

I hadn't seen Gramma Elizabeth's body after she died. She had simply ceased to exist. But this was different. No longer an abstract concept but a frightening absolute, death was an arbitrary stalker who could come in the night, swift as a punch, and take you out. One minute you could be a healthy, living, breathing person and the next, a corpse in a casket, as empty as the shells we collected as kids.

In the coming days, a powerful existential dread came over me. The capricious nature of life was terrifying. The unfolding of each day could not be trusted, and the magnitude of facing my own death hurled me headlong into panic mode. At night in bed, I panted to catch my breath, certain I was having a heart attack.

Gram had never shed a tear in our presence, and now she spent days weeping and sobbing. As if trying to dim the shock, she repeated the story to anyone within hearing range—how Mac had jumped from bed around midnight, grabbed his stomach, and groaned. She tried to hold him, but he collapsed on the floor and died before the ambulance arrived.

"What could I do?" she said to us. "What could I do?"

This different Gram shook our foundation. How could Pam and Freddy live there now with our grandmother alone and with no transportation of any kind? My mother was surviving from pillar to post, drinking more than ever, and Daddy didn't want them. Added to that scalding pot of worry was the question of where I would live after graduation.

I hadn't spoken to Charley since the double date, but he called two weeks later and apologized for hurting me. He said he had needed time to himself. Although a blow, we agreed he should skip my graduation. If that's what it took to keep him in my life, then that's how it had to be. Soon it would all be over, and we could be together whenever we wanted.

To compensate for a lack of skill in typing and shorthand, I had borrowed money from Gram to enroll after graduation in a three-month cram course at a business school downtown. Going away to college had been my dream, but when Daddy disappeared, that possibility left with him. In that pre-community-college era, the private and pricey Jacksonville University was the only choice in the city. Despite lecturing me through the years about the importance of an education and insisting I fill my curriculum with college-prep courses in high school, Daddy wanted nothing to do with me now. Money? No, that wasn't the issue. He had plenty, he just didn't want to spend it on me.

But, no matter where I ended up living, transportation would be vital. Gram suggested I call my father.

"It's about time Jim Knoche stepped up and became a father," she said. I rejected the idea outright—Daddy and I hadn't spoken since he dropped me off at my uncle's, and I would not call him groveling. "He lives on the bus line and you'd have transportation to your business school," Gram persisted. "Pretend you're renting a room."

In the days that followed, I mulled over her suggestion and came up with a plan to shame my father into letting me live with him. Uncle Norman and Daddy shared an interest in boats and all things marine, and although not friends, they did speak from time to time. Summoning my courage, I asked my uncle if he could suggest to Daddy that he take me in for a short time, three months, until I finished business school. Daddy wouldn't hesitate to turn me down, but he might want to save face with Uncle Norman. My uncle agreed that it sounded like a good plan, and he would give it a shot.

June 6, 1964. For most, the day came and went without fanfare, but not for the over four hundred students graduating from Robert E. Lee that evening. I swooned with joy walking down the long aisle, a tuxedoed boy to my left, listening to the sweet sounds of "Pomp and Circumstance." Against all odds, I had done it. Standing on the risers as the valedictorian spoke, trills of excitement raced up and down my arms. The fact that soon I would leave my past behind eclipsed everything else… I was getting out!

After the ceremony, my friend Joney and I snapped pictures while her mom and dad looked on with pride. She'd also lost a great deal of weight and looked stunning in her fitted white dress. Her parents took the two of us to dinner to celebrate, and we returned to their house where Joney and I talked and laughed into the wee hours.

The diet pills had become a way of life now, and I held to the belief that bingeing and purging had been a phase, a closed chapter from a turbulent childhood. But soon enough, I would discover that emotional problems have a way of festering; you can say you're done with them, but that doesn't mean they're done with you.

A few days after graduation, Charley and I met for dinner and a stroll in the park. Walking on the sidewalk holding hands, I brought up the subject of marriage and waved my ring at him.

"You know, we can get married now. I've graduated and I'll be getting a job soon," I teased. "We could get a little apartment and be together all the time. Wouldn't you love that?"

He smiled as we walked over to sit on a bench. Taking a breath, he looked out into the dark night sky, then looked back at me. "I love you, you know that, but you're too young, babe. You don't want to get married at seventeen. Let's wait till you're twenty." He shifted on the bench and lit a cigarette.

"But you could re-enlist in the Army, and we could travel and get out of this dead-end hick town."

He shook his head and chuckled. "I wasn't cut out for the Army. I'm lucky I didn't get kicked out."

Watching the shimmering fireflies dance in the violet-black sky, I let his words settle in my mind. *Maybe he's right. Seventeen is too young.* But would he stick around until I was twenty, or was he stalling, postponing an inevitable breakup? Our relationship was not as red-hot as it had once been, and his disappearing acts troubled me. I'd impressed on him that the passive-aggressive way he handled his doubt was cruel. "If we can't be one hundred percent honest with each other, how can we build trust?" I had asked him. We dropped the marriage conversation and cuddled together, each lost in our separate concerns.

A week later, my father called with the formal pronouncement, "Norman thinks it would be a good idea for you to come live with me for a short time and I agree. Get your stuff packed and I'll be over on the weekend to move you."

I sat at the small telephone table at the end of the hall after we hung up. *Hmmm. I hope this isn't a case of "be careful what you wish for."* There were lots of hidden land mines in this arrangement, but the wild card was the wife, seven years older than I was, and her preschool-aged daughter from a former marriage. But at least I'd be able to get to my classes since Daddy's house was a mile from the bus line. The skills and certification from business college would prove invaluable in getting a job. Once employed, I'd be on my own.

Coughing Up Dust - Sherry O'Neill

COUGHING UP DUST
Jacksonville
June 1964

"I am done looking for love where it doesn't exist. I am done coughing up dust in an attempt to drink from a dry well."
—Maggie Young

*I*loaded my clothes and books into Daddy's car and said goodbye to my aunt and uncle and cousins. I would miss the security of knowing that each day was the same—no surprises. My sixth move since leaving home held layers of unknowns, but I vowed to make it work.

We remained mute on the ride to his house, sitting next to each other but miles apart. The house sat toward the back of the development on a tree-lined cul-de-sac. As Daddy pulled his Caddy into the garage, my heart began to race. *Calm down and blend in; don't rock the boat. You have three months here. You can take anything for three months.*

Joy, who was standing in the kitchen, gave me a nervous smile when we came into the house carrying boxes and bags. "Jim, put her things in the blue bedroom," she said by way of greeting.

I tried not to stare, but it was difficult to pull my eyes away. Dressed in a diaphanous, color-splashed silk muumuu that hung to the floor and wearing a pink silk turban, Joy had translucent, flawless skin and long, pearl-pink, manicured nails. Tall and as thin as a zipper, she had the air of a high fashion model, someone entitled to the finer things in life, one too delicate to lift a finger. *This is where all my father's money is going.* I carried my garbage bag of belongings into the house.

The blue bedroom was a *House Beautiful* showcase. Daddy put the boxes down, closed the door, and left the room without a word. I sat on the floor and unpacked. I opened the closet, but Joy's clothes, shoes, hats, and accessories filled the space. I jammed my clothes in and shoved my books and shoes under the bed.

From the bedroom windows, I could see lush, green grass, tall trees, flower beds, and a slate pathway leading to a large, sparkling swimming pool. I pictured Pam and Freddy splashing in the water, but in an instant, I discounted that possibility. *Joy doesn't look like she could take the commotion.*

Expensive, heavy fabric and leather furniture decorated the house, mixed with weird, futuristic wood tables and snow-white, fluffy carpet throughout. It looked more like a display than a place to kick back and relax. Staying for three months would be tricky for me, and I wondered how Joy's daughter, Valerie, handled this kid-unfriendly place.

"She stays with my mother. I'm not strong enough to care for her right now," Joy purred in a baby-soft voice when I inquired about her.

Hmmm … sounded suspicious … like another parent shirking parental responsibility. I nodded and made a mental note not to ask any more questions. I would put in my time and leave.

Each morning, I walked a mile to the bus stop and rode downtown to business school. Half the day I sat learning to type, and the other half I spent practicing the cryptic, squiggly symbols of shorthand, almost like learning a new language. I'd already reached sixty words per minute on the typewriter, but shorthand took constant practice at home. One of my high school friends was in the class and we added a new friend to become an inseparable threesome, having lunch together and hanging out before and after school.

Joy remained in her bedroom if I was around, but one afternoon I came in from school and found her out in the den.

"Hi, Sherry. Why don't you come in here and talk to me for a while?"

After putting my books away, I came back and took a seat on the couch. Approaching the conversation like a friend, she asked all kinds of questions—what was I studying, did I have a boyfriend, what were my plans for the future, and did I want to go to college. Although she spoke in a congenial, gracious tone, my guard went up. Experience with interrogations had taught me circumspection, but I did answer the one about my boyfriend.

"You must have him over for dinner sometime," she said. "I'd like to meet him."

What the hell—more mind games? I smiled and nodded and reminded myself to avoid getting too comfortable with her.

After the first time, Joy often invited me to sit with her and chat. She spoke about all her illnesses—gallbladder surgery and a few other minor problems, none of them life-threatening or even serious. She dramatized and exaggerated her poor health, and it didn't take me long to size her up as a malingerer, a phony, and a gold digger. But I could be a phony too, and in an attempt to keep her on my side several more weeks, I smiled at the appropriate times and sympathized with her aches and pains. I even made some sappy, disingenuous comment about how kind and caring she was, joking that she was "too good for my dad."

Joy told Daddy about Charley, and he approached me one morning while I was having breakfast.

"You're an adult now, capable of making your own mistakes. If that's what you want, it's none of my business." What had caused his change of heart? Did he feel too hypocritical to forbid me on the grounds of age differences? Whatever the reason, I was thankful he'd removed himself from that part of my life.

A few weeks later, one evening when my father and Joy were going out, I asked if I could invite Charley over. Joy didn't answer, but Daddy agreed, saying in a gruff voice, "I'm trusting you and I expect you to behave like a lady."

"Always," I responded, thinking how artful and straitlaced I sounded.

Charley feared a confrontation with my father, but the idea of being alone together was worth any price we'd have to pay. I ran to the door when he arrived and pulled him into the house. Since we'd lost the love nest on Forbes, times like these were rare, and our wild longing drove us to take full advantage of the time we had.

My father and Joy returned home around midnight to find us sitting on the couch watching TV. After a quick introduction and a few awkward acknowledgments, Charley bolted for the door. Daddy would have blown a gasket if he'd suspected what I'd been doing, but my chafed face and red lips didn't set off any alarms.

CRUEL WONDERS
July 1964

"I abided in the unshaken belief that the time of
cruel wonders was not yet over."
—Stanislaw Lem

Joy watched me, sneaking furtive glances, like maybe she feared I would abscond with her treasured heirlooms. If I caught her snooping in my room or whispering about me, she smiled and said something like, "Oh, there you are. I was looking for you. Why don't we sit down and visit?" Unable to figure out her level of harmlessness, my first impulse was to decline, saying, "Sorry, I'd love to, but I've got a ton of homework."

During the time I lived with them, I put in a herculean effort to be pleasant and quiet, asking for nothing, accepting whatever rules and schedules they had without question. I didn't need to be told they expected me to be a potted plant, but even so, the atmosphere still vibrated with an unspoken hostility, a bristling at my presence.

My father left around the same time I did in the morning, but not before he found me and demanded to know what effort I was putting forth to find a job.

"Daddy, I'm waiting until I finish classes and have my certificate. Since I'll be applying for office work, I think it will be easier if I can type faster and include that on my application." I kept my voice modulated, even though I'd explained this to him several times.

After a month, he burst into my bedroom one morning.

"Here!" he shouted, as the classifieds came sailing toward me. "I don't want you waiting and sitting around on your butt. You need a job.

I want proof you're going on interviews every day. Circle at least two a day and report back to me."

Taking a deep breath, I stood there holding the paper, reeling at his illogical and cruel demand. He made it clear that I'd disrupted his life; my presence galled him, and one small infraction on my part would give him cause to throw me out. But I remained unwavering in my resolve to stay the course, and rather than argue, I swallowed my angry retort and sat on the bed to study the want ads.

Each morning I circled several jobs in the paper and followed up with calls. The next day after class, I walked the sidewalks of Jacksonville, going on interviews and being rejected. Due to my father's unrealistic demand, I applied for positions that required copious experience I claimed to have but didn't, hoping I could somehow finesse my way in.

Sitting in an architect's office one afternoon, waiting to take what I presumed was a typical typing test, I had to admit, shamefaced, that I had never seen a machine like the one in front of me. A typewriter? Well, kind of, except for the mysterious symbols on the keyboard replacing all the letter keys.

Similar scenes played out often in different arenas in my quest to have two interviews a day. Even as a seventeen-year-old kid with no qualifications or experience, I wanted something better than a menial, dead-end job, something with room for advancement.

After school, I wandered around the huge downtown area, map in hand, trying to locate various offices in the sweltering summer heat. At the end of the day, after clocking miles in heels on concrete, I stifled a groan on the bus as I removed my shoes and reached down to rub my screaming feet. To placate my father during his daily cross-examination, I exaggerated by saying, "This one looks promising," or "That one said I had a good shot." Holding him off too much longer would present a challenge.

Daddy's parenting skills had gone from cold and detached to merciless and tyrannical. Most mornings he came into my room, bathroom scale under his arm, and demanded I weigh myself in front of him. Aware I had lost sixty pounds, he fixated on keeping me thin. If my weight fluctuated up a pound, he warned me to get control; he wouldn't tolerate fat and lazy. Since I still took one or two of the magic pills every day, there was little chance of that. In the past, I would have refused this bizarre, vengeful treatment, but now I obeyed, repeating my mantra, and adding, *Only one more month.*

Joy offered to buy me a suit for my interviews and at one point told me how glad she was I'd come to live with them. Her words prompted me to let down my guard and ask if I could invite two girlfriends over after school for a swim. "Sure," she said with a warm smile.

To this day, I still question why I fell for it.

Karen and Gail jumped at the offer of an afternoon swimming. On the bus home the next day, in high spirits at the prospect of cooling off in the pool and hanging out, we chattered nonstop. Walking from the bus stop to the house, I reminded the girls to be quiet and calm in the house. I had already explained the weird vibe there, how I couldn't be myself, how I was always tiptoeing on eggshells.

We splashed around, diving and zipping down the slide for a few hours until it began to get late. After drying and wrapping in towels, we walked down the slate path to the sliding-glass doors and into the den, a veritable mausoleum, freezing cold and deathly quiet.

"I'm starving," Karen whispered. "Do you think we could have a snack?"

Aware that rummaging around in the cabinets or the refrigerator for something to eat would be seen as an unforgivable breach of decorum, I gave the girls each a glass of water and a few pieces of stale bread that were lying on the counter.

"Here, we can each have a piece or two," I said, as we giggled at the jailhouse hospitality of bread and water.

After changing, we sat around on the floor in the bedroom talking for another hour. As the girls were packing up to leave, I heard loud voices outside my bedroom, but before I could investigate, the door flew open, and my father's furious, knotted face filled the doorway.

"Get out! Get your ass out here now!" he bellowed.

The color drained from my friends' faces and they grabbed their books, bathing suits, and flip-flops and scrambled to leave the room. I rushed past my screaming father.

"Don't you dare walk away from me!" he yelled as he reached to grab me but missed.

I ran to catch up with the girls to apologize. "Oh god, I'm sorry. I'll see you at school tomorrow," I whispered as they ran out the door.

"Get back in here this instant," Daddy continued raging as I came back toward the dining room. "How dare you come in my house and think you can do whatever you want, destroying my furniture, eating my food without asking, having a gay old time! I'm not putting up with it! You're a spoiled, lazy brat, and I'm going to straighten you out." He whipped his belt off and came at me.

Through tears, I yelled, "I hate you! I hate you! I hate your stupid, ugly house." I started running and he chased me around the large formal dining room table, red-faced, yelling, snapping the belt at me, and trying to grab me.

"You get back here and take what's coming to you. I should've put you in juvenile detention when I had the chance. You're nothing but trouble, you ungrateful, rotten punk." My father appeared rabid; the veins in his neck protruded and his eyes had turned to burning, black orbs.

"You're a shitty father!" I retaliated. "Why don't you put me in juvie? It'd be better than living in this hellhole!" I screamed. Cursing in my father's face, something I'd never done, was cathartic and gave me the courage to let it all out. "You're no father to me. You couldn't be, you're too hateful and mean." Beyond constraint now, I let it rip. But my words only fanned the flames of his wrath. Determined to give me a beatdown if he could catch me, he skittered one way and ran another, but his moves couldn't compete with those of an agile seventeen-year-old. As I neared the hallway on one of our chases, instead of circling the table, I tore off down the hall, slammed my door, locked it, and pushed the heavy dresser in front of it. If he could get to me, I knew he would hurt me.

We engaged in a standoff the entire evening as he came and went, berating me and emphasizing how unappreciative I was, how he'd put himself out for me and all he'd ever gotten from me was disrespect and sass, and that I was a juvenile delinquent, as were my friends and lowlife boyfriend. He called the information operator for the official phone number of the Duval County Juvenile Detention Center, raising his voice so I could hear. After he hung up, he screamed through the door, "Good, I'll call them in the morning and arrange for you to be taken away. It's where you belong."

On one of his rants, he referred again to my ruining his furniture and eating without permission.

"What are you talking about?" I wailed, sobbing. "I've never done anything to your furniture, and are you talking about the stale bread we ate off the counter today?" I heard the absurdity in the question, but I still wanted to find out the origin of this unbelievable fury. Not one word of what he said was true.

"You or one of your good-for-nothing friends left a wet towel on our Luigi sofa. And that bread you helped yourself to was intended for a meatloaf the housekeeper had planned for dinner. But you and your grubby friends made sure that wouldn't happen."

No one would believe this! I was speechless. Illogical accusations didn't deserve a logical answer—that I didn't know the bread was going to be used, or that I'd tried to respect his kitchen, or that the towel wasn't wet but barely damp and couldn't have damaged his couch. Burning with rage and indignation, I would not give him the satisfaction of pleading my case.

He kept it up. "You're spoiled and you think I'm going to give you a free ride, but you're mistaken. You're getting nothing from me."

"Ha!" I yelled. "That's all I've ever gotten from you—nothing."

Then the final piece of the puzzle fell into place. "And how dare you disrespect me by telling Joy that she's 'too good for me.' I'm going to teach you a thing or two about bad-mouthing me like that. You're going to be sorry for that one," he threatened.

There it was! I would never know if Joy engineered the entire drama to get me out, but I was convinced that she had instigated this. Sitting on the floor, crying and resigned, the bitter injustice of it all consumed me. Daddy cared so little for me that casting me aside for that vapid, manipulative woman had been all in a day's work. My father's rejection, fresh and razor-sharp, still had the power to eviscerate me.

As the night wore on, he made threats to break the door down if I didn't open it. Certain he would not destroy his own property, I ignored him. Finally, he went to bed, and I fell asleep as the sun began to rise. After he left the house that morning, I found a suitcase in the back of the closet and packed my clothes, a few necessities, and my books. I got dressed and walked out the door for the final time. Joy and Daddy would be divorced a year later, having survived a mere two years together.

Walking to the bus stop with the heavy suitcase, a buoyancy infused my mind—I had left that poisonous environment behind for good. But where would I go now with two weeks of school left? As I contemplated my next move, a strange calmness came over me.

The typing teacher glared at me, then up at the clock as I eased in the door an hour late. Karen and Gail stopped typing and came over.

"Oh my god, are you okay?" Karen whispered. "We worried maybe he'd killed you."

I hugged them and apologized again for my father's behavior. Placing the suitcase in a corner, I sat down at my typewriter and went to work. Over lunch, we discussed the turn of events and my dilemma. Since it was Friday, Gail invited me to spend the weekend with her and decide what to do.

Sunday night, after sleeping at Gail's for two nights, I did my laundry, washed my hair, and tried to accept that I might be living in a park for the next two weeks. Charley suggested I stay with him and his family, but his mother, Lottie, didn't approve. Living together without the benefit of marriage was verboten in that era, especially in a conservative, backward town like Jacksonville. I couldn't bring myself to disrespect her after the kindness she'd shown me. Jane Ann and her husband had moved to Lake City a month ago. I was on my own again.

Mother and I hadn't spoken in a while, and I called her from Gail's. Foreclosure proceedings had begun on the house on Forbes, she said, but the process could take months, maybe even a year, and she intended to live there until the bitter end. I explained I was no longer living with Daddy and told her what he'd done.

"That son of a bitch! You can come and live with me till you get straightened out," she offered.

"No. I'm fine," I lied, "I'm living with a friend."

"Well, I want to take you out to dinner to celebrate your graduation since I wasn't able to attend. Can you come over Monday at about six? I'll be home from work no later than six-fifteen."

She sounded sane and sober, but I hesitated. *Maybe one dinner would be okay.* "Can I invite Charley?"

"Sure. I like Charley. You know where the spare key is. See you tomorrow."

When we spoke on the phone that night, Charley agreed to meet me at Mother's at six the next evening. Monday morning, Gail and I caught the bus for school, with me lugging the suitcase.

"Where will you sleep tonight?" Gail asked. "What will you do? Where are you going to live?"

211

"I have no idea. Maybe I'll sleep in the school building. I can wash up in the bathroom and sleep in the teacher's lounge." Classes were held in the evening until nine, and I could hide in the seldom-used third-floor bathroom until they locked up. Gail shook her head and remarked how spooky that would be. The business college was housed in an old, rambling government building, and although I didn't relish the idea, it would tide me over till school ended.

After filling out a few job applications on Monday afternoon, I walked back to school to retrieve my suitcase and took the bus to Forbes Street, landing on Mother's couch at 6 p.m. Bad energy filled the house, setting off a gerbil-scrabbling frenzy of memories, and I flipped on the TV to shut out the ghosts. A gentle rain started falling and the drops rolled down the windowpane like tears. With each passing moment, unease began to build into anxiety.

We'd have to cut dinner short if she was late because the success of my plan rested on returning to school before nine that night. I checked the clock—6:30. Maybe the rain had held them up, but a stab of fear made me turn up the volume on the TV. As the last scene of the program played out, I questioned how it was possible to stare at a television screen for over an hour and see or hear nothing.

Eight o'clock. The light outside had bled into darkness, and it was happening again. My mother ... I expected this treatment from her, but how could Charley do this to me? Well aware of my dread at being with her and spending any time in this geographical epicenter of intense misery, he knew how much I needed him. But he hadn't even bothered to call. In a matter of two hours, the last seven months of ground I'd gained were wiped out. That same frightened kid looked out the window again, crying and wondering why. Watching the hours tick by, I ping-ponged from deep hurt and anguish to trembling, knife-wielding fury, until at around 3 a.m., I curled up on the couch and fell asleep.

Streaming sunlight from the long, thin window next to the sofa woke me. After taking a bath, I dressed and left. Despite, or maybe because of the effects of the last twelve hours, I sensed a new power forged in the fire of my anger. Giving myself to cruel, heartless people, and expecting love and care from those unable or unwilling to give it would stop today. Charged with a new resolve and mental toughness, I vowed to somehow make it on my own. And I would never, ever open the door of that house again, no matter what. *I have to keep going.*

Exhausted from sleep deprivation and emotional upheaval, not to mention the simmering August heat, after school I skipped the job hunting and walked to Morrison's Cafeteria downtown to sit with a glass of tea. I needed to kill several hours before I could go back to school for the night.

As I moved down the line, smells from the fresh, tasty food stirred hunger pangs and made my mouth water, but my money had to last, and it would go fast now that I was homeless. Standing in the line waiting to pay, glass of iced tea on the tray, I turned at the sound of my name. Scanning the diners, I saw Allison waving and motioning me over. We hadn't spoken since that day at school when I had told her she needed to forget about me, that she couldn't understand my problems. Pride had prevented me from allowing her or any of my friends to see what I'd become. But today, she looked like a long, cool drink in a scorching desert, and I hurried over with the glass in one hand and suitcase in the other. We hugged and laughed and cried as if we were back in high school, best friends again.

Allison glanced at the suitcase and said, "What's with that? Going somewhere?"

We sat and I related my ordeal over the last year. She looked at me with tears glistening in her long lashes and said, "I can't believe you've been through all this since you left our house. Where are you going to live now?"

I explained my tentative plan to sleep at school for two weeks till I graduated. Almost choking on her pudding, she yelped, "Oh my god. You don't have to—my parents left today for a three-week trip. Just this morning I wished you were still here, how we could have fun like old times, and here you are!"

"Really? I can stay with you?"

"Oh yeah!" she yelled. "We'll have a ball." Our squealing and excited shouts had drawn the attention of several people in the restaurant, but I didn't care—nothing mattered now except that I had a safe, comfortable place to live for the next twenty-one days. At least for the time being, my worries were over.

Walking toward Allison's car in the parking lot, we jabbered and laughed, excited to have three weeks together without parents. Memories of all the times we'd spent together came rushing back. Oh, how much I'd missed her!

She explained she had a job at Family Finance Company, a few blocks away, and had been having a late lunch at Morrison's. Loading my suitcase in the trunk, we agreed to meet back in a couple of hours and go home together.

"At least you'll have a place to stay for three weeks," Allison said as she slammed the trunk closed and we hugged again.

Meeting at Morrison's that afternoon at the exact moment I stood at a precarious crossroad—was it kismet? A miracle? At the time, I accepted the gift at face value, but years later, reflecting on my life, I allowed for the possibility that maybe someone up there *had* been looking out for me.

Those three weeks were the most fun I'd had in years. We gathered our old friends and celebrated by throwing slumber parties, gossiping, laughing, and reveling in general mayhem. Allison and I fell into our familiar closeness and talked about how great it would be to get an apartment together and become swinging bachelorettes, but her parents insisted she wait until she was twenty-one to move out. The first few days I missed Charley and grieved his betrayal, but with each passing day, the ache lessened as I considered a life without him.

I received my certificate from CBJC, a rather banal accomplishment, but noteworthy considering the circumstances. The disheartening job hunt, the many dead ends and strikeouts, might at last yield gold. Before I had a chance to find out, my friend Gail called two days later to let me know she'd gotten a job with the welfare department as a clerk typist. She suggested I call for an interview.

The next morning, dressed in my starched and pressed white blouse and tan straight skirt, brown pumps, and stockings, I rode the bus downtown to Bay Street. The drab old buildings that had once housed the Jacksonville Shipyards were now home to the Florida State Welfare Department. Walking toward the front door, I stopped to look up at the shiny state seal of Florida, sparkling in the morning sun. *This will be the most adult, knowledgeable interview I've ever given.* I took a deep breath and squared my shoulders as I entered.

The receptionist at the front desk pointed me to the director's office, and I walked down the hall to a symphony of snapping typewriter keys and the whooshing sound of return carriages with their tinkling bells. The offices were standard government-issue—black, gray, or drab olive-green, austere, and metal. The secretary motioned for me to take a seat and said the director would be with me in a moment. I fiddled with my purse zipper and crossed and uncrossed my legs, correcting my posture in an attempt to convey an air of confidence. The intercom buzzed and a tinny voice said, "Please send her in, Barbara."

Sitting behind the enormous, mirror-shiny desk was an angel in the person of Director Pansy Mattair. Beautiful, tall, and thin, she looked to be about forty and was dressed in elegant attire. Her soft, welcoming demeanor radiated understanding and compassion. She gave me a warm smile and said, "Have a seat and tell me about yourself."

Words tumbled out in a breathless stream. I was a high school graduate, I'd completed a certified secretarial course at CJBC, I could type eighty words a minute, my shorthand was about 120 words a minute, and I needed a job.

She sat back in the chair and her dazzling eyes twinkled. "Take a deep breath and relax," she said in a soothing tone. "We have a job for you. You can begin as a Clerk-Typist II, provided you can type fifty words per minute, but from what you say, you can far exceed that. The beginning salary is two-hundred-thirty-two dollars per month, but you will be eligible for raises in six-month increments. There is room for advancement here as well."

Tears sprang to my eyes and I brushed them away. Sitting on the edge of the chair, I said, "Thank you from the bottom of my heart. I will work harder than anyone else here and make you happy you hired me."

Her laugh was full and genuine as she rose and extended her hand to me. "It's been a pleasure meeting such a bright, ambitious girl. My secretary will administer your typing test."

I aced the test, typing over eighty words per minute, and Barbara smiled at the results. "Impressive," she said, handing me a stack of papers to fill out. "You'll start on Monday at eight. We work until five with an hour for lunch. When you come in on Monday, report to me and I will take you to your office."

I struggled to sit still on the bus back to Allison's, anxious to tell someone the thrilling news. But now I faced the huge challenge of where to live. No question I had to be on the bus line, but the idea of living alone frightened me, and could I afford to live in a decent apartment without a roommate? I had a few days to come up with an answer.

"Yes! Yes! You got a job. Way to go," Alli said as she hugged me. Grabbing the phone in the kitchen and grinning, she said, "Let's have one last big party—we have to celebrate."

I called Gram the next day to tell her I'd gotten a job. She didn't miss a beat. "I talked to Gladys Hopkins at church last Sunday and her grand-daughter, Sandra, lives about a mile from here," she said. "She drives into town for work every day and Gladys said Sandra would be happy to take you to and from work for a few dollars a month in gas money.

I told Gram I'd think about it, and we hung up. I had no other choice, but I needed a day or two to accept it. I planned to leave Allison's before her parents came home, mostly to avoid Jake's "I told you so."

My mother phoned Gram for Allison's number and called me the next day to tell me Charley had called asking for me. We hadn't spoken since the night he stood me up, and I had no urge to talk to him.

The freedom I'd tasted over the last three weeks had awakened my desire to experience life as most seventeen-year-olds. But I *was* bewildered it had taken a meager three weeks to get over the love of my life. What did that say about me?

In truth, our relationship had died the night he stood me up at my mother's. No matter what his excuse, tying myself to someone who could hurt me in a cruel and purposeful way opened the door to more of the same, and I'd had enough of that to last a lifetime.

PART V

Without A Map- Sherry O'Neill

WITHOUT A MAP
Jacksonville
August 1964

"My sun sets to rise again."
—Robert Browning

Allison drove me to the bus stop, and we hugged and promised to keep in touch, maybe get that apartment together one day. I held her tight and said, "You'll always be my best friend. You saved my butt again."

"I hope the next time I see you, you'll be rid of this damn thing," she joked, retrieving the now battered suitcase.

"Me too," I said, taking it from her. I crossed the street to the bus stop, and we waved goodbye as she drove away. After a twenty-minute ride downtown, I walked to the Greyhound bus station for the trip to my grandmother's.

An hour later, the Greyhound deposited me at the corner of Normandy Boulevard and Lenox Avenue. I stepped from the curb, crossed the street, and went into the 7-Eleven, the last sign of modern existence for miles. After paying for a Tab cola, I stood outside under the awning and drank from the cold pink can, fortifying myself for the final leg of the journey—a hot, two-mile hike to Gram's.

Hurling the suitcase into the dumpster flitted through my mind, but it contained the few remaining possessions I owned. I tossed the empty can in the trash and started out, putting one foot in front of the other, lugging the suitcase and shifting it from hand to hand. Despite facing the inflexible religion regime at my grandmother's, I was filled with relief to have a home again.

At long last, I arrived at the creaky screen door. Pam and Freddy rushed me, and I bent down to share a three-way hug. As I stepped into the living room, the familiar earthiness and mustiness of the house, combined with the aroma of cooking and baking, took me back to family gatherings and summer fun. But most of all, they conveyed a profound sense of stability. The suitcase landed on the floor with a thud, and I collapsed onto the sofa's clammy plastic covering. Gram came toward me from the kitchen wiping her hands on a dish towel. "Where's the rest a yur things?"

"That's it. I haven't got anything else."

"Well, put that suitcase in the front room. You and Pam'll sleep there. Then come in the kitchen for dinner." I liked the way Gram referred to lunch as dinner—one of many old-fashioned, quirky twists in her speech pattern. The cuckoo clock crowed one time, and I smiled as I looked around the room. With few exceptions, time had stood still. The TV in the corner of the living room was bigger now, but that was about it.

Lofty oaks towered over the house, providing a coolness that neutralized the September heat. I glanced around the dark, fusty bedroom where Pam and I would sleep, remembering this was the room Jo and I had slept in when we were small. My grandparents' house was as familiar to me as my own face, but today I looked around with fresh eyes—the cherry veneer dressing table dwarfed by the oversized, round mirror where my mother and aunt used to sit and apply makeup as teenagers; the ancient, monolithic chifforobe that stood across from the bed, rooted in its original spot. Then my eyes landed on the door connecting the two bedrooms and that perfect, round hole where the doorknob should've been. Years of fingerprints circled the hole. I'd never contemplated it before, but now it took on a poignant note as I remembered my grandfather and the hands that built this house.

We sat down at the kitchen table to Gram's savory "dinner"—fried chicken, white rice, gravy, collard greens, sliced tomatoes from the garden, and cornbread—hot, salty, greasy, and delicious in the fine Southern tradition. My grandmother had a passion for baking and today she'd made my favorite—a tall, fluffy-frosted red-velvet cake.

After we finished, Gram took out her dentures, rinsed them in the sink, and went to lie down for a nap. Pam and I cleaned up, washing and drying the dishes and wiping down the table and stove. The kitchen was ripe with the odor of sulfur water from the well, mixed with an enduring veil of grease and the pungent aroma of baking supplies and spices from the tall, metal baking cabinet—smells that were unique to one place on earth.

I spread out across the bed in our room, and for the first time in months, I fell into a deep slumber. After church on Sunday, Sandra and I spoke on the phone and ironed out the logistics of our agreement for transportation.

"Thank god," I said when we hung up. "She seems solid and trust-worthy." My work life depended on it.

Within a short time, the untenable situation of living in isolation with no car, no bus line, and nothing but Griffin's within walking distance became claustrophobic. After Daddy Mac died, Gram gave his car to my mother, who turned right around and totaled it. Since it wasn't her first DUI, she spent a short stint in the prison farm as a result. A driver's license and a car now took first and second place on my list of goals.

Monday through Friday, I typed case reports from a Dictaphone recording. Boring, you might say, but having a job and working toward my objectives gave me a deep sense of accomplishment. Each month I walked into the bank, pulled out my dog-eared passbook from its cover, slid it across to the teller, and deposited my paycheck, minus a few dollars for expenses. Over the months, the passbook became my holy grail of success as I watched the number grow. The discipline of delayed gratification imparted a feeling of control that was absent in other areas of my life.

Daddy promised the kids he would be there on Saturday to take them for a ride, but instead, he left them waiting on the porch without even a call. His disgraceful treatment of my siblings added salt to the open wound I carried for what he'd done to me. When I answered the phone a few days later, a cold silence greeted me, and then my father demanded, "Put Pam or Freddy on the phone."

Determined to hold him accountable, I said, "You know, you are a rotten father. You don't deserve kids. How can you be this self-centered and mean? Don't you know they look forward to your visit for days? What is wrong with you?"

His fury burned through the phone line as he shouted, but this time he couldn't terrorize me with a belt, and I gave him an earful. "You're going to die all alone, an old man with no one to love or care about you."

Freddy ran into the living room and begged me to stop talking to Daddy like that. "He'll *never* come see us again if you're mean to him."

As I handed my brother the receiver, I reassured him that Daddy was only mad at me. That was the last full sentence I spoke to my father for years.

Charley didn't have Gram's phone number, and I let a few more weeks pass before I called him.

"Oh god, it's good to hear your voice," he answered. "I miss you more than I ever dreamed I could miss anybody, and I'm so ashamed and sorry for letting you down. Please, please forgive me." His voice cracked when he said, "I need you and I want to see you. We have to talk." In an emotional turmoil, I agreed to meet and have coffee downtown after work.

On a blustery day in late October, I sat down in the vinyl booth at The Toddle House to wait for Charley. As I looked out the plate-glass window, my breath caught in my throat. Crossing the street, thin trench coat flapping in the wind, the love of my life looked unkempt and too old for me. The magic spell he'd cast had been broken. Dumbfounded, I tried to take in this bizarre shift; it was like seeing someone you know, only to realize you've mistaken them for a stranger.

He slid in the seat across from me and grabbed my hand. There were droplets of rain in his dark hair and rolling down his coat. He leaned over the table, stared into my eyes, and said, "How have you been? You look wonderful, beautiful."

"I've been okay, I guess," I answered, blushing and looking down.

The waitress stood tapping a pen on her green pad and asked if she could take our order.

"Coffee for me, and water, please," I said.

Charley kept his gaze on me, caressing my hand and said, "I'll have the same." After she moved away, he said, "I love you beyond words. I can't live without you. I'm ready to do whatever you want, get married, move away, anything." The intensity of his neediness made me cringe inside.

The waitress brought two steaming white, ceramic cups and placed them in front of us. Charley released my hand, sat back and stirring his coffee, said, "Tell me, how's the job going?"

"Great. I like it a lot," I answered, relieved to be on more neutral ground.

"And life at your grandmother's?" he asked, smiling.

I told him about all the forced religion and being without transportation, but said otherwise it was fine, that I was happy to be living with my little sister and brother again. In the past, we'd been able to read each other's minds, and he had to see my hesitation now. His handsome face had taken on the look of a wounded puppy, and his plaintive gaze drove a stake into my heart.

"How is JCPenney these days?" I asked, hoping to keep the conversation light.

"I've almost got enough for a down payment on a car, but the work is mind numbing. I'm going back to get my degree as soon as I can. I've put in paperwork for a government loan."

"Oh, Charley, that's terrific!" I said. "I know you'll do it—you have to." I squeezed his hand.

The more we talked, the more conflicted I grew. Why couldn't I love him like I had before? Overwhelmed with a storm of emotions, I cursed myself for the inability to return his passion. He was pouring out his feelings, and all I could think of was escape. When we finished our coffee, I touched his cheek, saying I had to get going and we would talk more on the phone. I brushed a kiss across his lips and walked to the restaurant to meet Sandra for my ride home.

Over the next weeks, speaking often on the phone, he tried to convince me, and I tried even harder to be convinced. After meeting again, it was plain to me I didn't feel the same; I couldn't conjure up those feelings again, and I had to tell him. But more than anything, I didn't want to hurt him. He had loved me when I'd belonged to no one. He'd given me back my life. But he had also destroyed my trust. It was over for me.

One evening on the phone, I found the courage to tell him that I had loved him and what we'd had, but I needed to move on. He was silent for a long moment.

"Charley, are you still there?" I said.

"If that's what you want, I'll let you go," he said in a quiet, somber voice. "But I want you to know I'll always love you." He hung up. Those were the last words I ever heard him speak.

Over the next two weeks, I grieved my decision, anxious that I had cut him out of my life and guilty for the hurt I had caused. The few times I phoned to see if he was okay, he refused to talk to me. I wanted to keep him in my life as a friend, but it was too late for that.

Two years later, I ran into his mother, Lottie, at the bus stop. We chatted and I asked her how Charley was.

"He's getting married," she sighed, "to a strange girl that none of us like."

"Why is she strange? Tell me about her."

She explained that the girl was the daughter of a city commissioner and had money, but she was snobby and peculiar and didn't like being around their family.

"Oh no, that doesn't sound like a good match."

Lottie shook her head and looked at me through Coke-bottle glasses. "When I asked him if he loved her, he told me he did, but not like he'd loved you. He said he would never love anyone like he'd loved you." Her sad eyes stared into mine, and a stabbing pang clutched at my chest.

Life was manageable as long as I had my diet pills, but around this time, Dr. Roach cut me off, saying, "You have to learn to do this on your own now. You've achieved your goal weight and maintained it. Now just watch your calories." But without the pills, the grinding fear and sense of worthlessness returned. I sought relief from these feelings in food.

It wasn't long before I found myself sitting in a new doctor's office waiting room filled to capacity, watching patients revolve in and out like Grand Central Station. Dr. Bennett appeared in name only. His nurse, a crotchety, no-nonsense woman, ran the show. She didn't waste time on niceties, explaining office hours were Monday through Saturday, nine to five, and shots were three dollars each. When I asked what was in the shots, she snapped, "They're diet aids. Isn't that why you're here?" Then she plunged the needle in my arm and handed me a prescription, ushering me out the door and demanding the next patient come through.

Walking onto the elevator, mere seconds later, a spectacular rush charged into my adrenal system, licking every nerve and cell along the way. A typhoon of bliss thrilled its way through me and I let the waves roll over—far and away the most glorious, off-the-charts euphoria I'd ever experienced. Sights and sounds expanded—I was alive! When the initial charge subsided, a glow of well-being circulated through me and a laser focus overtook my brain, a focus that would be wasted on typing. I should be discovering a cure for cancer or expanding the concept of relativity. Revved to the max, I couldn't believe how *good* I felt. Eating anything was a repugnant idea. After that first experience, I trembled with anticipation on my way to the doctor's office for my thrice-weekly injections.

Unaware of what was in the pills and shots or if they were safe, I took them anyway. I was in the hands of a legitimate physician who had sworn an oath to "First, do no harm," and in the early 1960s, most of us still trusted doctors. However, I should have known that nothing that good comes without a hefty price tag. The truth is, I didn't want to know; I was waging a wide-open attack on my flesh, and the drugs were a means to an end—thinness at all costs.

The black capsules kept me sharp, energized, and hunger-free; I had to remember to eat. The chemicals did a masterful job of masking the obsessive-compulsive relationship I had with food and weight. But like a game of Whac-A-Mole, the obsessions began popping up in other forms, from my crushing need for perfection that never failed to leave me defeated, to anxiety about my mother, or fear of death and fury at my father—any of my hot-button topics. I found it impossible to enjoy any of the ways my life had improved as mental and emotional wellness slipped further from my grasp.

Allison and I spoke on the phone often and met downtown on Fridays to spend the weekends together. She was in love, and a veil of rapture spread across her face when she spoke of her boyfriend, Jerry. His family had money and we took advantage of the perks—spending the weekend skiing at their lake house, going to fancy restaurants, and tooling around in his British sports car. They set me up with blind dates, but most of the boys were shallow, immature, and raring to make me their conquest. Charley had set the bar high for finding someone sweet, loving, and intelligent.

I dated all types—older guys, college students, blind dates—and after several months, I began dating a guy I'd met through a friend. Matt, a few years older, was easy to be with and dependable. One Sunday afternoon, he came over to take me for a ride in his new Chevy Malibu. As I slid across the black leather seat, admiring the smooth fabric, I said, "Hey, do you think you could teach me to drive?"

We ended up in an isolated farmland area and he put the car in park and jumped out.

"Scoot over. I'll tell you how the stick shift works. Relax and get the feel of it. Don't jerk the clutch out; ease it out like this," he said, as he motioned with his hand. Patient and laid-back, he sat in the passenger's seat smoking as we lurched and skidded along country roads, stalling and jolting until I began to catch on. After several more lessons, I pronounced myself ready to take the test.

The following week, Matt dropped me off at home and I burst through the screen door and into the living room waving my new driver's license overhead. "Hey, everybody! I can drive now!" Pam and Freddy came at me like kids running for the ice cream truck, and Gram nodded her approval. Now I just needed a car.

VAGARIES

"It's your road, and yours alone. Others may walk it with you,
but no one can walk it for you."
—Rumi

My sister Jo and her husband moved to Gene's hometown in Wisconsin after his discharge from the Navy. She had two more babies in quick succession, and at twenty-one was the mother of three toddlers under the age of four. On an afternoon in late spring, I went to the mailbox and recognized her handwriting on one of the envelopes.

"Gram. You got a letter from Jo," I hollered to her out the back door.

Sitting at the kitchen table, she put on her glasses and read the letter. "Well, we're gonna have five more living here for a while. You and Pam best gather up your things and take them to the little house."

Jo and Gene were moving back to Jacksonville. Now I could thank her in person for the gold bracelet she sent me for graduation—the only gift I had received. The letter said they would stay with us for a week or two until they found an apartment.

A few weeks later, Gene's long, black-and-white Buick pulled into Gram's dirt driveway, and we scurried out to meet them. We peeked through the window at three little towheads spread out on a blanket-covered palette like puppies, sound asleep in the back seat.

I ran around to the passenger's side and hugged Jo, telling her I was overjoyed she was back home. There were dark circles under her eyes, and she didn't hug me back. She acknowledged Pam, Freddy, and Gram with half-hearted hugs, then set about getting the babies from the back seat. Rebuffed, I stood to the side while Gene unloaded the car.

Over the following weeks, Jo told me of her deep unhappiness, confiding that her husband, a selfish womanizer, gave her scant help

231

with the kids. They never had enough money, and her resentment toward Gene grew every day. The bitterness had altered her personality. She was snappy and mean, especially to me, the obnoxious little sister. She rolled her eyes and made snide comments, putting forth no effort to hide her antipathy or envy of what I had—freedom. I sat alone in a field one afternoon and cried.

Two weeks later, they moved to an apartment in Riverside. When not working, I often took care of the boys, sometimes staying overnight, allowing my sister and her husband to enjoy a night out. Over the weeks, Jo softened toward me, but her role of condescending big sister lingered. Gene went to work for The B. F. Goodrich Company, and they began to resolve their financial problems. For the sake of the kids, they agreed to stay together and work on the relationship.

After seven months at my job, I'd saved enough money to pay cash for a car, and my brother-in-law agreed to accompany me to a couple of dealerships. The next Saturday, we drove downtown to find a car. I would have been easy pickings for the slick salesmen had it not been for Gene. I assumed, as with any other commodity, that the price tag dictated the cost, but when the salesman inquired if he could help us, the dickering began.

"Yeah, okay, but what is your rock bottom price today? C'mon man, you can do better than that," my brother-in-law wheedled and cajoled, enticing the salesman with the tidbit that we had cash and intended to buy a car that day.

Gene bargained the dealer down from the list price, and I ended up with a car and $200 for my savings. The spanking-new Plymouth Valiant, a stripped-down model with a stick shift, had no heater or air conditioner, but at least it had a radio.

As the salesman handed me his card and the keys, he said, "Enjoy your beautiful new car and be sure to come back when you're ready for a trade-in."

"Wow. I did it. I bought a car," I said, beaming.

Gene and I walked over to the gold-and-beige Plymouth, laughing and joking as I thanked him for his help. Out of the blue, the realization hit me—I'd have to drive the car all the way home alone, through downtown traffic and over expressway thoroughfares. I panicked. Back roads for short distances hadn't prepared me for an obstacle course of traffic.

"You'll be fine, kid," Gene reassured me, patting my shoulder.

Trying to finesse the tight clutch, I jerked the car through the parking lot as I caught a glimpse of Gene in the rear view mirror, doubled over with laughter. Pulling into traffic, I popped the clutch and stalled. Terrified, my slippery hands wobbled on the steering wheel as drivers zoomed around me, blowing horns, gifting me with middle fingers and menacing stares. By the time I rolled into the driveway two hours later, my hands had seized up on the wheel and my armpits were soaked. Everyone came running out to celebrate.

Mother came for a visit only once while I lived with Gram. She arrived on a Saturday morning with a woman she introduced as her boss, explaining that the boss was training her in a new sales job. I remember little about the visit, only the heartbreak in its aftermath. She couldn't hide the red blossoms of broken veins that filled her swollen face, nor her yellow-tinged skin. The phony optimism and quick laughter didn't disguise her shaky hands and wild gestures as she fidgeted with her purse like a trapped animal. Self-destruction had ripped away another chunk of her soul.

I longed to wrap my arms around her and tell her I loved her, and then yell, "Look at yourself! You're destroying your life! Why can't you see that?" It took all I had to sit and pretend with her. AA had educated me as to what lay ahead and the depths to which she would sink before dying. After she left, I went into the bedroom and lay on the bed sobbing into the pillow.

A few minutes later, I came out and sat on the couch to talk with Gram. For the first time, I witnessed an agony equal to my own in my grandmother's face; it was a mother's pain for her daughter. I asked if she had heard where Mother was living, and in a whisper, my dry-eyed, stoic grandmother replied, "I think Christine's staying with Cecil's brother, Bud, and his family."

Taking care of my mother and protecting her had been my life's work growing up, but there was nothing I could do now. Relying on the kindness of others, she was homeless, living a marginalized life. I sat there, letting the grief bore into me. Watching a person you deeply love destroy themselves will slice you open.

On the other side of town, my father went back to a carefree bachelor life after divorcing Joy. He had a big yacht and a sailboat he raced in different competitions up and down the state. Living in an apartment somewhere in Jacksonville, he partied and wined and dined his lady friends, out on the town most nights. The kids told me he said bad things about Joy and how she'd taken him for a bundle. *Ha! Couldn't have happened to a nicer person.*

I met Lacy Anderson in our Christian youth group, and despite that, we became friends. She didn't parade around in a cloak of religiosity and spared me all the phony Jesus talk or questions about why I hadn't been "saved." She lived nearby with her divorced mother who, rumor had it, was a call girl. The idea that Lacy's piety was a quiet rebellion against her mother did cross my mind, but we never became the kind of friends who had those conversations.

She called one Saturday morning and asked if I'd like to accompany her to the USO that afternoon to decorate and set up for an open house. Her uncle, a naval officer, worked with the USO, and she lent a hand with their receptions.

"This one should be interesting, though," she said. "Two French naval ships arrived in port and we're hosting them this weekend.

The evening turned out to be more fun than I expected. Although unable to converse at length, we used my small translation book to break the ice. The French sailors were charming—young guys away from home in a strange land. Lacy and I agreed that the USO had what we needed: a wholesome environment to meet guys and practice the art of flirting.

A month later, we agreed to help out again at the USO. After arriving that Saturday afternoon, we decorated, put out snacks, and chatted with some of the young men who'd drifted in. The large room held tables and chairs, a jukebox in one corner pumping out Top Forty, two Ping-Pong tables, a couple of pinball machines, and a pool table. Free refreshments were served from the kitchen at a pass-through window.

Lacy and I were in the middle of a Ping-Pong game when I whispered, "Don't look now, but a couple of good-looking guys just walked in." She giggled and we feigned absorption in the game. They headed in our direction and the tall one walked up to me.

"Hey, I'm Jim," he said. "How are you? Can I play a game with you when you're finished?" I smiled at him and nodded. *Hmm, this character is someone who sees what he wants and goes after it.*

Brad, the other guy, approached Lacy with a shy dip of his head. We played a game of doubles and Jim, almost tall enough to reach across the expanse, swamped the table with his long, graceful moves. Placing our paddles down, we went over to one of the tables to sit and chat. They were stationed at Cecil Field, a Navy base close to where we lived on the West side, Brad explained, adding that he was from Vermont and Jim was from Ohio.

Jim was a good-looking guy with big, sparkling aquamarine eyes and broad, muscular shoulders. He was open and sincere and endearingly unaware of his good looks, but there was no denying his appeal. As we sipped our Cokes and talked, I learned that he had enlisted in the

Navy out of high school on something called a "kiddie cruise"—join before you turn eighteen and get out at twenty-one with full GI college benefits.

"That's a great deal," I said, remembering I'd toyed with enlisting in the Air Force after graduation.

"Yeah, I'm starting college as soon as my tour is over," he said, piercing me with those baby blues.

Jim came from a large family, four boys and two girls, with three of his siblings still at home with his parents in Cleveland. They were devout Catholics, and his older brother was a priest. I spoke of living with my grandmother and told him about my siblings and where I worked, but I omitted any mention of my parents. We danced and talked the rest of the night. At closing time, Jim asked when he could see me again. Smiling at his straightforward approach, I scribbled my phone number on a piece of paper and handed it to him.

The next few weeks were filled with a whirlwind of double dates to the movies, the beach, and an excursion to St. Augustine. We took Pam and Freddy to Gold Head Branch State Park for the day and to a local carnival. Jim made no secret of his fondness for me, and we talked for hours on the phone in the evenings. I found him guileless with a wicked sense of humor. He was intelligent and sensitive, and my impression of his goodness squared well with the stable, traditional upbringing he described. On top of that, he was far and away the best-looking guy I'd ever dated; he was tall and slim with just the right amount of muscle and was always impeccably groomed. With shiny, wavy, golden-blond hair and a fresh, clean-scrubbed smell, he reminded me of a brand-new, unopened present.

After a couple of months, sitting in my car kissing and talking at our favorite parking place in Riverside Park, he took my hands in his and said, "You know I'm crazy about you; I think I may even be in love with you."

"Wow," I said, surprised. It had been a year since I'd broken up with Charley, and I didn't trust my feelings of love, not even sure what it meant. "Are you crazy enough about me to go to church this Sunday and get to know my grandmother?"

"Sure," he said, as a slow smile curled his lips, but I could hear the apprehension in his voice.

After that first Sunday, he became a fixture around our house, sometimes spending Friday and Saturday nights in the little house with Freddy and accompanying us to church on Sunday. He joshed with Pam and Freddy like a big brother and listened, attentive and patient, as Freddy told his stories. Seeing how my little brother hungered for a male role model only increased my anger toward Daddy.

Jim's genuine charm won my grandmother over too, but I'd warned him never to mention his Catholicism around her. She was convinced, as were many uneducated Southern Baptists of that era, that Catholics were satanic, that they worshipped idols, and that the priests had babies with the nuns and buried them. All of us were aware of her morbid enmity toward the Catholic Church and how apoplectic she would be if she found out about Jim's ties to it.

Accompanying us to church Sunday mornings, Jim listened with respect, but the faint expressions that flitted across his face indicated he had never experienced a cast of characters like those that worshipped at Macedonia Baptist. After services one afternoon, as we sat on the porch rocking and talking, I asked if he'd like to go with me to a revival the following Friday night.

With a serious expression and a slight nod, he stared at me and asked, "A revival of what?"

I laughed out loud. "A religious revival, goofy. Haven't you ever been to one?"

"No, never," he said and shook his head. "Catholics believe it's a sin to go to another church or service."

"Well, I think it will give us golden points with Gram. What do you say?"

"Sure, I'm up for it," he said, reaching over to take my hand.

The following week, we sat in a sweltering tent for two hours listening to a pounding, near-hysterical preacher rave about the flames of hell, the wages of sin, and the wicked nature of our souls without Jesus. When the call to be saved came, we watched one after another congregant prostrate themselves on the makeshift altar, wailing and sobbing as they begged for the mercy of the Lord.

Most of the participants had left their seats in search of salvation, and I feared we would be singled out by the preacher any minute. I nudged Jim and pointed to the flap in the side of the tent next to him. He looked at it and back at me with a quick nod. A few minutes later, I squeezed his hand, tilting my head toward the flap. We ducked out and ran to the car, breathless with laughter.

Talking on the way home, I asked what his take had been on the experience.

"Whew!" he said, shaking his head. "That was something. I don't know what to think. I hope that was my first and last revival, though." After attending my first Catholic mass, I realized how disturbing the experience must have been for him.

In September of 1965, we were wallowing in bottomless heat—the kind that bathes you in languor and never dissipates, even in the early-morning hours. Forecasters were talking about a strong hurricane barreling toward us in the next few days, but native Floridians, having endured many storms, didn't take much notice.

"What preparations should we make, Gram?" I asked.

My grandmother shrugged her shoulders and said, "Nuthin' to do, I reckin,' but hunker down."

Gram's neighbor across the street, Miss Annie, asked Jim and me to help her put up plywood on the big, plate-glass windows of her sprawling brick house. After we finished, she insisted we all ride out the storm in her solid, concrete home. After the hurricane passed, we crossed the street to assess our damage. A tall oak tree had upended and smashed onto the front porch, ripping screens and taking down part of the roof, while Miss Annie's fortress went unscathed.

The next day, I watched Jim work for hours in the heat, lifting the heavy pieces of wood off Miss Annie's windows and carrying them to the garage. Unlike the other guys I'd dated, he had exceeded my expectations of a boyfriend and a partner; his devotion and constancy never wavered. Maybe one day the two of us could build the amazing life I'd sworn to have. And it was possible I could even glom onto some of his normalness. We spoke of getting married in four years after he graduated from college.

Jim planned to attend a junior college an hour from Jacksonville then transfer to the University of Florida, also an hour away. We'd still see each other on the weekends, maybe even some evenings, and I'd stay at Gram's, saving money for our future. As much as I wanted this authentic, adult life with Jim, my ever-present fear and doubt didn't let me trust anything, let alone a fairy-tale ending.

Bits and pieces of my past were all I shared with Jim, but as we sat in the car talking and kissing one evening, a strong need to tell him everything came over me. He had a right to know and understand what he was getting into. Having spent years tamping down my memories, shoving them away with drugs and food, I assumed I could relate the details in a calm, detached way. But as I spoke, the scar tissue tore away, and tears crested and rolled down my cheeks. I buried my head in his neck.

He held me tight, caressing my hair and kissing my head. "It's all over now and you can put it in the past. I will never let anyone hurt you like that again," he whispered. In the moonlight, I could see glistening tears on his cheeks.

That night changed me. I had never been understood or validated in that way, and my heart broke open with a deep love that went beyond infatuation, need, or even sexual attraction—it was profound and sacred.

Sitting on the couch sewing a button on one of my shirts, I heard Aunt Corrine's car roll into the driveway. They had moved from our first tacky neighborhood into a big, rambling house near Cedar Creek, a few miles from Gram. Most of her visits took place when I was at work or out with friends and I'd been spared her judgment, but today I braced myself for the insensitive or nasty remarks I could count on.

"Mama, I'm here," Corrine called out, crossing the porch and stepping into the living room. She looked over at me and by way of greeting, said, "Oh, you're here," and walked through to the kitchen. She and my grandmother stayed in the kitchen, talking and drinking coffee for a while, and I eased into the bedroom to wait her out.

Assuming she was gone, I came out just as she was reaching for her sunglasses and saying goodbye. She looked at me, and in a childish, taunting voice, *sang*, "I know a secret about Sherry," like a bully, teasing a weaker adversary.

"Oh ... what's that?" I asked in a nonchalant way, trying to ignore the screeching alarm in my head.

A malicious smile crept over her face and with all the drama of a forties film star, she proclaimed, "Jim's a Catholic! Did you know that, Mama? Ha!" she snorted. Turning to Gram, she said, "I bet she never told you *that*!" She swung her head back to me. "Did you, Sherry?"

Blood pounded in my temples as I tried to swallow the boulder in my throat. Gram gave me a hard, sideways look but said nothing. Corrine sashayed out the door, calling "Bye!" as she left.

How had she found out? The answer came in an instant. It must have been during one of her clandestine interrogations of Pam or Freddy.

My grandmother didn't bring up the subject again, but the coldness in her voice when she spoke to me indicated it wasn't over. I pretended nothing had happened and relied on my ace in the hole—the car—to keep me out of trouble.

Not long after that on a Sunday, Jim and I were in the kitchen washing dishes and putting food away. He finished and went to sit at the table while I dried the last dish. Setting the dish towel on the counter, I walked over to him, sat down on his leg, and put my arm around his shoulder.

"I love you," I said, and in that instant Gram appeared in the doorway, angry and glaring. I jumped up and said, "Come on. Let's go sit on the porch where it's cool." In the shade of the oak trees, sitting in the rockers that afternoon, an ominous foreboding hung in the air.

A few days after the incident, Gram came into my bedroom, her stony face set with a look of pure condemnation. "Either you get rid of Jim, or you'll have to go. I can't have you behaving the way you were in front of my face."

Stunned, I looked at her in disbelief. "Go? Where?"

"I don't care, but you can't stay here," she said as she turned to walk out.

A tightness in my chest made it hard to breathe as I sat down on the bed and tucked my shaking hands beneath me, replaying the scene in my head, trying to understand her reaction. We'd been careful to keep our affections private, and the scene she'd witnessed had been so chaste it could have graced the cover of *Christian Monthly*. There was little doubt in my mind this was retribution for Corrine's revelation. I was convinced there would be no changing Gram's mind or having a civil discussion. It was her house—she could choose who stayed and who went.

Where will I go? Maybe I can keep seeing him on the sly and continue our relationship in secret. Could I fool Gram? I rejected that idea immediately. I'd done nothing wrong, and I wouldn't be forced to sneak and lie.

I called Jim and asked him to meet me at the base the next afternoon.

"Are you okay?" he asked, hearing distress in my voice.

"No, but I can't talk now. I'll tell you tomorrow."

Awake all night, I kept going over the shock of my grandmother putting me out on the street. Gram's had been my last refuge; there was nowhere else for me.

I picked Jim up the next afternoon and we drove to Riverside Park. On the way, I recounted my grandmother's ultimatum. The more I spoke of it, the angrier I got.

"My aunt is a bitch and I hate her. But how could my grandmother be that heartless? She doesn't care what happens to me, and that hurts more than I can say."

We walked around the pond holding hands, bathed in the waning light of early October, the heat of the day having given way to autumn air. The path took us away from the water and into the wooded glen where trees whispered as a breeze circulated, lifting the leaves off the ground. Circling the park, we came out on the other side of the pond and walked over to a bench to sit down.

"I refuse to live where I'm not wanted again," I said, wiping away tears. "But I don't know if I have the courage to take off, to live in another unfamiliar place and try to figure out my next move." Jim held me, kissed my tears, and reassured me we'd work something out.

Sitting on the bench in the serene quiet of the park, watching the ducks paddle around in the water as nightfall approached, Jim squeezed my shoulder. "Why don't we just get married now?" he said. "I don't want to live without you, and although it's sooner than we'd planned, it's a perfect solution. With both our salaries, we can afford a small apartment and share the expenses."

"Married now?" I said, looking at him in surprise. "At nineteen and eighteen? Isn't that too young? And besides, we've only been dating four months. What will people say?"

"Forget about the numbers. We're both much more mature than kids our age, and we've spent the last four months together almost night and day."

True, my experiences had matured me quite a bit in the last few years. Plus, we were good together, and I'd seen enough to realize that kind of compatibility was rare.

"You're right. This could work, but are you sure it's what you want? What about your plans for school and getting your degree?"

"I want it more than anything in the world. I love you and I know we can have a good life. As for school, nothing will change except that we'll be doing it together. That's even better." He bent down and kissed me and pulled me close. I nestled my head into the crook of his neck and pondered his proposal.

The flaw in this plan was the age requirement for marriage in Florida. Georgia, a half-hour away, might be the answer. But if that didn't work … the scary threat of living in my car would be a certainty.

"I'll find out tomorrow what the age requirement is in Georgia," Jim said. "Rest easy, I'll work it out even if we have to go to Alabama. I think the legal age there is twelve," and we both laughed as the night shadows danced on the lit pavement.

Gram, 73 years old (1965)

A watercolor I painted years ago from a photo taken by my cousin.

7750 Lenox Avenue (Gram's house), with the A/C unit added in the 1970s.

My graduation picture,
1964

Me and Charley after graduation, 1964

Joney and me posing minutes before
graduation

Joney, her boyfriend, Charley, and
me after graduation (1964)

Jim and I on one of our first dates (1965)

L to R: Freddy, Jim, Me, Gram, and Pam (Al—in front of me—is my father's stepson from his third marriage)

L to R: Jim, Me, Mom, and Kenny Heffner (soon after she moved back to Jacksonville from Miami)

L to R: Eddie, Ricky, and Mike, 1965

Jo's boys and me (babysitting and bathing)

Jim in the living room of the trailer (1966)

Mother, me, and Freddy in front of Jo's house (just after Mother's stint in Avon Park Rehab), 1967)

Jim's official Sears picture (1970)

In front of our apartment at Pompeii Gardens, Opa-locka, Miami, Florida (1970)

Just after moving into the apartment in Hollywood, 1971

FINDING MOTHER
Jacksonville
1965

"If I know what love is, it is because of you."
—Herman Hesse

I circled apartment rentals in the newspaper and previewed them after work. It took a week to locate a cute two-story fourplex. Newly furnished and clean, the apartment was a couple of blocks from the bus line and within our budget. Jim walked through the front door the next afternoon and declared the apartment perfect, adding, "Just bring your toothbrush … oh, and maybe some sheets and towels and dishes."

The marriage age requirement in Folkston, Georgia, was nineteen for the male and, with parental consent, eighteen for the female, doubtless a holdover from days when women were chattel. But who cared? We could work with it if we could locate my mother and prop her up long enough to go with us and sign. But finding her might be a problem. Gram and I weren't speaking, but I informed her I would be out the following week.

The last location I had for my mom was the home of the Langfords, her first husband's family. I'd start there. Jo might be a help since she used to visit her grandmother Langford as a young girl. After work, I stopped by my sister's house to talk it over.

The next afternoon, we loaded my nephews into the car and set out for the east side of Jacksonville. After driving around for an hour, ready to give up, Jo yelled, "Stop! That's it," and she pointed to a sagging, two-story Victorian. "I'm sure of it. I recall the gingerbread architecture on the front porch and that rusty turbine on the roof."

I held my breath as I ran across the street and bounded up the steps. A loud knock on the rickety screen door brought a frail, elderly lady shuffling to greet me.

"Yes?" she whispered.

"Are you Mrs. Langford?" I asked, out of breath.

"Yes. Who are you?"

"I'm Christine's daughter, Sherry, and I wonder if you know her whereabouts?"

She looked at me with milky eyes and said, "Why, yes, she's staying with us at present, but she's not here right now. She's at work."

Yes! "Can you tell me when she'll be home?"

"I suspect around six."

"Okay, thanks. Tell her I'll be back tonight," I said and dashed down the porch steps, across the street, and into the waiting car.

Later that night, Jim and I went back to the house. Mother answered the door wearing a red cotton robe and fuzzy slippers. "C'mon in," she said, smiling up at Jim.

"Mom, this is Jim and we're getting married."

"Wow," she said as she sat down on a battered, sagging sofa, her eyes brightening. "Tell me all about it."

"We're going to Folkston, but we need you to go with us to sign for me. Do you think you can do that?"

She lit a cigarette, exhaled, and gave me a broad smile. "Yes, indeed I can. Sit and tell me what led up to this monumental decision. When is the big day?"

I explained our story and what Gram had done. She pursed her lips, nodding a few times, and said, "Yep. That sounds like her."

Purulent sores, some bandaged, ran up and down her arms and legs, and I asked about them. "Oh, a little case of impetigo, but I've got it on the run now. It'll be gone soon."

The shabby living room smelled of accumulated grime, decay, and cats. My mother had been a meticulous housekeeper when we were growing up; in those days she wouldn't have touched a surface in this house. An unspeakable sadness came over me as I looked at my once glamorous and accomplished mother, now bloated, glassy-eyed, and emaciated. I had to get out of there before I broke down.

We hugged goodbye, and I begged, "Mom, please don't let me down. If you do, we can't get married and I will have no place to live. Please, please, Mom. We'll pick you up."

"Don't worry about it, Sherry. Sonny (one of the Langfords' grown sons) will drive me there, and I'll make sure he gets me up early. I'll see you Tuesday morning at eight-thirty at the courthouse in Folkston." I could tell she was about half in the bag, and my insides fidgeted at the likelihood of pulling this off.

In the car on the way home, silent tears slipped down my cheeks as Jim caressed my shoulder. "It's okay, babe, I understand," he said. The scenario had gotten to him too.

"I wish you could've known her before this. Before everything, she was lovely and funny. My god, she's such a wreck now," I said, blowing my nose. "I can count on the fingers of one hand the times she's come through for me in my entire life, and I don't have any faith she will now. What will we do if she doesn't show up?"

"We'll figure it out, honey. Don't worry."

I explained to Pam and Freddy that Jim and I were getting married and would be living in Riverside. I would still come over to take them places, and they could spend the weekends with me if they wanted. Freddy hugged me and said he was happy for me, that he couldn't wait to spend the night in our new apartment, but Pam spurned my overtures.

"You're leaving us again," she said. "And this time you're taking the car." Then she tossed her hair, put her nose in the air, and said, "Anyway, you should have a proper wedding in a church." I almost burst out laughing at the little diva she'd become.

The next day on the way to work, I sat at a traffic light daydreaming about our future. Jim and I could live in peace, love and care for each other, and choose the people we wanted in our lives. Out of nowhere, a slithering shadow of guilt wound its way through me like a viper, reminding me I was leaving Pam and Freddy behind once more. I burst into tears as I watched a pathetic, lost soul in filthy, tattered clothes cross the street in front of me.

The night before our big day, too excited to get much sleep, I rose at five in the morning and tiptoed around getting dressed, putting on makeup, and styling my hair. I hadn't told anyone this was my wedding day, and I wanted to slip out without any drama. I picked up my suitcase, looked at Pam snuggled in a sound sleep, blew her a silent kiss, and slipped out the door into my new life.

PART VI

Rising - Sherry O'Neill

THE BIG DAY
Jacksonville 1965

"Love is the only way; through it you find
the way to all other things in life."
—Rumi

Tuesday, October 12, 1965 arrived with heavy ground fog and an accompanying coolness in the air. As I pulled up to the entrance of the base, my soon-to-be husband, dressed in a sport coat and tie, waved to me. Through the haze, his outline reminded me of a dreamy, impressionistic painting. I parked the car and slid over as he jumped in the driver's side and grinned at me.

"Are we really doing this?" I asked, excitement filling the air.

"Oh, we're doing it. This is going to be a day we'll never forget. The best day of our lives," he said, bending toward me for a quick kiss and handing me a perfect white orchid. Once on the road, Jim glanced over, took my hand, and kissed it. "You okay, my little bride?"

"Much better than okay," I answered. My entire body hummed with nerves as I smoothed the creamy, pale yellow dress and fluffed my hair. Mother had sworn to me the night before on the phone that she'd be there. If our plan worked, we would be husband and wife by noon.

"There she is!" I yelled as we pulled into the parking lot of the City Hall. She was leaning on a car, smoking a cigarette, and talking to a young man. We parked beside them and I hopped out. "You made it! You made it! Thank you, thank you, thank you," I said as I hugged her close.

"Oh, come on. I wouldn't miss the marriage of my own daughter," she answered without a trace of irony. Dropping her cigarette on the pavement, she ground it out with her shoe, and introduced us to Sonny, the nephew from her first marriage. I was overcome with gratitude that even in her present circumstances, she had not let me down.

Two couples waited ahead of us for their chance to say "I do." We sat down on the long church pew outside the chambers for our turn. The walls of the room were papered in a stylized version of the Constitution and I read and re-read the lines in an attempt to calm myself. When the previous couple came out hand in hand, I jerked to attention. Jim stopped pacing and stared at the clerk. Glancing at her clipboard, she called our names, and I grabbed my mother's hand.

"This is it, Mother." The clerk reached behind a counter and handed me a large, clear plastic bag containing miniature boxes and bottles of laundry detergent, cleanser, spray starch, and the like—a wedding grab bag. I erupted in a crazy case of the giggles, and Jim smiled.

"Let's do this," he said, taking my hand. I put on a serious face, and the three of us walked in together.

Inside the chambers, the judge looked over the paperwork and asked for proof of age. I handed him our birth certificates. He studied them as I explained that my mother was there to sign for me. He looked over his glasses from me to her.

"Where is the father?" he asked.

Unrehearsed and in unison, my mother and I said, "He's dead." The judge nodded, looking back at the papers. Later, we had a good laugh about how great minds think alike, how easy it was to kill Daddy, and how convincing we must have been.

Hearing the words, "Mr. O'Neill, you may kiss your bride," I let my shoulders relax for the first time in days. Jim leaned in and gave me a sweet, chaste kiss on the lips, and Mother and Sonny clapped and congratulated us as we all embraced.

"What a happy day," my mother said, brushing away tears. "I'm glad I could be part of it."

Stepping outside into the glorious sunlight, I inhaled, taking in the moment. The fog was gone, and the streets and buildings radiated joy in the clear, fragrant air. The gods had smiled down on us. We walked around the corner to a small restaurant to celebrate with a three-dollar bottle of champagne and leathery steaks.

After spending one night in a motel in Folkston, Jim and I were anxious to get to our new place and set up housekeeping. The ringing phone in the motel room startled me. I snatched the receiver up and put it to my ear.

My mother's low, sultry voice said, "Well, how was it—your first night together?"

My face flushed. Did she expect me to explain the details of my wedding night?

"Fine, Mother," I said, brushing her off. "We're packing right now and heading to our apartment. I've got to go. I'll call you when I get home."

Jim came out of the bathroom with a towel around his waist. "Who was that on the phone?"

"Oh, just my mother, wanting to know how our honeymoon sex was."

He stopped toweling off and stared at me. "Did she say *that*?"

"No, those are my words, but she asked how our first night together was. What else was she asking?" I knew Mother started every day with a big glass of vodka now—the binges with days or months of sobriety no longer existed. I wanted to believe my *real* mother would never have asked that. The sound of my breathing and a low hum from the TV filled the silence as I sat on the bed thinking about her and that unseemly question.

Arriving at the apartment, we walked up the stairs to our door and Jim carried me over the threshold. When he put me down, we looked around the little apartment in awe.

A Love Story - Sherry O'Neill

A LOVE STORY
October 1966

"I have for the first time found what I can truly love—
I have found you."
—Charlotte Bronte

We were in love, flush with happiness and hope. We held the notion that our dreams were there for the taking; nothing was beyond reach. We'd been reborn as husband and wife.

Sex, in all its mysterious ways, was new too, and we couldn't keep our hands off each other. Sometimes, lying in bed together, holding one another, we marveled at our luck in finding such happiness. As the days went by, we grew closer, sharing a newfound intimacy and aching for each other when we were apart.

Twice a month, Jim had to spend two or three nights on base, leaving me home alone. I dreaded those nights as fear and deep sadness—a feeling of abandonment—filled me. In my logical brain, these emotions were unwarranted, but knowing that didn't make them less scary or sad or lessen the tight grip they had on me. I didn't understand—I was a different person now, all grown up, a married woman. Where was all the grief and fright coming from?

Freddy came to stay sometimes on Friday night, and he entertained us with imitations and funny stories. Even at that age, he was a keen observer and had a gift for creating humor from the mundane. A large neon sign of the jolly king with his crown could be seen from our bedroom window, and my brother, noticing we were a street over from Burger King, lit up with excitement. "That," he said, pointing. "That right there is where I want to eat supper. Can we go, can we go, please?"

I smiled. A fast-food meal would seem exotic after living a few years at Gram's.

"You bet, and you can get anything you want, including a milkshake," I said, tousling his hair.

Pam, true to her word, refused my invitations. But Gram, magnanimous in victory, had allowed me back in her good graces while never mentioning my marriage or anything related to the incident. When I came over on the weekends to take her for groceries or an errand run, our relationship slipped right back into the place it had been before my aunt's revelation.

Lacy Anderson, my USO friend, threw me a post-wedding shower at her house. As I welcomed friends from work and reconnected with old friends from high school, a familiar voice from the open front door rang out, "Sher-er-ry Baby... Sherry Baby ..." I ran to greet Allison. We laughed and hugged, and she held her left hand up to show off her diamond; she and Jerry had set a date. The news called for another round of hugging and squealing.

"I want you in the wedding. Will you be a bridesmaid?" Allison asked. Her sister Georgia would be the maid of honor.

"Oh, Alli, you know I will. I'll be anything you want me to be. I'm excited for you—you're going to love being married." The house resounded with laughter that afternoon as about twenty-five women reminisced and shared stories. Thanks to the generous, loving sisterhood that surrounded me, gifts were stacked to the top of the car in both back and front seats and loaded in the trunk.

A few weeks later at a visit to Gram's, an unfamiliar, expensive-looking car sat in the driveway. Letting the screen door slam behind me, I crossed the porch into the living room and flinched at the sight of my father sitting on the couch. We stared at each other for a second and I offered a stiff greeting.

"Hello, Daddy. How are you?" I couldn't read his expression behind the large, reflective aviator sunglasses.

"Oh, hello," he said, leaning his elbows on his knees and looking up.

I kept walking through the living room and dining room into the kitchen to find Gram. Handing her the drugstore purchases she'd asked me to pick up, I pointed toward the living room and whispered, "How long has he been here?"

"Not long. He dropped in to take the kids for a ride." She called in the direction of the bathroom, "Hurry up, young'uns. Yur daddy's out there a-waiting."

When I went back to the living room behind Pam and Freddy, Daddy stood up from the couch and handed me a check.

"I heard you got married. Here's something for you." He stayed at arm's length and kept his face stony. As I reached for the check, I had the peculiar sensation we'd wrapped up some kind of business deal.

"Thank you, Daddy," I said, not looking at the face of the check. He ushered my sister and brother out the door and to his car, and Gram shook her head, mumbling something about what a strange man he was. Looking down at the check, I didn't know whether to laugh or cry. He'd made it out to my maiden name in the amount of ten dollars.

In the evenings, Jim and I sat at our small Formica table adjacent to the kitchen, eating the meal I'd cooked and sharing the events of the day. I listened to my soft-spoken husband, astonished at my good fortune in avoiding the common trap of choosing an angry, hard-drinking cheater like Daddy. But once in a while, a voice reminded me that nothing good lasted, and betrayal was the result of trust.

The black beauties and shots were still keeping my weight down and erasing any temptation to overeat or purge in my alone times, but they'd become less effective. I doubled my dosage and upped the shots to four times a week. Alone at night, I began to unravel. Fears and anxieties grew to an apex of eye-burning, all-night vigilance. Convinced that I wasn't safe, I listened for sounds from outside and sat up in bed gripping a large butcher knife and resting a baseball bat beside me till light came peeking in the windows. During those two or three nights alone, rest was impossible. I might doze for ten minutes, then shudder awake and resume sentry duty. When Jim returned, I'd crash for twelve-hour stretches.

The drugs had been a constant for three years by then, but *addiction* never entered my mind. In 1965, drug addicts were jazz musicians in smoky clubs in New York City. My drugs were medicine, prescribed by a doctor, I told myself. But somewhere buried beneath layers of denial was the knowledge I was in trouble; I just couldn't face it. The amphetamines or whatever was in the shots and pills had something to do with the intensity of my fear and paranoia, but my dependency had deep roots, and breaking free of them would be unbearable.

Saturday afternoon at the laundromat, I watched our clothes twirl and flop in the dryer and picked up a *Reader's Digest* from the table next to me. Opening the magazine, a headline screamed from the page: "The New Diet Drugs and Their Life-Threatening Side Effects!" My stomach dropped as I read the article and learned how damaging amphetamines were for your body and mind when taken for longer than a week or two, how adverse side effects could become permanent, and how addiction was a predictable outcome. And, yes, raging paranoia was a well-known side effect of abuse. Overcome with panic by the time I finished the piece, I made a stone-cold resolution to clean up my system that minute, to stop the pills and shots at once.

The first days without them were torture—a harsh desert of concrete I scraped myself across. Every movement took energy I didn't have, and the mental fog left me disoriented and unable to concentrate. I had fits of itching and scratching till I drew blood. One minute I was a puddle of tears, and the next, furious at the world. Bone-tired, drained of get-up-and-go for even small tasks, I hungered for sleep that wouldn't come. The cravings were intense, sometimes tearing through me with a feral longing; I was glad I'd flushed the pills down the toilet. I called in to work with the flu and stayed in bed, tossing and turning until my skin was raw. Jim did the best he could to ease the misery, assuring me we'd get through it together, but there was little he could do. Each hour hung back at the doorway of the last, dragging out the torture. On the fifth day, I got up, got dressed, and pushed through, arriving in my office, shaky and bleary.

My supervisor, Mrs. Fenton, said, "You don't look well. Do you need a few more days off? You can have a relapse with this flu, you know?"

"No, I'll be fine. I'm still a little slow."

Over the next weeks, little by little, I regained some energy, and my head began to clear. Most difficult was contending with the realization I would *never* have that much energy, focus, or euphoria again without the drugs. It was like facing a death of sorts. The physical addiction passes, but the mind never forgets. Once you've experienced that extreme high, that quivering rapture, your normal state of mind, even in the best of times, can't compete. It's like opening Pandora's Box— you can't go back. Allowing time to make a ghost of the artificial, chemically induced feelings enables the brain to eventually accept your natural state, but that takes a long time.

Mrs. Mattair, the director, looked up over her reading glasses and smiled as I entered her office. "Sherry, how are you? Take a seat," she said, motioning to the leather chair facing her desk. Awaiting the reason that I'd been summoned to her office, I fidgeted, smoothing my navy-blue skirt and rubbing at scuff marks on my blue pumps.

Rifling through a stack of papers, she extricated one, removed her glasses, and looked at me. "An opening has become available upstairs in the Independent Adoption Department and we feel your skills would be put to greater use there," she said. "This promotion comes with a sizable raise, and we hope you'll accept it. You will be working for Katherine Wells as her assistant, and you'll have your own office. It's quite a plum position." She put the paper down and waited for my reply.

"Oh, that's amazing. Thank you, Mrs. Mattair. I would be honored to accept."

Smiling, she extended her hand to me. "Congratulations, Sherry. I know this will work to everyone's benefit."

In the new position, rather than typing all day, I conducted initial client interviews and worked in tandem with Katherine to ensure that deadlines were met and necessary documents landed on the judge's desk in perfect order. Much to my relief, the pace was slower and the workload less demanding than downstairs. Without the pills and shots, I was no longer a quick-firing sprinter, but more like a methodical long-distance runner.

Standing in the break room one afternoon sipping a Tab and reading the notices tacked up on the board, one caught my eye: *Mobile home for sale. Great condition, $1,200.* The trailer belonged to our mail girl, Marie Daniels. She and her husband had lived in it all through college, but now they'd bought a house. Maybe this could be an alternative to the high rental prices in Gainesville.

When I told Jim about it, he agreed that perhaps the trailer answered the question of affordable housing; our nest egg held more than double the sale price, but we'd have to check it out thoroughly before we made a decision.

After a comprehensive inspection, we deemed the trailer to be in impeccable condition and pulled the trigger, becoming first-time homeowners at the ages of nineteen and twenty. Our sweet little tin can was eight feet by thirty-six feet—cozy, to say the least, with two miniature bedrooms, an eat-in kitchen, living room, and one bathroom. We converted the second bedroom into a study area (calling it an office would be grandiose) and added a large window-unit air conditioner to take us through the long, brutal Florida summers.

For the first time in five years, I was drug-free, binge-free, and purge-free, proud I'd been able to white-knuckle my way to freedom. But without something to blunt the emotions that bubbled up and overflowed, I struggled to maintain equilibrium.

The Power of the Past- Sherry O'Neill

ANCHORED TO WHAT WENT BEFORE
1967

"The scars you've inflicted are here to stay."
—Ridgley Torrence

We celebrated Jim's discharge from the Navy and finalized our moving plans. Palatka, Florida, one of many small, sleepy backwoods towns stuck in time, was populated with a brotherhood of openly racist good ol' boys who clung to their rifles and Confederate flags. But it was also the location of the area's single junior college, St. Johns River Junior College. We would bide our time there for a year and a half until Jim received his associate of arts degree, then transfer to the University of Florida in Gainesville. After working at the welfare department for three years, it was bittersweet to leave all my friends, but I told myself this new chapter would be an adventure.

Relocating and all that it entailed triggered a swirl of emotions with anxiety at the center. On moving day, driving from Jacksonville to Palatka behind the truck towing our trailer, I worked to stay calm. Outside the city limits, we crossed Rice Creek and drove into a cloud of putrid rot and decay, the kind of smell that overpowers the atmosphere.

"Oh my god! What is that smell?" I screamed as I clasped my hand over my nose and mouth.

"That's probably the runoff from the paper companies," Jim said, smiling as he glanced over at me.

A knee-jerk fear shot through me, and I screamed, "Oh no! No! We can't live here! I can't stand this god-awful smell. This was a huge mistake. What are we going to do? Where can we go?" Tears welled up and a sob escaped. My heart pounded and hands shook as full-blown panic took over. I couldn't breathe.

Frustrated, Jim sighed and said, "Stop. Calm down. Get a grip. Everything's going to be okay."

How could everything be okay? We had no one to turn to. All our plans ... everything ruined. I swallowed my sobs and tried to calm, but it was no use. Once the old undertow of panic took over, it had a life of its own. I gulped for air, certain I was having a heart attack.

When we pulled into the Oak Haven Trailer Park, the air was sweet with clean, fecund scents from the ancient spreading oaks, dark soil, and jungle-like gardens. Embarrassed by my crippling fear and overreaction, I sat in the car and cried.

Here I was, extricated from my parents and all the past troubles, ensconced in a loving, stable relationship, but something was still wrong with me. Fear and mistrust dominated my mind, panic attacks were set in motion at the slightest provocation, and each day presented the possibility of uncontrollable catastrophe.

"Why can't you relax, take things in stride, and enjoy our happiness?" Jim asked. "It's like you don't want to be happy. Why is your first response negativity and unrealistic fear? You melt down over the most insignificant things. You have to change—look on the bright side."

Defensive, I'd claim I was *realistic*, not negative, but he was right. I didn't have it in me to be like Jim, confident and untroubled, and I had no idea how to change. At nineteen, unborn yet to consciousness or introspection, I was a long way from understanding the reasons.

Palatka, 1967—we watched as LBJ announced he would not seek reelection. Within the next three months, two of the most influential men in the country, Robert Kennedy and Martin Luther King Jr. were assassinated. A war halfway around the world in a mysterious country called Vietnam was killing and maiming our soldiers by the thousands, and despite a huge groundswell of calls and protests to end the war, it raged on. Like most Americans, we watched from the sidelines, trying to understand what it all meant.

Jim came home bursting to tell me about his classes and teachers. We were a team, working together as I proofread his writing and helped with his projects. I'd had no trouble locating a job in Palatka, but the position of receptionist at Central States Paper and Bag Company meant mundane workdays. I relied on the constant gossip and scandals of who was sleeping with whom to keep me entertained.

Residents of Southern backwater towns are preternaturally cliquish and distrust strangers or newcomers. It stood to reason they would exclude me from the partying and "hell-raising," as they referred to what happened after work, and for the first time, I didn't mind not fitting in.

In June 1968, after a year and a half in Palatka, Jim received his associate of arts degree. We hitched our trailer to the back of a rental truck and didn't look back.

Gainesville is one of the prettiest, most eclectic, and vibrant small cities in the state. It has a beautiful, venerable Southern feel with a canopy of imposing, ancient, moss-draped oak trees existing alongside palms and myriad evergreens. Summers are hot and sticky, but in fall, ruby-red and bronzed gold leaves blanket the city, and the stifling heat gives way to clean, crisp air.

A melting pot of old-time residents, intelligentsia from the university, students, hippies, artists, farmers, and entrepreneurs populated the area. Shands Teaching Hospital and the world-renowned J. Hillis Miller Health Science Center were staffed with scientists, specialists, researchers, and geniuses. Owing to the impact of a major university, the area teemed with culture, including music, theater, improv, art, funky shops, and galleries. Top-notch local entertainment performed in restaurants and on the streets. As with most Southern towns, it had its share of rural, politically reactionary types too, but they blended into the bustling mix.

Walking around the university's two-thousand-acre campus, I admired the historic Gothic architecture. Covered in climbing vines, the buildings mirrored those of Ivy League schools in the Northeast and sat next to Frank Gehry-style modern buildings, somehow elegant and odd. The size and awesome nature of the campus slammed me back to the paralyzing experience of enrolling in my senior year of high school, and I asked Jim if the huge campus intimidated him.

"A little," he said, but with a grin, added, "I'm more excited than afraid, though."

I envied his courage and cool self-confidence. My workaday experience as a receptionist at a five-name law firm downtown couldn't compare to his days, but the salary was more than double what I'd been making in Palatka.

Over the next few months, we wove ourselves into the fabric of college life in a college town. Jim settled into his class workload and campus geography. Although routine, my position as receptionist kept me busy greeting a steady stream of clients. A promotion to legal secretary came within a few months, and I left the cushy front desk to work for two junior partners, fresh from law school on a crusade to impress the senior partners. They cranked out motions and pleadings like a winning slot machine, and I dashed back and forth from my office to those of more experienced legal secretaries, asking about interrogatories, pleadings, time limits, statutes—something new every day.

My mother and her ever-deepening problems cast a long shadow on the days. She was out there suffering and destroying what was left of her soul, and her misery clung to me like a wet, cold fog. I didn't reach out to her for fear of what I might hear. The last time we had spoken, she told me she'd been raped by a man who pulled her over into the bushes. As we talked, I learned she'd been walking on the dark, dangerous streets of northeast Jacksonville in the middle of the night—drunk, I'm sure. The assailant bruised her up and slapped her around but ran as oncoming car lights approached. I was sick for days thinking about what she'd gone through.

Bouts of anxiety, grinding dread, and hypochondria plagued me. No matter how often I told myself to snap out of it, I couldn't. These feelings seemed so real and deeply ingrained. That something else was going on, something at a deeper level, never crossed my mind. Instead, I focused on the physical—do I look good, am I thin enough, do I measure up? And the answer was always no.

September arrived, and with it, football mania and parties. Alcohol lubricated the gears of the party scene. Certain I would never allow myself to become my mother, I swigged, sipped, and guzzled along with everybody else. The next day, wallowing in a hangover, an ominous darkness filled me as I feared I *was* my mother, destined to follow her path. I couldn't unwind my drinking from hers.

"But, babe, you're *not* your mother; you're no different than all of us, working our way through campus life, partying and having a good time. You only drink socially and don't crave alcohol, do you?" Jim tried to comfort me.

"Not at all, I don't even think of it," I replied. "But that doesn't mean I won't one day." Holding me in his arms, he assured me that I was a normal drinker and he would tell me if he saw the slightest indication to the contrary. Though desperate to escape her fate, I feared the die had already been cast.

A SECOND CHANCE
Gainesville, 1967

"Hope springs eternal in the human breast..."
—Alexander Pope

I visited the kids once in a while on the weekends, taking them places and catching up on their lives. According to Jo, Mother had been living on the street for a short time but was now staying in the garage apartment of St. Mark's Episcopal Church. Father Damon had been our pastor in Panama City years ago, and unbeknownst to us, he'd been transferred to Jacksonville. I remembered him as a good man and said it had to be a positive sign that she had reconnected with him.

Walking up the creaky wooden stairs of the garage apartment, I didn't know what to expect. "Mom, it's me," I called, after lightly tapping on the door.

"Come in. It's open," a raspy voice replied.

In bed with a blanket up to her shoulders, she had a box of Kleenex on the bed and prescription bottles lined up on the tiny nightstand. Pneumonia, she said, but assured me she was getting better thanks to the care and concern of Father Damon and his wife, Mary. Gray and shaky, her face bore the trauma she'd been living.

"I was staying across the street from this church, and I happened to see Father Damon one Sunday greeting his congregation," she said. "I recognized him and went over to say hello." Between wracking coughs, she explained that her situation had been desperate at the time, and Father Damon and his wife had offered help and a place to stay.

The apartment was one large room with a small stove and refrigerator in the corner. A table and two chairs, the bed, dresser, and TV took up the rest of the space. The only other room was a tiny bathroom. Light streamed in through the two windows and the television flickered and hummed in the background.

"Come sit by me. I have some exciting news and I want you to be the first to know." She smiled and patted the bedspread. My mother was a flame I couldn't stop touching, and as much as I loved her, I'd sworn I wouldn't let her burn me again. I stood rooted to the spot. She tapped the bed again and said, "Well, come sit on the bed and I'll tell you."

I eased onto the end of the bed, half standing.

"With Father Damon's help, I'm going to a place called Avon Park for thirty days. It's a rehabilitation center in southern Florida.

"Oh Mom, that's great news. I'm happy for you. When will you go?"

"As soon as I'm well. Maybe in a couple of weeks."

Her voice carried a longing tremble as she continued filling in the details. We spoke about the future and good things to come, meticulous in our avoidance of the past. She promised to stay in contact and we traded numbers.

"Take care of yourself and do what the doctor says," I said, telling her goodbye. "I'll be in touch, Mom, and call me whenever you feel like it."

Our dance of devotion and betrayal carried deep pain and fear that didn't allow me to trust this time would be different. All the way home, I mulled over the visit. What would happen to her? Could she do it this time?

Once home, I tried to focus on pressing issues. The Valiant had begun to give us problems and we talked about buying a new car—what kind, how much, pros and cons of new versus used? It wasn't the first time I'd longed to pick up the phone and speak to a caring, knowledgeable parent for advice.

Standing in front of the picture window in the trailer, ironing and watching TV one afternoon, I looked out as a shiny red Volkswagen Beetle pulled into our driveway. Jim jumped out of the driver's side as I was opening the front door. Grinning, he waved his arm at the Bug and said, "Well? What do you think?"

I walked around the beautiful, gleaming car. "Can we afford this?"

"The dealer is giving us a good trade-in and payments are $30 a month," he said, radiating excitement like a kid at Christmas. "We haven't bought it yet, though; they let me take it for a trial run and now you can test-drive it and we'll decide. Come inside and I'll explain all the details."

That little car brought us campus status and solid dependability. Jim would tell anyone within earshot that the day we bought the Volkswagen was one of the happiest of his life.

"Gram, have you been able to reach Mother?" I asked as soon as I arrived at her house. I'd tried calling my mom, but the phone in the apartment rang and rang. She nodded, and I could tell there was a story coming. As was her custom, before she started, she walked over to the screen door, opened it, and spit a slew of snuff juice into the bushes. Situating herself back in the rocker, she tapped her mouth with a lace-edged hankie and began.

Mother was down in Avon Park, Florida, at the first alcoholic rehab center in the state. After recovering from pneumonia, she'd left Father Damon's and disappeared—maybe for one last bender. When she resurfaced a month later, drunk and in awful shape, Father Damon went to work clearing the way for her admittance. There was one hitch: She had to dry out and remain sober for a week to be accepted. They agreed she would enroll in the Get Clean Program offered by the city jail. If an addict checked in to jail voluntarily and signed an agreement to remain locked in a cell for a full seven days, the jail program would provide meals and medical attention if needed free of charge. Upon release, an employee would accompany the newly sober addict to the Avon Park facility.

Christine checked in, signed the form, and began detox. Convulsions, fevers, hallucinations, and delirium tremens brought her to death's door, and at one point, the jailers called an ambulance to rush her to the hospital. A few days later, she was released and taken to rehab.

In the car on the way home, thinking of what she'd been through, I whispered, *Please, please, help my mother.* She'd bravely put herself through hell to get sober and wanted it so badly. Gram had given me her address and explained she was allowed to receive mail and parcels now that she'd been there a week. As I meandered through the aisles of the drugstore collecting fancy soaps, good shampoo and conditioner, lotion, and anything she might need or want, a tiny seed of hope began to take root. It was possible my mother might receive the help she needed. I couldn't wait to share the news with Jim.

A week later, Mother called to thank me for the package. Clear-headed, positive, and rational, she said she was physically and mentally healthier than she had been in years. The poor-me attitude was gone, as was casting blame or making excuses. Our conversation bolstered my conviction that she was on the right track at last. I told her how proud I was of her, and we discussed her future plans once the thirty days were over. She reiterated the warnings the counselors had given against going back to the same environment.

"I'm thinking about my options," she said. "Maybe I'll relocate to Miami for a while, get a job and an apartment, and you all can visit."

"Oh, Mother, that sounds ideal, and we'll visit often." I was committed to anything that would keep her sober.

The treatment at Avon Park was based on the Twelve Steps of AA. In the program, I'd heard stories of people bearing deeper scars and despair than we had; their tales of the healing power of the twelve steps convinced me that my mother could do it too. For the first time, she was accepting advice and thinking through her plans.

After we said goodbye, I hung up the phone and, staring upward, whispered, *Thank you, thank you, thank you.* When Jim came home that afternoon, I met him at the door with a kiss and the big news. "I think she'll do it this time," I said. "This Avon Park place is a light at the end of a long, dark tunnel—the answer to my prayers."

He nodded at each revelation and said he was happy for me; he knew how much I loved my mother. But he added, "Be careful of letting your expectations climb too high. I don't want to see you get hurt again. Let's take the situation one little piece at a time."

"Why do you have to cast a shadow on my news, on my mother's success? This time is different. Can't you see that?"

"I don't want you to be blindsided or devastated if this doesn't work out. I'm only trying to protect you—can't *you* see that?"

My mother and I spoke often, and I celebrated with her. There was laughter and we were old friends again. My spirit lightened and I was certain she'd made a lasting change. I could almost reach out and touch our new relationship—sharing the future together and growing closer through the years.

In anticipation of her release, I mailed her a package of new clothes I'd purchased. She called to thank me and we made plans to be together again soon. Her salvation was tied to mine in a complex, inextricable way.

The phone rang as I stood drying dishes and putting them away. Before I could say hello, Mother's breathless voice rang in my ear.

"Guess what? I'm moving to Miami next week. I have an apartment and with the help of the people at Avon Park, I've gotten a job at JCPenney in the ladies' department." Her excitement was contagious.

"That's wonderful. This is a brand new start."

"I'll call you as soon as I'm settled. Can't wait to see you and Pam and Freddy."

The next call from Mother came a week later. "I've got a fantastic surprise. You won't believe it. I got married!"

The blood drained from me and I sat down. "What? What do you mean? When? Who?"

"His name is Kenny Heffner and he's a chef working at the Four Seasons Hotel here in Miami Beach." She admitted he'd been a fellow patient at Avon Park and they'd fallen in love.

"But Mother! You've known the man all of thirty days! Why would you jump into marriage?" A painful tightness squeezed my chest as Jim's words resounded in my head. I took a mental step back—even sober, my mother's decisions were as capricious as the wind.

Assuring me it was a solid decision, she said they worked hard to keep each other on the straight and narrow, attended meetings together, and supported each other. "You'll love him," she said. "He's sweet and kind and hard-working and nothing like your father."

We hung up and I paced the tiny living room. Her marriage to this man she didn't know made my hair stand on end. But maybe a strong, determined man was what she needed. They could share their sobriety together. When Jim came home from the library, I told him the latest surprise. We agreed it wasn't ideal, but we'd have to accept her decision and hope for the best. The next few nights I tossed and turned, mind churning. What if she'd blown the sole chance she would ever have at a lasting recovery? I had to let go and live my own life. At least she was sober …

We met Kenny Heffner a month later on a trip to Miami with the kids and found him cordial but guarded. I delighted in my mother's sober smile and voice, reflections of a time long ago before the madness. She said she was happy, but the losses, sorrows, and vulnerabilities she still carried were apparent to me.

Their apartment was located on the Intracoastal near the Playboy Club on the 79th Street Causeway. Our three days were taken up with swimming in the pool and sightseeing. In the evenings, we sat in hard, fold-out chairs in a room choked with smoke as the evening's speaker began his saga. "Hi, my name is [fill in the blank] and I'm an alcoholic." As I looked around the room, all color was drained from the scene; everyone appeared to be cast in sepia, and there was a palpable desperation in the air. My mom sat next to me and we held hands.

In AA, the consolation prize for not drinking is the chance to tell your story. These tales describe misery and heartbreak, but the underlying message of each speaker is one of hope—"If I can do it, you can too." And this is what keeps people all over the world coming back.

After three days, we gathered at the car to say goodbye. Mom brushed away tears as we hugged and promised to see each other soon. On the seven-hour drive home, while the kids slept in the back, Jim and I talked softly so as not to wake them.

"I think Kenny is a decent type, and your mother is settled and sober, so that's all good news," Jim said.

I agreed, "But I have reservations. Her new husband is also skittish and closed off, like someone with a past to hide. And I'm especially troubled that Mother dismissed one of the main AA tenets for continued sobriety after rehab: no new relationships for a least a year. She married a man she doesn't know, when they were both fresh out of rehab, after only a month. A person committed to the program wouldn't have done that. It's not a good way to start her sober life, but I hope she proves me wrong this time."

The days passed like pages flying off a calendar and Jim registered that summer for his senior year. Allison and Jerry got married in June, and the wedding, my first bridesmaid gig, occasioned much laughter

and reliving of old times. I'd made some solid friendships in Gainesville, but I missed Allison, and we vowed to stay close, no matter what.

We sold the mobile home and moved into the luxury of a standard
one-bedroom, one-bath apartment for our last year in Gainesville. The
sale netted us the exact amount we'd paid for it, saving the cost of rent
for three years.

That last year in the apartment was fraught with my struggles. The
familiar dark cloud of doom and the undertone of anxiety I'd had since
childhood dogged me. I compared myself to other women, noting all
the ways I was wrong, and I took out my feelings on my body, starving
again for days, then eating everything I'd denied myself. I watched
others eat normally, casually, and hated myself because I couldn't.
Looking back years later, I could see the slippery slope I was traversing.

Against my advice, Christine and her husband bought a house a few
blocks from Gram, moved back to Jacksonville, and brought Pam and
Freddy to live with them. Her blatant disregard of the three absolutes
in AA's recovery plan concerned me, but she assured me that she was
strong and had been sober for six months. She wanted to right all the
wrongs as soon as possible and make a proper home for her remaining
kids.

Pam and Freddy, now fifteen and fourteen, had lived with our grandmother since they were six and seven. Any contact with Mother during
those years had been limited and sporadic. Now they were living with
two strangers. At least they were at the same school with their friends,
and Gram was nearby. Mom was working as a hostess at an upscale
restaurant and stayed busy pulling the new house together. Jo and
Gene bought a small house in the same subdivision within walking
distance. For the first time in years, we all congregated at Gram's or Jo's
for Sunday dinners and holidays.

Now that my mother was sober, I longed for her to offer regret, to say she understood the devastation she'd caused me. I wanted an acknowledgment, an apology, but it didn't come. One night, the realization landed with a thud in my chest—*She's not working the program.* The ninth of the twelve steps is to make amends to those you've hurt. The AA slogan, "It only works if you work it," alludes to working your way consistently and repeatedly through the twelve steps. I couldn't stop thinking about it. I had never seen anyone as far gone as my mother get sober and stay that way without AA. Keen to believe there would be a happy ending, I had blinded myself to the obvious.

Two months before Jim's graduation, Gram called. My mother's husband Kenny was drinking again. He'd gone down fast, becoming violent and abusive. We worried Mother would be next. Before I could call to see how she was, she phoned me in a panic. They couldn't stay in the house any longer. Kenny was violent and dangerous and had threatened to kill all of them and himself. He had disappeared, but she was sure he'd be back, and they had to get out of there.

"I'll be there in an hour and we'll figure something out," I said.

When I arrived, Gram, Aunt Corrine, and Uncle Leon were there with Mother. The kids were at school. We sat at the kitchen table as she cried and explained that her husband's drinking had been going on for a few weeks, and he'd become a different person—vicious and threatening. My mother, who was afraid of nothing, trembled fiercely as she lit a cigarette. I'd never seen her like that. She was terrified for the kids and repeated she had no choice but to move to a new location where he couldn't find them. "We've got to get out of here and we've got to get out of here *now.*"

Aunt Corrine paced around, rolling her eyes and shaking her head. "What a complete mess you've made of your life. We're not getting involved in any of this. We'll help you move, but that's it. You made your bed, now you can lie in it." Considerate and helpful, as always.

Noticing the packed boxes, I asked where she was going.

Bracing the coffee cup in both hands, she took a sip. "I've found a small house closer into town and signed a one-year lease. I need your help with the move." Half-baked, spur-of-the moment decisions, the same ones she'd made in the past, had put her in this situation, but she was adamant. "I've got it under control, and this is all I can do."

We finished packing and taking boxes to the U-Haul my brother-in-law Gene had rented, and he and Uncle Leon moved all the furniture into the truck. After spending the night with Gram, the next morning we began the process of moving them to the new place.

The rental house had been neglected for years and was in filthy, appalling condition. It was located in an industrial part of town on a four-lane street, and the noise was deafening as cars, trucks, and semis whizzed by. The roof sagged and the floorboards were either loose or warped and popping up. In the bathroom, the wood at the base of the toilet had rotted away, leaving gaps that exposed the ground under the house and made easy access for roaches, rats, and snakes. *What was she thinking?* I stayed one more day to help, but I had to get back to work.

"I'll be back on Friday," I said as I hugged Mother and slipped fifty dollars into her hand. Pam sat on the couch with her arms folded across her chest, face red with fury. Freddy's sad, forlorn look made me want to cry. I hated leaving them in that nasty house, but I would return in a couple of days and stay the weekend. At least Mother was sober, and if she could stay that way, maybe she could salvage the situation. My sister and brother were at stake now and I'd have to make sure they were safe.

I drove over as often as I could on Saturday or Sunday and left my mother money each time. She still had her job, and the house was clean, but the kids were never there. She claimed they were spending the night with friends, on a camping trip, or at a sports or school event. If I did see them, they looked shell-shocked and were non-communicative.

With graduation a few weeks away, the university sponsored a job seminar for eligible seniors, and Jim fielded offers from several large companies. We talked it over, trying to decide. With a Bachelor's in marketing, he leaned toward the offer from Sears, Roebuck and Co. in their fast-track store manager training position. In 1970, Sears was king of retailers, a paradigm for success, and the lure of moving to a large, glamorous city like Miami was strong. The salary and benefits were well above average, and we already had friends living there, including Allison and Jerry. I wanted to be more excited, but with the troubling situation in Jacksonville, the idea of being far away unnerved me.

Just before Jim's graduation, a wicked case of the Hong Kong flu kept me in bed for two weeks, leaving me depleted, weak, and emaciated. The illness had also taken away my appetite and sense of smell; bird-like portions were all I could tolerate. I was ecstatic to see my bones in the mirror again—concave stomach and spare arms and legs. I didn't recognize this as the warning sign it was. To me, at the time, it was a blessing.

PART VII

Reckoning- Sherry O'Neill

THE DEMONS ARE WINNING
Miami
June 1970

"How could it be a cure, when it was killing me,
this disease of my soul that masqueraded as the answer."
—Ernest Dowson

We rented a furnished, one-bedroom apartment in Opa-locka, an urban community in northwestern Miami. With little time to find a place in an unfamiliar area, after previewing the apartment one night with a flashlight, we signed the lease. The grounds were lush and manicured, and a large, sparkling, sapphire-blue swimming pool sat in the center of the U-shaped building. But when we opened the door on moving day, blinding sunlight danced off nauseating orange shag carpet and a bright-neon blue-and-green sofa.

"Whoever decorated this place must've been color blind," Jim said, looking around and chuckling. I stood in the doorway and sobbed. My husband put his arm around my shoulder, saying, "Hey, hey, this isn't the end of the world. We can get a throw for the couch and put a big area rug over the carpet. Try to get a grip."

Once the job of moving in was completed and we began to acclimate to the surroundings, something strange caught my attention. The complex itself was surrounded by an eight-foot decorative iron fence with sophisticated, coded locks on all entrances and exits. The rental office was locked day and night, and the elevator was locked after 6 p.m. Tenants were given a code to enter both. I'd never seen an apartment complex guarded like Fort Knox.

On a beautiful, balmy Miami evening as the last bit of daylight drained from the sky, I sat alone by the pool reading. A security guard walked through the area with his German shepherd. I smiled and he came over to chat. I asked if there had been a problem in the area, and he explained that he patrolled the apartments every evening, maintaining security. We conversed about the weather, then I mentioned we were new tenants and commented on the many unoccupied units in the complex. He asked if I was aware that we were one block from Liberty City, some of the roughest real estate in Miami, with a violent crime rate that approached the highest in the country.

"No, we had no idea."

As he said good evening, he added a caution about not going anywhere in the area alone, day or night.

Oh my god. Pounding fear shook my hands as I collected my things. I wanted to run or hide, and going up to the empty apartment terrified me. Jim would be home from work late, and there'd be no point in trying to sleep until I heard his key in the lock. I despised being alone and now it would be worse. But alone was how I spent most of my nights in Opa-locka.

Jim and I had been married for five years and we'd been together every one of those days, fulfilling goals together, taking care of each other, and growing as close as two humans could. He had loved and comforted me through my neurotic fears and anxieties, and as long as he was at my side, I could feign normalcy. But this new career kept him working late into the night. His six-day workweek included long, demanding hours, and on his one day off, I was working as a legal secretary at a law firm on the outskirts of Hollywood, about ten miles from home.

Jim was devoted to his new job, considering it a culmination of the hard work in college and an opportunity to move up the golden ladder to success. The young guys he worked with, managers-in-training, were fresh out of college, much like him, and they formed a fast bond, playing cards on their nights off or grabbing a beer after work. We spent little time together. I felt like a baby ripped from her mother's loving breast and handed a cold plastic cup of milk. It hurt that my husband would rather be with his new friends. He didn't need or miss me like I did him. Over the long nights, familiar feelings of rejection came creeping back, and before long, I was swimming alone in a pool of darkness. The setting and the people were different, but the effect was the same as living with my mother. Depressed and angry at Jim, I wallowed in misery. When I tried to talk it over with him, he was either too weary to listen or not interested.

Today, I look at that young girl and ask her, "What did you want him to do? He had a job that required long hours, and he, like you, was anxious to prove to the world he was different than his father who'd stagnated in a low-paying job all his life."

After we'd been in the apartment a few months, my sister Jo called with shattering news. My mother had started drinking again mere days after Kenny's relapse. *What? How could she have hidden it from me all those months?*

They had been evicted from the ramshackle house, and she'd moved them to the bottom floor of a decrepit rental house in Riverside. I fell into the chair and let my shoulders sag. My poor siblings! Fire poured into my stomach, and I kneaded it with the heel of my hand. *What a pushover I've been.* Thinking back to the times she'd taken my money, faking sobriety, a wave of anguish rolled through me. Trusting her had been a rookie mistake for someone as jaded as I was.

"I need you to come home and help me with this," Jo said. "The living conditions are deplorable. Freddy's sleeping on a back porch and Mother is drunk, jobless, and delirious much of the time and leaves Pam and Freddy alone at night. Gram and I agree they have to go live with Daddy now. There's no other way." It all sounded achingly familiar.

"I'll be there. When do you need me?"

"As soon as possible. I'm afraid for the kids. We need to get them settled as soon as we can."

"Agreed. I'll call the airlines now."

The next afternoon, I sat waiting at the gate for my flight to Jacksonville. The scene suddenly turned surreal as Allison walked toward me. We hugged and moved over to a row of seats away from the other passengers. She was sobbing and held a wadded tissue to her eyes.

"Allie, what's wrong?" I asked, putting my arm around her shoulder.

She whispered, "My mom is gone. She took an overdose of sleeping pills. Jake found her this morning."

I was stunned. Allison had shared her concern about her mom's bouts of depression, but no one had expected this outcome. The family immediately split down the middle as to why; some said the cause of her suicide was depression, but the others blamed the stepfather, Jake, for driving her to it. I remembered how insufferable he'd been when I lived there, and I grieved for what Vivian must have endured to lead her to such a desperate act.

We talked all the way to Jacksonville on the hour-long flight, and I tried to comfort Allison as she had me years ago. It seemed preordained that I would be there for her in this desperate time. Vivian was the heart of their family, and the devastation would be irreparable. Waiting at the curb for our respective rides, I hugged Allison and said I would call her that night. As they drove away, her anguished face through the car window brought a fresh wave of tears to my eyes.

Jo picked me up and we headed for her house. On the way, we discussed the plans to confront Daddy. She favored both of us presenting the proposal. I agreed that two would be more persuasive, but I cautioned her again that Daddy hated me. She should do the talking.

My nephews barreled from the house when we arrived and threw their arms around me. All three boys chattered at once as we made our way into the house. My sister and Gene, her first husband, had divorced after nine tough years of marriage. Soon after, Jo had married a man several years younger. They were living in a new house in the Southside with the boys—ten, nine, and seven years old. She looked beautiful and told me she was crazy in love and had never been happier. I smiled, acknowledging her joy, but I silently questioned her impulsive decision and how long it would last.

Our meeting with Daddy the next day didn't go well. Still bitter and self-absorbed, he fumed about Mother, casting himself as her victim, saying he hoped she got what she deserved. Those words cut straight through me, but I kept quiet, hoping to facilitate a smooth transition for Pam and Freddy.

Even though he and his third wife, Lucy, were living in a large house with two unoccupied bedrooms, he balked at the prospect of taking Pam and Freddy. After much back and forth, he agreed, but his state of mind didn't bode well for my sister and brother. *Please at least allow them some peace to finish high school.* Pam was a sophomore and Freddy a freshman.

After getting my sister and brother settled, Jo and I went to visit Mother at the address Gram had given us. The old Victorian house downtown appeared to be some loosely run halfway house and was as sad and down at the heels as its occupants. My mother came out on the porch to greet us. Years of alcohol had rendered her previous vanity futile; the makeup and polished nails were gone. She looked sick and weary, but sober. No hellos or hugs. She began a well-worn tirade.

"I will never forgive you for doing this to me. How could you take my kids away from me? We were happy together. They loved living with me. And now you're giving them to their father, a man who doesn't want any of you? He's a horrible person," she sobbed. After living with all her delusions and denials, she couldn't confront the truth anymore. I suspected she could no longer differentiate the truth from what she invented. She'd lost touch with any sliver of reality. We turned to leave, and I reached to hug her, but she resisted. "You'll live to regret the terrible things you've done to me," she called out as we walked down the steps. That was the moment I had to accept that my hopelessness for her was no longer a feeling but a hard reality. I swallowed back tears and promised myself not to cry.

Back home, I told Jim about the meeting with Daddy. After hearing the details, he said, "I hope you don't ever hold this against me, but I detest that man for what he's done."

How could I hold that against him when I wanted desperately to sink into a blissful apathy toward both of my parents, to live in a place where they couldn't reach me? *What the hell was wrong with me?* My mother and father still had the power to wound me, to impale me with their words and actions.

The long, solitary nights in the apartment resumed, and I moved deeper into a black hole. Soon after we'd gotten settled, my appetite had returned, and with it, all the weight I'd lost when I was sick. I obsessed about being thin at any cost; I had no respect for my body as a life-giving miracle. It was an enemy that needed to be conquered. If I were thinner, maybe Jim would come back to me. If I were thinner, people would love me, revere me. Positive emotions—happiness, excitement, enjoyment, or even peace—were blocked by a never-ending glut of negativity.

To dispel the anguish, I turned to food. Self-deception is the beginning of any binge. *I can handle it in moderation this time. I won't let it get as bad as it was before.* But I fell fast after the first time. Mindless gorging and vomiting left me numb. Buying and consuming vast amounts of dense, rich foods and hanging over the toilet disposing of the calories filled the empty hours and granted me a temporary reprieve from pain.

Although fearful that what I was doing was hurting me, possibly even killing me, I deluded myself that it would hold me together. Each day I vowed to stop, but willpower didn't stand a chance in the face of long nights alone. *Why, why can't I stop? I got off the pills and shots; why can't I stop this?*

As before, when I lived with Allison, asking for help or confiding in anyone was inconceivable. I'd spent my life worrying about the opinions of others and trying to make people love me. Besides, if I couldn't understand this, how could anyone else? I had created an abysmal, invisible dimension of hunger and addiction, a secret place that I protected with scrupulous precision, including scrubbing the toilet and hiding all wrappers and containers in the dumpster.

A wealth of knowledge about bulimia exists today, but in 1970, it was unheard of. I considered myself damaged goods, out of my mind. As I cried myself to sleep many nights, fear of what I had become and how it would end held me in a death grip. Maybe my stomach would burst and I'd die. Maybe Jim would find out and leave me. Maybe I would succeed this time in ending my life.

I hoped to find answers at the library, but my research yielded no information on people who gorged and vomited, with the exception of references to Roman vomitoria[2]* in the fourth century that had nothing to do with eating or vomiting. It confirmed what I had suspected—I was a freak, alone in this insane practice, broken beyond repair at only twenty-four.

At night, I lived at the edge of consciousness, baffled by what I was doing. But during the day, I strove to look normal, pleasant, and competent at work. I'd become adept at hiding the truth, and none of our friends suspected anything either. But in my alone times, the curtains came down and I was swathed in darkness as I sat trying to fill a cavernous hunger, spending endless hours in a food-induced stupor.

Hungover one workday morning after a night of purging, I stood in our parking lot looking around. Where was the car? *I know I parked it here last night; wait, maybe I parked somewhere else? Think, Sherry! Where is the car?* A shiny little red jewel twinkling in the empty parking space caught my eye. I bent down and picked it up. The piece

---

2 *There is a common misconception that ancient Romans had spaces called vomitoria for the purpose of vomiting after gorging. However, the word in fact refers to Roman architecture designed to provide rapid egress for large crowds at amphitheaters and stadia; the Latin word vomo means to spew forth. There were no places to binge and vomit and it is unclear how this urban legend began.

of a taillight rested in my palm. Despite all the security, our beloved Volkswagen had been stolen.

"You'll never see the car again. It's already broken down for parts and is on its way to Mexico or South America," the policeman said as he wrote up the paperwork. We replaced the VW with insurance money, but no successive car ever held the sentimental attachment of the little red Volkswagen.

Thanksgiving and Christmas passed in a blur. Jo and I spoke often, but I hadn't been in touch with anyone else since we'd moved the kids to Daddy's. My mother was gone again. Pam and Freddy, although still with Daddy, were surviving in a toxic household. Daddy and his wife drank to inebriation in the evenings and fought—the family tradition. "Juicy Lucy," as Freddy called her, had taken an immediate dislike to my brother, claiming he was a delinquent troublemaker, which I assume she based solely on the length of his hair. She tolerated Pam, but Daddy's playbook hadn't changed; he treated her like he had treated me. Drowning in my own swamp, for the first time, there was nothing I could do to help. *If they can just hang on till graduation …*

In April of that year, Jim completed his training and received his next assignment to the Hollywood Sears store. We'd lived in Opa-locka almost a year and witnessed its breakdown. The last few weeks, I watched out the window as riots broke out and looters smashed windows. Smoke billowed and flames leapt into the sky while helicopters whirred overhead, and sirens wailed.

Exiting I-95 at interchange 1A and driving down Hollywood Boulevard, I was struck by the blinding brightness. The stores and buildings, painted a super white with shiny mica flecks, reflected the intense sunshine. The town shimmered with a vivid brilliance. Hollywood was a small, picture-pretty, oceanside hamlet less than ten miles from Opa-locka, but it existed in a different universe. It was clean—pristine even—and safe.

Our new, airy apartment was located on the second floor of a two-story building. Twelve units, six on each floor, all faced a common pool, and plentiful palm trees and vegetation provided welcome shade.

On the weekends when Jim was off work, we visited Allison and Jerry in their new house. Thanks to the generosity of Jerry's parents, they were our sole friends who owned a house, which seemed like a mansion to us, and a shiny, spotless Lincoln Continental.

Combining the friends we had made with Allison and Jerry's, our big crowd socialized at dinners and parties where the booze flowed and the pot smoke drifted from room to room. (It was 1971, after all.) We went club-hopping on Lincoln Road in Miami Beach and took in concerts and shows all over Miami. Picnicking on Haulover Beach, we listened to the lilting sounds of Spanish in the air—*"Mira! Mira!"*—and breathed in the smoky, sensuous smell of roasting pig while bongo drums played in the background. The Cubans really knew how to have a picnic.

After Allison had her first baby, Adam, I watched my friend with her little boy and my heart melted, the pull of motherhood undeniable. I wanted what she had—pure, unconditional love. Jim and I talked it over and made the decision to give it a try. Dispensing with my birth control pills, I assumed I'd be pregnant the next month.

Six months passed and my periods came and went, though not regularly. Each month I got my hopes up, only to be let down. The bingeing and purging continued, but at a slower pace than they had in Miami.

I don't recall consciously believing a baby would fix my problems, but maybe I did. For the most part, I compartmentalized the bulimia, blocking any images of a *bulimic* mother holding her baby and what that would look like.

After a year, we visited a fertility specialist who tested both of us and declared us healthy and able to conceive. A prescription for the drug Clomid to induce ovulation should do the trick, the doctor said, and I relaxed in the knowledge that I would soon be pregnant. Eight more months passed with no pregnancy. At a final appointment with the doctor, he took a conciliatory stance, recommending we research adoption possibilities; for whatever reason, it didn't look like a natural birth was in our future.[3]*

When he left the room, I ripped the paper off the exam table and threw it on the floor, sobbed, and slammed my fists on the table. How could this happen? No one in my family had had the slightest problem getting pregnant. Still crying as I left the office, I drove home totaling up all my misfortunes and wrestling with this latest news.

Over the following weeks, a dreadful, gnawing, unnamed need sent the eating disorder into overdrive, and within a short time, it took over my life with a self-destructive fury. I consumed enormous volumes of food and vomited seven and sometimes eight times a day, every day. I purged in the office bathroom, in public restrooms, at friends' houses. No food went into my mouth without the prearranged knowledge of how and where I could throw it up. On the nights Jim was at work, I brought home cream pies, ice cream, potato chips, candy—forbidden foods—and began the process with the eagerness of an addict readying his works for a hit. The fear that I might have a heart attack from the pressure of all that food didn't stop me. As weird as it sounds, I couldn't stop any more than I could stop breathing. The force of the compulsion

---

[3] *According to studies, bulimia interferes with the balance of hormones needed for conception.

was more powerful than anything I'd ever experienced. At times, I was overcome with an out-of-body feeling, looking in the mirror at the face of a stranger or watching from a distance as an unknown girl shoveled food into her mouth.

Now grim and exhausting days centered on food: gorging, vomiting, weighing, and obsessing. These acts defined me—they contained all the hurt, self-hate, and rejection of my past that made me who I was.

After the fright of vomiting blood several times, I admitted that whatever this was, it had reached a frightening point, but my need was stronger than any fear I had. Bulimia had ceased to be about anything but *addiction*. Nothing and no one could change the fact that I was beyond saving.

At my nadir, going through the motions of trying to look normal, I sat in a small bistro a few blocks from work having lunch with the receptionist from our law firm. I confided to her I suffered from depression and was struggling. The conversation turned to her past and she revealed that she was an agoraphobic.

"Isn't that someone who can't leave their house, afraid of crowds?" I asked as I stirred sweetener into my tea.

"Yes, exactly," she said. "I spent years suffering and terrified of venturing away from home. It was awful. I couldn't even get to the driveway before a panic attack set in. It destroyed my marriage and all my friendships." She explained that, despite a master's degree in economics, answering phones and greeting clients was as much responsibility as she could endure. Taking a drink of tea and dabbing her mouth with a napkin, she went on, "But my life changed the day I met Dr. Anopolus, my psychiatrist. I can't tell you how great he is. He's a miracle worker at uncovering mysteries and making sense of emotional and mental problems. He gave me back my life."

I made a decision that instant. She went on speaking about her recovery, how it had taken a long time, but the condition was behind her now. Her voice faded to the background; I had to get back to the office and call for an appointment before I lost my nerve. A life preserver had been thrown my way.... maybe my secret hadn't been that well-hidden.

When Jim arrived home that evening, I was sitting in the dark, crying. He flipped on the light and came over to me on the couch. "Hey, what's wrong?" he said, sitting down beside me. He was aware I'd been depressed and withdrawn.

"I don't know where to start. I have an appointment with a therapist this week to try and figure out why I'm such a mess."

"You are not a mess," he said as he put his arm around my shoulder. "You're a beautiful person who sometimes struggles with events from the past." He almost sounded like a therapist himself. We sat on the couch, and he held me while I cried.

After making the appointment, I worried—would I be able tell another individual all my dark secrets? I was desperate to unburden myself, but the past was fraught with pain, and I questioned if digging around in it might make me worse. But if I didn't stop, something dire was going to happen. I had no choice. More than anything, I wanted to break the hold this compulsion had on me and regain my sanity, and for that, I'd have to reckon with my past.

SEARCHING FOR ANSWERS
Hollywood
1972

"The only journey is the journey within."
—Rainer Maria Rilke

I sat on the soft brown leather sofa in Dr. Anopolus's office and gazed at the wall of books to my right. The dark mahogany woodwork and muted light from half-closed blinds gave the room a cloistered effect, but the silence was discomfiting. I breathed in the smell of furniture polish and old books as I studied the framed collection of diplomas and honors hanging on the wall next to his desk. A tall, shedding ficus tree stood in front of a long, narrow window, and a large box of Kleenex rested on the end table next to me. Picking at my nails and chewing the inside of my lip, I looked at the well-worn leather chair facing me. *Boy, if these walls could talk.*

A few minutes later, Dr. Anopolus opened the door and walked to his desk. Picking up a legal pad and pen, he moved over to the chair in front of me. Dressed in a rumpled suit, he wore metal-rimmed glasses and a wide, gold wedding band. Even though he appeared younger than I'd anticipated, somehow there were eons of care etched on his face. His Greek heritage was apparent in the dark complexion and grayish-black hair.

Studying me with piercing, dark eyes, he said, "Hi, how are you this afternoon?"

I answered, "Okay," and looked down at my shaking hands.

He shifted in the chair and crossed his legs but kept his eyes on me. A gulf of silence hung in the air for an excruciating time until I could stand it no longer.

"Well, how do we start?" I said.

"Any way you'd like," he said in a soothing way.

Again, not what I'd expected. Alarmed, I groped with how to explain the reason I was there. After a deep breath, I said, "I need help to stop eating and vomiting. I don't know why I do it. The shame I feel is unbearable, but I can't stop, no matter how hard I try. I hate myself and wish I could put an end to it all."

I'd never said those words out loud before and they sounded shocking. Tears sprang to my eyes and I grabbed a tissue, but a comforting balm of relief infused my mind and the nervousness was gone. His eyes bored into me, and he said, "Tell me about that."

I spent the next half-hour talking and crying as he jotted notes and seldom spoke or took his eyes off me. When, finally, I'd exhausted myself and stopped to take a deep breath, the silence was back. We stared at each other for a few minutes while I sniffled and blew my nose. He leaned forward, shifting in the chair.

"Let's talk a little about your early childhood and upbringing," he said.

At the end of the session, Dr. Anopolus put his pen down, leaned toward me again with a serious, concerned look and said, "I cannot, in good conscience, let you leave the office without a commitment from you to resume therapy three times a week for the time being. Otherwise, I would like you to enter full-time, in-house therapy right away, tomorrow if possible. You are suffering from a mental illness, an eating disorder that is imminently life-threatening. Eating disorders have a higher mortality rate than all mental illnesses combined."

Stunned, two thoughts collided: *Thank God I'm here*, and *I'm going to die*. I agreed to therapy three times a week and left the office, assuring him I would see him in two days.

Driving home, a hollowed-out exhaustion came over me, but I was calmer than I'd been in a long time. Although wrenching, the session had been cleansing. Facing difficult truths brings with it the gift of freedom. For the first time in my life, I was talking, telling the truth about everything, and someone was listening. In the coming months, I would discover the amazing healing power of that.

Over the next sixteen months—two hundred hours of dissecting my life—I didn't miss a session. Starting from the beginning, we worked our way through the neglect, emotional abuse, torment, and self-abuse. I found feelings I didn't know I had. Most surprising was the deep anger I still held toward both my parents. In time, I began to see how growing up in an unstable, uncaring environment explained my deep-seated fear of rejection and abandonment. My mother's victimhood mentality taught me from a young age to take on the role of the parent, protecting her and trying to assure her well-being. I had learned from the beginning that my feelings didn't matter, and in order to receive my parents' fleeting love and attention, I had to be the person *they* needed. Left unexpressed, my emotions had piled up and not only created negative thought patterns but triggered mental and physical symptoms.

Dr. Anopolus was a brilliant and skilled therapist. Although intense, he was also kind and genuinely engaged. His silence prompted me to talk more, facilitating those light-bulb moments, epiphanies that had heretofore been hidden. He said I had a right to feel the psychological injuries, to express the hurt out loud, but that instead of feeling disgust and hate for the person I'd become, I needed love and compassion for her.

Still bingeing and purging, albeit much less, I brought up my concern with Dr. Anopolus. He explained that the eating disorder was merely a symptom of much deeper issues, which was why we worked every session to uncover and gain insight on childhood experiences and emotions. "But," he said, "the bulimia is getting better, and that is all we can hope for at this juncture. I expected it to get worse as we began our work, so I'm more than relieved to see it diminish, even a little."

Thank God. I trusted Dr. Anopolus, and my fears were lessened by his upbeat assessment. I longed for a time when the condition would fade to a faint memory.

Answers I'd been searching for all my life were revealed in therapy. I learned that compassion was the sole emotion that could engender forgiveness and that, in turn, facilitated deep healing. Dr. Anopolus cautioned that if I held onto guilt, shame, anger, and self-hatred, compassion and forgiveness were impossible, and without them, healing couldn't happen. He encouraged me to explore my own parents' upbringings to comprehend how that undoubtedly affected their actions. In small increments, I began the process of understanding causes and effects, but it would take years to reach the point of genuine forgiveness and detachment.

One afternoon, I asked Dr. Anopolus how I could stop attaching past trauma onto events in my current life. Since it was all I had ever known, I questioned my ability to move past an intractable fear of instability and a phobia around abandonment.

"You are no longer a child at the mercy of abusive adults, and in order to achieve the wisdom and healing you seek, you will have to gain mastery over the past by judging each new experience from a mature, adult perspective," he said. "Today you have reason, reality, and experience on your side. Your life is your own."

Jim was still in the dark about the bulimia—I'd covered my tracks that well—and I was afraid to tell him.[4*] We did sometimes discuss the discoveries I'd made, and he listened with rapt attention trying to understand the new landscape of this big, scary thing called therapy and how it affected me.

---

4 * In the course of writing the book, I asked Jim if he remembered when I told him about the bulimia. We concurred it was around this time, but neither of us recalled exactly when.

"I'm proud of you for ripping off the Band-Aid," he said one night as we talked over that day's session.

I'll be honest—therapy, if done right, is painful as hell, like spending time with someone who wants to crawl inside your skin, but for me, it was my last hope and I embraced it with the zeal of a born-again convert. I read all the books Dr. Anopolus recommended, kept an exhaustive journal, dissected hidden corners, and fearlessly exposed embarrassing and excruciating memories. During the process, in a nonthreatening way, Dr. Anopolus would suggest how the pieces might fit, asking me to look a little closer. Slowly, an understanding began to emerge. I wasn't a lost cause; maybe I could learn to forgive myself and others and find my way back to health. Dr. Anopolus cautioned it would remain an ongoing endeavor for me for many years. There wasn't a quick fix.

During this time, Pam packed her things and moved in with Jo, sleeping on a hide-a-bed in the family room. When I asked her what prompted the move, she said the final straw came when Daddy, irate at her laziness, demanded she come home from school and clean all the windows in the house, inside and out. He wasn't going to put up with entitled teenagers who wanted a free ride. Pam, neither lazy nor entitled, worked a job after school and maintained a consistent presence on the honor roll. She'd only lasted six months with Daddy.

Freddy stayed for three years, but the day after graduation, he packed up and moved in with Pam into the apartment she rented after her graduation. My brother had been subjected to the same treatment we'd all suffered, but he chose to deflect the hurt with humor and hilarious stories of their drunken idiocy. But beneath his spot-on imitations and comical delivery, a valley of pain existed.

I only spoke to my mother sporadically during this time. She would disappear from the radar for long stretches, and each time I assumed the worst, walking a tightrope and waiting for the call.

My periods were never regular, but it had been quite a while since I'd had one. I left my urine sample with the nurse at the doctor's office and rushed back to work. Convinced that the pregnancy test would be negative as they'd always been, I put the whole matter out of my mind. Swamped at work for the next few days, I sat at my desk proofreading a contract I'd completed when my intercom buzzed with a call for me.

"Hi, Mrs. O'Neill. This is Stephanie at Dr. Morrison's office. I wanted to let you know your pregnancy test came back positive. You are definitely pregnant."

I squeezed the phone in a death grip as arcs of excitement charged through me like lightning. "Are you sure?" I said.

She chuckled and assured me the test didn't lie—I would be holding my newborn in less than six months. We made an appointment to see the doctor the next week and hung up. *How did this happen?* We'd been told we couldn't have babies. Pure joy warmed me from head to toe.

Jim and I sat on the couch talking that night. His first question had been the same one I'd asked the nurse. "Are they sure?"

"The nurse told me the test doesn't lie. I'm over three months pregnant."

He said he was happy, but worry creased his brow. A problem solver by nature, he wanted to talk about the logistics: *Where will we live? How will we survive on one income after the baby comes? How will a baby change our carefree lives?* For the first time, I was the confident one; I promised him we would work it all out. After all, as he'd once said, people did it all the time and we were no different.

In bed that night, I pictured the tiny embryo growing inside me and the miracle of it. I would love this baby unconditionally; it would have a real family, nothing like the one I'd had. At last, I would have someone to fill the gaping hole in my soul, someone to bond with me the way I'd yearned to bond with my parents. As I drifted off, the certainty that my life would be perfect created a downy pillow for my mind.

The next day in therapy, I blurted out the news. Dr. Anopolus smiled, congratulated me, and asked me to give him my thoughts. I spoke about how excited I was, how I would never binge or vomit again—I had to protect the baby. I said I would be a perfect mother, nothing like mine. I'd be loving, caring, attentive, and most of all, stable. I wanted to take parenting classes and read everything I could find on the subject. I would break the emotional abuse pattern in my family, and along with it, all the dysfunction. This was my chance to redeem us.

A shadow crossed Dr. Anopolus's face, and he looked at me, perplexed. Sitting back in his chair and holding his pen horizontally between two fingers, he said, "I know that you are aware there is no such thing as a *perfect* parent or family. If you cling to that illusion, you will miss the lessons your child can teach you. There are ups and downs in raising children and you must be kind and gentle with yourself." He went on to say it was a profound mistake to ask my child to fill the void left by an absence of love and care in my own childhood. I let his advice settle, but I wasn't ready to receive it; I was too entwined in my romantic image of mother and child.

He spoke to me more than he had in previous months, going on to say he was sure I would be a good mother, but that I had spent a lifetime castigating myself for not being good enough, trying to please those around me, and denying myself the right to be human. He assured me I would make mistakes as a parent, everyone did, but the love I had for my child would supersede any perceived mistake on my part.

This theme ran through the next four months of therapy—my obsessive need for perfection, the black-and-white mindset, and my overall unrealistic expectations of motherhood. He allowed that he had three children of his own (the only personal information he ever disclosed), and although he considered himself a good father, there had been times in the past when he had failed his children.

"As humans, we are all flawed individuals prone to error. You are no different; it would be foolhardy to try to be better than human," he said. "The key is to lovingly forgive yourself and forge ahead."

Wise words. I would go on to forget some of them in the heat of motherhood, but more often than not, his words came back to me time and again and helped me gain perspective and let go of unrealistic expectations. Through the years, I found that the experience of psychoanalysis remained with me, aging as I did and sharing deeper insights as I grew in wisdom.

Most days, I was overjoyed to be pregnant, but there were times of fear. *What if I'm not up to the job? What in the world made me think I could be a good parent with all my baggage?* I poured over Dr. Spock's *Baby and Child Care* with hair-raising intensity, taking notes and highlighting important passages. I scribbled copious notes in my *Parent Effectiveness Training* class and quizzed my parent-friends ad nauseam. The heavy responsibility of raising a child still overwhelmed me at times.

Acting on an impulse, after undergoing therapy for sixteen months with Dr. Anopolus, I told him one afternoon at the end of our session that I was strong enough to take a break. I had not binged or vomited since the day I learned of my pregnancy and hoped I could handle life without it now.

He smiled and stared at me for a moment. Nodding slightly, he said it was a good idea. He cautioned me again that like any other human, I would face challenges in the future, times of stress and struggle, but if I ran into any problems, he would be there for me, only a phone call away. I had grown fond of him, and it would be bittersweet to end therapy, but my mind was on the baby and my new role.

I got up to leave, and he stood and walked me to the office door.

"I'm pleased with the progress you've made," he said. "You've put in a lot of hard work to get where you are, and you should be proud of yourself. Not everyone is able to see it through."

I shook his hand, and tears rolled down my cheeks as I told him how grateful I was for the time I'd spent with him, how much he had helped me, and what a wonderful therapist he was.

"Best of luck," he said as he patted my arm. "Call me anytime."

The cool December air caressed my face as I walked to the car. The buildings sparkled in the sun, and the lush, emerald-green palm trees circling the parking lot were laden with coconuts. Through the windshield of the car, I watched the turquoise ocean undulate with white, cottony waves. Winter in South Florida lasts about three weeks, but it is the most beautiful three weeks you'll ever experience. *What a perfect day for my graduation from therapy.*

As I rounded the first of two circles on Hollywood Boulevard toward home, an odd, untethered feeling swept over me; the sessions had become a huge part of my life. In an instant, gratitude replaced it as I remembered the frightened, miserable, self-loathing girl I'd been the day I met Dr. Anopolus. Without his help, I wouldn't be enjoying this spectacular winter day. My past emotional and mental difficulties hadn't disappeared—they never would altogether—but I'd managed to find perspective, forgiveness, and for the first time, a bit of peace.

Bounding through the front door, I sang out, "Hey, honey! Guess what? I graduated!"

Lest I leave my readers to assume that my life was a straight, smooth line ever after, let me assure you it wasn't. The good news is that after my son was born, excepting three or four small slips in the ensuing five years, I never purged again. It took me longer to release bingeing as a way to cope, but I worked at being careful and mindful with myself, taking time to question what emotions were driving my compulsive actions. Change is slow and painful; it's taken many years to know myself, to understand my mind and emotions, and it's an enduring pursuit. I still disappoint myself, but now the feeling evaporates like a dandelion in the wind.

The bulimia, a faint shadow now from so many years ago, seems like another lifetime. But there is no question it is a part of me, etched and immutable—a part I can't and shouldn't ever forget. There would be many challenges to overcome in the following years, lots of good times and some bad ones, and at one point, I went back into therapy for a time.

Age and time have bestowed on me the ability to swim *gently* down the stream and mostly accept the inevitability of life with a loving detachment toward myself. I've learned to tolerate discomfort and uncertainty and have also learned that holding on to a sense of grievance is a monumental waste of time and a detriment to healing. In the end, I alone am responsible for my own journey. Today, I am strong, at peace with my memories, and profoundly grateful for my health.

AFTERWARD

Some have asked why I was able to overcome a turbulent past when others in similar situations aren't. As the Zen proverb points out, "The farmer casts his seeds evenly on the fertile soil and cares for them lovingly, but no one can say why some flourish and produce succulent vegetation while others wither and die." For me, despite his flaws, my father loved me in the early, formative years and gave me a sense of worth and safety before he lost his way. A handful of people in my life reached out to help, and they made all the difference. The phenomenal gift of a brilliant, patient, and insightful therapist helped me find a passageway toward healing. And, lastly, I can't overestimate the blessings of a stubborn, tough mettle and a little bit of that most fickle emotion, hope, for where there is even a flicker of hope, there is life.

I never spoke to Charley again, but many years later in Jacksonville at a chance meeting with his brother, I learned he'd received his doctorate degree in English and was a college professor in Memphis. He had remarried and had two little girls.

My older sister Jo died of lung cancer at the early age of sixty-five. We were never able to transcend the roles we had growing up to become simply friends. We were close, but our relationship remained a complicated one. She led a tumultuous life, marrying several times, searching for the love and validation she'd been denied in childhood. At least at the end of her life, she was married and settled. Of her three boys, only one survives. The other two died in their early forties of addiction.

The remaining three of us maintain the deep bond we forged in childhood. Pam is a retired attorney and has led an interesting life. She, too, has struggled deeply with issues relating to our childhood, but that's her story to tell. Married for twenty-five years, she chose not to have children but is a loving aunt and a devoted dog mom. Since retiring, she has worked tirelessly as a guardian ad litem in an effort to help abused and abandoned children. Pam is my best friend and confidante—we speak once a week and visit each other regularly.

Freddy fulfilled his dream of living in the mountains when he retired. He's had his ups and downs but today is happily married. My brother is still kind and funny, not a lot different than the little kid he was, and although he rarely shares his wounds from childhood and how they affected him, a dive into the past can bring them bubbling to the surface. He has one son who's grown into an amazing, successful husband and father of three adorable girls.

We checked off one of our bucket-list items by hiking the Appalachian Trail together, camping in the woods for a week at a time. I was fifty and he was forty-two—our family and friends said we were crazy, but we loved the experience, and it remains a cherished memory for both of us.

My father and I never mended our broken relationship on any deep level. Only once as an adult did I ask him about his rejection of me when I was nine. At the time, desperate to understand, I wanted to find a way to forgive. He reacted with puzzlement and denied it ever happened.

Daddy's story through the years had been that he'd tried to regain custody of Pam and Freddy after the courts *removed them and placed them in the custody of my grandparents.* Telling this lie often enough, preempting reality, he had come to accept it as fact. In therapy in her thirties, Pam made an unannounced trip from her home in Houston to Jacksonville and appeared at our father's door to confront him and this lie. She brought along the entire divorce file she'd obtained that outlined our custody through the years, and she tearfully told him of the pain and suffering she had endured due to his neglect and cruelty. Faced with the truth, my father listened, dry-eyed, and said little. There was nothing to say, except for maybe, "I'm sorry," but he was never able to do that.

In his last years, Daddy mellowed somewhat, sharing with me that he had changed; he no longer hated everyone. When I asked what he meant, he didn't have an answer. He never discussed his role as our father or understood what he'd done. The topic rarely came up and when it did, he chose to absent himself emotionally or lash out. One afternoon, in the middle of relating a story from his past, he mused, "I guess I wasn't much of a father to you kids" (the closest to an apology we ever received), but he had no desire to face the depth of that statement. In my thirties, after an extended estrangement, we forged a relationship based on a kind of amnesty, allowing for socializing on holidays and birthdays. I forgave Daddy, but even the passage of time couldn't restore our once loving father-daughter connection.

Daddy died recently at the age of ninety-eight. He retained the blessing of a sharp mind till the end. Divorced from Lucy in the late eighties, he remained alone for over thirty years. Through a sequence of illnesses during the last seven years of his life, Pam, Freddy, and I drove and flew thousands of miles to minister to him and make sure he was aware that we cared. Those cognizant of our childhoods didn't understand our devoted effort to be there for him. The three of us agreed—we did it for ourselves and each other as much as we did it for him. For the most part, we'd come to accept the person my father was, narcissistic to the end, but also a vulnerable human being alone in the world. We were with him in the last moments of his life. I hope he has found love and acceptance wherever he is.

My mother was never sober again, and her life continued to disintegrate in terrible, degrading ways. She married a fourth time, and although life with another alcoholic gave her little solace, at least there was a roof over her head at the end. After years of drinking, an empty shell existed where she had once lived, and she continued to insist she'd been a victim of her children's abuse.

I was never able to see into the heart of my mother—that's the thing about people who lack self-knowledge; how can you know someone who doesn't know themselves? The last time we were together, at my sister's wedding, Mother was drunk, and her shattered visage couldn't be disguised by a heartbreaking attempt at buoyancy. I could no longer hold her hand as she slowly killed herself, and I chose distance in the last two years of her life. A year after my son was born, in 1974, she died at the age of fifty-two in a head-on car collision. No one knows if the accident was a suicide or a horrific, drunk-driving catastrophe. The article in the newspaper stated that "a white Torino [her car] *mysteriously* drove directly into the path of an oncoming car at a high rate of speed." The two young men in the other car were critically injured but eventually recovered.

I'd been preparing for her death for years, and I didn't expect the fact of it to be so devastating, to plunge me into a subterranean state of grief. I wept for all she'd missed, for all her brokenness and pain, for the tragedy of her life, and for all I had wanted for her and from her, all too impossible in the end.

Trauma and grief carve themselves into our bones and cells, our very essence, to remain throughout life, but so does love. Strength comes from the moments of kindness, affection, and compassion we've known, the tenderness and stroking we received as babies etched deep within an unknowable place.

I've spent my life unraveling the past in an attempt to live an authentic life and find a deeper understanding of myself, but it has taken me years to accept and internalize the truth that we are all faulty in some way. No one escapes the human condition, and there is no payoff in making hard work of perfection. It is liberating to understand and accept with unwavering certainty that the best I can ever be is flawed, no better or worse than my fellow human beings.

The road I traveled after therapy took me over some bumpy terrain to bring me to the place I am today, but I've always had a companion. Jim and I celebrated our fifty-fifth wedding anniversary this year and we are closer than ever. Through the years, his support was steadfast. He encouraged me to reach for the stars and offered love and stability to make that possible. Native Americans say that when nature gives you one burden, it also gives you a gift. Jim is my gift.

I left the legal world in 1982 to start my own business (a domestic employment agency) that succeeded beyond my wildest dreams. I tried my hand at selling real estate, wrote curriculum for trade and secondary schools, including for the education program at The Federal Correctional Institute in Miami, where I taught for three years. But in 1991, at the age of forty-four, I graduated from college with highest honors and embarked on my heart's calling—painting and creating. Working steadily through the years, I enjoyed a twenty-three-year career as a professional artist and teacher, conducting art workshops and classes stateside and internationally. I continue to have affiliations with several art galleries, and much of my work is in collections all over the world. In 2002, I was inducted into The National Association of Women Artists at the Metropolitan Museum of Art in New York City.

But, by far, my children are my greatest accomplishment and the dearest part of my life. They survived a mother still wrestling with her past, but one who loved them fiercely. Today, my sons are kind, well-grounded, educated men, successful in their careers and, most gratifying to me, present and loving fathers. Raising them taught me more about myself and gave me a well of patience and perspective to draw from the rest of my life. They presented a million reasons to be the best I could be, and I wouldn't trade the experience for anything on earth.

L to R: Back row—me and Jo; front row—Pam and Freddy
(1989—I'm 42)

LOVE WINS

I searched blindly in the dark, groping and grabbing
for some undefined something.
What was it and how could I find it?

Wisdom landed on my shoulder one day and whispered,
"Love wins." A glimmer of light spilled into the dark corner of my life
And illuminated the words, Love Wins.

At journey's end, one question persists.
Was I loved, beloved on this earth?
The answer warms my aching heart. Yes! I was loved
And there is nothing more…to love and be
loved in this life. Love Wins.

Sherry O'Neill

A NOTE ABOUT THE PAINTINGS IN THIS BOOK

My latest painting series, "Strong at the Broken Places," received its name from this memoir and represents certain periods of my early life, as well as the most influential characters, my mother and father. The texture and muted palette convey the rugged, dark emotions and tonal quality of life before I began, slowly, to heal.

Author's website: www.sherryoneill.com

REFERENCE

Bulimia, or for that matter, any eating disorder, is difficult for many people to understand. We've come to accept alcoholism and drug addiction as complicated diseases, but an addiction to food is as unfamiliar to many as an addiction to gambling or shopping is to me. But it is real, self-destructive, and devastating.

Over the years, the curtain of secrecy has lifted on eating disorders, and they've escalated in numbers. Those who study and treat the illness have learned a great deal about it since 1973, when Hilde Bruch published a groundbreaking book called *Eating Disorders: Obesity, Anorexia Nervosa, and the Person Within*. Although bulimia was first erroneously linked to the Middle Ages, the initial clinical paper on it called "Bulimia Nervosa, An Ominous Variant of Anorexia Nervosa," was published in 1979.

It is now known that bingeing and vomiting triggers an endorphin rush that can temporarily mask anxiety and depression. Researchers have proven there are similar biological abnormalities in the brains of those suffering from alcoholism, drug addiction, and eating disorders. This fact was reinforced by the discovery of an identical neurological pattern in those with eating disorders and those of the hard-core drug addict.

Scientists discount purely innate neurosis as the cause and believe culture and family are equal contributors to the development of these conditions. Childhood emotional abuse, trauma, and life transitions such as moving, experiencing a divorce, or the death of a loved one are major contributors, as are psychological conditions that include low self-esteem, depression, anxiety, and fear. Ongoing studies show that if you are bulimic, familial chaos was an element of your environment, and, if anorexic, a rigidly controlling parent or parents were there.

A strong leaning toward academic achievement and excessive,

self-imposed pressure may be noteworthy in the development of eating disorders in young women. Most eating-disordered people are extreme, tending toward excess, incredibly self-critical, and over-achieving.

Bulimia is a seductive, terrifying addiction. It brings a constant roar in the mind and a chemical and emotional imbalance, as well as a deep, almost obdurate self-loathing. It is no easy addiction to overcome. Today, there are at least thirty million people of all ages and genders suffering from eating disorders in the United States, and every sixty-two minutes one person dies as a direct result of this disorder.

Fortunately, in the twenty-first century, there are many organizations,[5]* groups, and rehab opportunities for sufferers, and scores of people are in recovery receiving help in understanding and overcoming this baffling condition.

---

5 *ANAD (National Association of Anorexia Nervosa and Associated Disorders) is a free, non-profit service that provides multi-pronged treatment possibilities. It assists people struggling with eating disorders and also provides resources for families, schools, and the eating disorder community, offering, among other things, peer-to-peer counseling, individual and group counseling, and in-house referral programs.

CPSIA information can be obtained
at www.ICGtesting.com
Printed in the USA
BVHW041405111021
618680BV00013B/373